TEN CI

Roger L. Brown is also the author of:

The Followers of Jeroboam, 1983
The Welsh Evangelicals, 1986
Irish Scorn, English Pride and the Welsh Tongue, 1987
The Tribulations of a Mountain Parish, 1988
Lord Powis and the Extension of the Episcopate, 1989
*Reviving the Clergy, Renewing the Laity: Archbishop
    Benson's Mission in Wales*, 1994
A History of the Fleet Prison, London, 1996
David Howell: A Pool of Spirituality, 1998
Llandaff Figures and Places, 1998
Pews, Benches and Seats, 1998
Reclaiming the Wilderness, 2001
A-Z of Welsh Clerics, 2002
Parochial Lives, 2002
The Letters of Edward Copleston, Bishop of Llandaff,
    1828-1849, edited for the South Wales Record Society, 2003.

TEN CLERICAL LIVES

Essays relating to the
Victorian Church in Wales

Roger Lee Brown

TAIR EGLWYS PRESS
WELSHPOOL
2005

ISBN: 0-948780-15-0

Published by the TAIR EGLWYS PRESS
Welshpool Vicarage, Powys, SY21 7DP

CONTENTS

ABBREVIATIONS:

CDH	*Carnarvon and Denbigh Herald*
CL	Copleston Letters at Llandaff Cathedral (these are the letters which were not included in my edition of his letters, published by the South Wales Record Society in 2003).
CMG	*Cardiff and Merthyr Guardian*
CPAS	Church Pastoral-Aid Society
EC	Ecclesiastical Commission
NLW	National Library of Wales
QAB	Queen Anne's Bounty
WM	*Western Mail*

INTRODUCTION

This book is a sequel to my *Parochial Lives*, published by Carreg Gwalch in 2002 with the assistance of the Arts Council of Wales. All the clergymen depicted in *Ten Clerical Lives* ministered either wholly or for a certain period of time during the reign of Queen Victoria. A number might be described, quite correctly, as Victorians, though some others were relics of a bygone age, and one survived almost into the mid-twentieth century. By writing their stories, I hope to illustrate something of the profundity and concerns of the Victorian Church in Wales.

The Victorian age was one of substantial change in both society and Church, though in many cases these changes were the outworking of events and issues belonging to a previous generation. New communities had emerged around the ever-developing iron works, woollen mills and coal-mines, pioneered by a new breed of entrepreneurs who often lacked the social concerns of the landed gentry. A new Empire was evolving, providing outlets for industry, opportunities for emigration, and encouraging a new emphasis on missionary zeal and labour amongst the churches. The various parliamentary reforms, slight though they were, encouraged reforms in other directions, especially within the Church. A new concern for the dignity of people, arising from the evangelical conviction that all people were created in the image of God, even though they may not be equal to one another, prompted a philanthropic desire for health and sanitary reforms, education of the masses, as well as the emergence of various civilising agencies such as libraries and organisations for young people. It was an age of communication: the penny post, railways, and the steamship and telegraph. Paradoxically, with these concerns for communication and education, combined with the implied belief that the Victorian age of progress was allied to the English language, a feeling arose that the Welsh language was inferior and fit only for a peasant people.

The Victorian age was also an age of conflict. The working masses, dissatisfied at their exploitation, looked firstly to the Chartist and then to the Trade Union movements for their salvation, and the upper classes, fearful of social unrest, looked to the Church (as well as to the newly formed police force) for their security. The Church was there, they believed, in both its liturgical and educational roles, to remind people of their God-given station in life, to encourage peace and harmony within society, and to uphold the status quo. Possibly much of the support given to church planting in the new industrial areas was provided to enhance this viewpoint. As a result, Nonconformity was placed at a discount. If some of the older generation saw it as aligned with the forces of destruction – witness the *Blue Books* report into Welsh education of 1847 – its leaders had to work hard to ensure their churches were seen as respectable elements in society. There was also conflict within the Church. If, on the one hand, there were some who wanted a more rationalised view of Christianity, seeing Christ as more of a human figure than divine, and finding support in the theory of evolution pioneered by Darwin, on the other hand there were some who wished to return to what they saw as the romantic age of Christianity, namely the medieval period.

Until the 1914 Welsh Church Act came into force on St David's Day, 1920, the four dioceses in Wales (with adjacent areas in England) were part of the province of Canterbury and within the Church of England. The terms used here, "The Church in Wales" or "the Welsh Church", for these four Welsh dioceses had no validity before that date, even though it is used for the sake of convenience. There was no official body to represent the four dioceses, though occasionally the four bishops met and informal links, such as a meeting of the four diocesan conferences called to prepare for disestablishment, were established. There was also an ambiguity here as well, for while some defined the Church in Wales as a geographical term, others seem to have used the term to mean the Welsh-speaking parts of the four dioceses. This ambiguity was not confined to the Church in Wales, however, for it was also exhibited in society at large. "For Wales, see England," proclaimed the *Encyclopaedia Britannica*!

A number of themes will be found in these ten biographical accounts, and it will be of value to identify them in this introduction. It will be noted that many of them are related to one another, so in a sense my own format is as arbitrary as my selection of these ten clergymen for my studies (in fact they were chosen mainly because there was sufficient information about them to justify their inclusion).

The Welsh Church, even more so than its counterpart in England, was in competition with Nonconformity. Mann's religious census of 1851, for all its inaccuracies and difficulties of interpretation, shocked the Established Church almost as much as the *Blue Books* report of 1847 had shocked Nonconformity. The Welsh Church had 29 per cent of the places of worship in Wales, 31 per cent of the sittings or seats, but only 19.31 per cent of the attenders, compared to the Calvinistic Methodists with 25 per cent.[1] Although Mann's estimate, using various devices to account for those attending more than once, and suggesting that about one-third of the population of Wales did not attend a place of worship, was ignored, the contrary view that Wales was one of the most religious parts of Great Britain, was equally ignored. The evidence of the Church's failure and Nonconformity's strength was seen as paramount. When this was coupled with another factor, namely the perceived failure of the Church to provide Welsh-speaking bishops and clergy for its members, the cry that the Church was alien received even more assent than previously. Wales, it was proclaimed, was the land of Nonconformity.

The Liberation Society, founded in 1844 to liberate the Established Churches from their state connection, appears by the 1860s to have concentrated its efforts in Wales, on the assumption that here the Established Church was weakest and most vulnerable. Founded by members of the older dissenting groups, the impetus of Henry Richard at its 1862 Swansea conference, organised to celebrate the 200th anniversary of the Great Ejection, persuaded the Calvinistic Methodists, the new dissent, to throw in its lot with the liberationists. Eight years later a bill to disestablish the Church of England in Wales was heavily defeated in the House of Commons, but in 1891 an alliance of Nonconformity with the Liberal party managed to place disestablishment and disendowment onto the Liberal party programme. In that same year a Church Congress held at Rhyl helped mobilise the wealth and power of the Church against these proposals. It is not the place here to relate the long and tortuous procedures which eventually led to disestablishment, which came about as a result of the curbing of the House of Lords after it had rejected Lloyd George's budget of 1911. What we need to note is that Church and Chapel were on a collision course from the 1880s onwards, and nearly every aspect of Welsh life was involved. It was the Church versus Chapel, Liberal versus Tory, temperance versus the brewery, Church schools (with the accusation of proselytising Nonconformist children) versus board schools, and the ballot box versus open elections. The churchyard also was brought into the affray with the demand that Nonconformists be allowed to have their own services conducted by their own ministers therein. Even the land issue was dragged in as so much of Wales was owned by Church landlords.

If the advocates of disestablishment suggested that the Church would be a better organisation when relieved of its state connection, the Church defenders alleged that for the Church to be deprived of three-quarters of its income would severely restrict its work and mission at a time when the forces of secularism were gaining the upper hand. The disestablishers argued that the Church, having lost its national constituency, had no right to retain endowments given to religion in general. In return Churchmen used emotional terms such as sacrilege and theft to describe disendowment, and pointed out that the attack on them only intensified when the Church had started to reform itself and had became a serious rival to Nonconformity.

It would be wrong to suggest that either side was unanimous about its particular concerns. There were many who deplored the bitter words used; the violence and disruption done to the spiritual life of the churches, and the sheer waste of time and energy involved, and who wished the various churches to unite together to face the common foe of secularism and religious apathy. Within the Church there were many who felt that the Church was making too much of its state connection and privileges, and would be far healthier if it compromised with its opponents and accepted terms rather than fight to the bitter end, or even, that it would be a far healthier church spiritually without the false trappings of endowment and establishment. Their concern was more about spiritual life than economic considerations. Sadly, these men were marginalised by Bishop Edwards of St Asaph and others, although, ironically, the compromise some of them proposed in the Bangor Scheme of 1895 bore an uncanny resemblance to the actual terms of the Welsh Church Act. By this the four dioceses were disestablished and separated from the Church of England, becoming a province in their own right, and disendowed, by which they lost their historic endowments.

It needs to be remembered that from the 1880s onwards the fear of disestablishment dominated the leadership of the Church. The Nonconformist taunt that this fear was forcing the Church to put its own house in order was an unjust one, but certainly there were many within the Church who argued that the real defence against disestablishment was a Church doing its proper work and giving a spiritual and pastoral ministry to the nation itself. At a local level clergymen had a real concern that one day in the future their endowments might be lost and their livelihoods forfeited, their churches secularised and their spiritual authority lost. By and large relationships between ordinary people, although separated ecclesiastically, remained good, especially as many families themselves were similarly divided. But any close or formal relationships between Church and Dissent were frowned upon by the Church leaders, as Archdeacon Griffiths of Neath discovered to his cost. Although the old attitude that dissent was evil and even seditious had long since evaporated, many in the Church considered Nonconformity to be not only inferior but also inimical to the Church itself.

The new industrial areas, particularly in south Wales, were areas where Church and Nonconformity were particularly seen as competitors, though in these areas the Church was generally the loser. A dissenting body was able to form a cause in a private house, use its own members in the work of ministry, establish a Sunday school, and finance itself from the contributions of its people. If the cause prospered it was able to build its own chapel and call a stipendiary minister. By contrast the Church was beset by legal rules and entrenched regulations. To establish a new church in one of these areas required the consent of the incumbent of the parish in which it was situated (even though the parish church might be miles away), probably a full-time stipendiary curate (as lay people were not permitted to take services), and substantial financial resources to pay the curate and provide accommodation for him. To go further, and create a new parish, meant in the earlier stages a parliamentary act, a church built in a particular style, a house with an appropriate number of rooms fit for a gentleman, and an endowment for his stipend. The legal work involved was costly and substantial. The result, hardly surprising, was that by the time the Church had got its act together in these areas Nonconformity was already established and had won the lion's share of the battlefield.

We need to remember too that until late Victorian times the Church was supported by the church rate, which faded into oblivion by the 1850s (and sometimes by pew rents), while the offertory at the Communion Service was devoted to the poor of the parish. It was not until late Victorian times that offertories were generally introduced. Nonconformity was self-financing, whereas after the 1840s the Church relied on the assistance of individuals, including the incumbent of the parish, for its financial support. It was the incumbent, in law, who was responsible for the payment of his curates, though grants were available from various sources, such as the evangelical Church Pastoral-Aid Society or the Assistant Curates'

Society.

Church planting, as it was termed, was not only to provide spiritually for the Church people who had moved into these newly industrialised areas, but also to bring back those who had strayed from the fold. This latter need was also evident in the urban areas of Wales, where the population of a town had outstripped the church accommodation available for it. In many of these places, as in some rural areas, the pews had been appropriated to private houses. The result was that people regarded themselves as having a proprietary interest in their pew, and believed they alone had the right to determine who should sit in it. Churches that might be half empty in reality would be regarded as technically full because of this reason. Some churches had galleries or new aisles built, others were repewed, and when the accommodation was still insufficient a new church might be built for the "labouring classes". There was a real fear that if accommodation was not provided, people would be lost to Nonconformity. At the same time there was a deep concern that pews should be free and open, that is, not appropriated or rented out, as was allowed in some churches in law and illegally practiced in others. As Archdeacon Wickham maintained, if the Church was the National Church, it was the Church of the poor as well as of the rich, and they were as much entitled to its ministrations as anybody else. It was seriously believed that free seats, a warm building, good preaching and lively hymns would bring in the lost working classes.

The various liturgical changes established by the tractarian movement had a much wider impact than amongst its adherents. The ecclesiological effect of the movement was to persuade people, even churchwardens, that a proper church was based on the medieval pattern of nave, chancel and sanctuary. The old churches, often dilapidated, were seen as insufficient, and an orgy of church building and restoration followed in both urban and rural areas. Victorian respectability and the availability of money for this work through agricultural and industrial prosperity assisted the process. Accompanying these rebuilds were often new or enlarged parsonage houses, church schools (for the teaching of church doctrine), and mission chapels.

All these matters were seen as signs of Church progress, outward no doubt, but often with a core of inner conviction. Though the Church's defenders described these matters, and others, as forming the Church's revival, their Nonconformist detractors pointed to their own conception of revival, namely a manifestation of God's extraordinary grace, and declared the former as man-made rather than

God-gifted.

Apart from the monies available from private individuals, there were also resources available from within the Church itself. There were a number of voluntary societies such as the Church Building Society, which gave grants for building churches in necessitous areas, diocesan societies, and the National Society, which while its grant aid was mainly for the work of Church education, also gave grants for the erection of schoolrooms which could double up as mission churches on Sundays. The two main grant-making bodies, however, were Queen Anne's Bounty and the Ecclesiastical Commissioners.

Queen Anne's Bounty, founded by the queen of that name, collected an old ecclesiastical tax imposed on some, though not all, of the clergy, called tenths and first fruits. Queen Anne, convinced that taking such monies into the royal coffers, as her predecessors had done, was sacrilege, decided to give it to the Church as a charity for the assistance of poor benefices. Those parishes which were given a benefaction by an interested party could have that amount doubled up to a sum of £200 by a grant from the Bounty. The money that was left over was divided into portions of £200, and all the parishes under a certain income, at first £10, were placed in a ballot. In both cases the grant, and the benefaction when given, were invested in land and the income arising from its rental added to the stipend of the incumbent. As parishes were assisted in turn so the qualifying amount was raised. In addition the governors of the Bounty were allowed to grant mortgages on a parish's (that is, the incumbent's) income for the cost of rebuilding or repairing the parsonage house. However, the Bounty was only able to assist parishes whose income was under £200, and as the contributions made to the cost of curates and other such incidentals was not allowed against this sum, its application, though significant, was limited.

The Ecclesiastical Commission had been established in 1835 in order to reform the administration of the Church, especially as it had no central body able to do this work. Indeed, each parish, cathedral chapter, and bishopric formed an ecclesiastical corporation in law. The Whig government of that day, deeply concerned about the unpopularity of the Church and its archaic structures, decided to stream-line both the bishoprics and the cathedral bodies. The incomes of the sees and cathedral chapters had enormous variations, from opulence to poverty, so that the bishop of Llandaff, in the latter area, comparatively speaking, needed to serve as dean of St Paul's, London, in order to obtain a proper episcopal income. The incomes of the bishoprics were equalised, with some variations, and a house provided where one was lacking, while the cathedral or capitular bodies were regulated, incomes again equalised, and the number of canons reduced significantly. The surplus income thus obtained was used to provide for parishes in populous areas, meaning in effect those parishes in industrial and mining areas. Existing interests were respected so that it took time before the commissioners were able to offer grants on any large scale.

Grants were available for vicarage houses, assistant curates, and the provision of stipends for incumbents by a permanent endowment. In addition, as time went on, the commissioners were able to offer benefactions to increase the stipends of clergy to a more realistic level, such as £300. In addition, because the commissioners had taken over the interests of episcopal and capitular bodies, they owned estates and property rights, such as tithe income, in various parishes. Here they would act as good landlords, offering assistance to the local church when required. The commissioners' income was never sufficient for the needs of the whole Church, for it was mainly reserved for the industrial and populous areas. In addition the commissioners positively disliked livings in private patronage, feeling that the patron, who claimed the right of appointment to the parish, should be assisting the parish himself. They would only assist such parishes if the patron himself made a benefaction to it.

If money was available from these central or diocesan funds, it was limited in extent and clergy often had to join a queue for their assistance. Most money for church projects had to be raised from local sources, and it was hard work to do so.

A further factor we need to note is the growing professionalism of the clergy. The "Church" was no longer a place for the younger son of the squirearchy, where long and comfortable years could be stretched out with some pastoral duties and a general benevolence towards one's parishioners. It was now a vocation, demanding total commitment and requiring, at a later period, professional training. This meant that the old *laissez-faire* attitude of ministry had to go, along with its accompanying characteristics of non-residence and pluralism. To be fair, some of the pluralism was by way of accommodation. Small parishes with inadequate stipends were linked together in plurality, and sometimes an incumbent looked after a neighbouring parish as curate to an absentee rector. In the diocese of Llandaff a number of these groupings had become almost traditional and it was probably so in other dioceses.[2] At a later stage the Church, and in particular the Ecclesiastical Commission and Queen Anne's

Bounty, endeavoured to unite such parishes into one, convinced that these small parishes could no longer support an incumbent on their own. On the other hand the pluralism noted in the careers of Thomas Stacey and Hugh Williams was different in character and was condemned by a later generation. Another reason for pluralism was the lack of a parsonage house. By the mid-nineteenth century, as more funding became available from central and diocesan sources, incumbents were being urged to build parsonages if their parishes lacked one. In several cases it was known to be a condition of appointment.

This new professionalism took a heavy toll of the clergy. By the end of the century a successful parish was almost required to have a full range of Sunday and weekday services, mission outposts, Sunday and day schools, benefit clubs, a mothers' meeting, youth work, district visitors, a parish magazine, and many other such organisations. In addition other work was done on a deanery basis, with clergy chapters, associations and the like. Whereas the eighteenth-century cleric lived a life of leisure, his counterpart a century later lived one of ceaseless activity. And, besides all this work, it was generally left to him to organise the fund-raising required.

This new concept of ministry, with all its ramifications, and the urge to have fit and "proper" places of worship, owed much to the Oxford or Tractarian movement. It had an impact hard to fathom, since most people suspected the theology which lay behind it, and yet were influenced by its more outward concerns.

By and large the Welsh clergy were evangelical or low tone in churchmanship. Their doctrinal beliefs were very similar to those of Nonconformity, though perhaps with a dose of episcopacy added! This is the reason, together with the use of the Welsh language, which restricted the growth of the Oxford movement in Wales. At first, old-fashioned high churchmen like Bishop Christopher Bethell of Bangor gave some encouragement, but in many cases this turned to rapid disapproval and even distaste, as in the case of Bishop Edward Copleston of Llandaff. This is because they realised the movement was endeavouring to revive the doctrine and practices of the medieval Church, and claimed that the Reformation settlement was concerned with the abuses involved in these practices rather than with the doctrines themselves. The emphasis on apostolic succession, for example, "unchurched" Nonconformity, and allowed the tractarians to state that as Nonconformity had no valid apostolic succession it had no ministry, no sacraments, and no spiritual validity whatsoever. While Copleston and others expressed their concern that the movement was straining the comprehensiveness of the Church and refusing to allow Nonconformists to have any share in Christ's redemption, there were far more people who shared his anger that Roman Catholic doctrines and practices were being introduced into the Reformed Church of England. At a time when it was said that the religion of the common man was "No Popery", and Nonconformity saw the Church as a bulwark against the claims of Rome, people now saw the enemy within the Church. Even worse, they discovered that because of the archaic nature of the Church there was little that could be done about it. Those clerics who taught these things possessed the freehold of their livings, and it was difficult as well as costly to charge a man with heresy in the ecclesiastical courts. As a result Welsh Nonconformity, believing that a Church relieved of its state connections might have more freedom to deal with these malcontents, reiterated its desire to see the disestablishment of the Church.[3]

The Oxford movement entered north Wales mainly because of the unofficial patronage or possibly the blind eye of Bishop Bethell. The autobiography of Robert Roberts, *Y Sgolor Mawr*, gives a vivid description of the way in which a number of individuals, many of them laypeople, helped forward this movement in this diocese during the early 1850s.[4] One of its leading practitioners in Wales, Griffith Arthur Jones, had his first incumbency in the parish of Llanegryn, in the diocese of Bangor, before he moved to St Mary's Church, Cardiff. Constable Ellis also served in the diocese of Bangor, where he was an *enfant terrible*. In south Wales, apart from Tenby under George Huntington and some isolated parishes in Monmouthshire, the movement spread because of the patronage of the Bute Trustees. The third marquess of Bute, who converted to Roman Catholicism at his coming of age, managed to evade the strict interpretation of the law, which stated that the ecclesiastical patronage of a Roman Catholic was to be exercised by one of the universities, by the appointment of patronage trustees. By ensuring these men were either tractarians or in sympathy with the movement, and believing that the Oxford movement would eventually lead the Church of England back into union with Rome, he managed to place prominent tractarians into some of the major parishes in the diocese of Llandaff which were in his patronage: St Mary, Cardiff, Roath, Neath, Aberdare, Merthyr Tydfil, amongst others. In each case a tractarian was appointed to follow noted evangelical ministries. These parishes all required a large staff of curates, which introduced even more tractarians into the diocese of Llandaff.

The effect of the Oxford movement, as it generally affected the Church over a number of generations, was to introduce a new style of worship within a re-ordered church. The priest was elevated in the sanctuary, and between him and the congregation in the nave was a robed choir in the chancel. Gradually the liturgy and its observance replaced the priority of preaching, and the pulpit was placed at the side of the church rather than in a more central position, while the altar was emphasised. The church band, generally placed in the west gallery, was replaced by a pipe organ, the old-fashioned pews by benches, the homely windows by stained glass, and the offertory introduced. The parish clerk was relegated to a back seat, so that the liturgy became the preserve of the clergy. Although hymnody was in use long before the movement, the tractarians managed to introduce their own hymnbook, giving a poetic form to their theology, *Hymns Ancient and Modern*. For some reason the book became standard in most churches. The old austerity of the church also had to give way to colour and ritual: altar vases for flowers, decorating the church at the seasonal festivals, coloured stoles, processions and sometimes genuflections, were all introduced, and in some advanced churches vestments as well.

One strange result of this was that as the Church advanced to a broader position, those who held to the old evangelical faith became identified with Nonconformity. As noted earlier, there was little doctrinal difference between evangelicals and Nonconformists, but as Nonconformity started to campaign for the Church's disestablishment, all those identified with them, even in matters of belief, became tarred with the same brush.

Finally, and perhaps most emotionally, there was the question of the Welsh language. From 1716 until 1870 the various prime ministers, in whom the patronage lay, did not appoint a Welsh speaker to any Welsh diocese. This was because of political rather than linguistic reasons. In turn, the Anglo-Welsh bishops, as these English-speaking bishops became known, used their own patronage within their dioceses to enrich their relations, and thus introduce English-speaking clergy into Welsh-speaking parishes. The excuses given, namely that bishops had no need to speak Welsh as all their clergy spoke English, and that as Wales was a conquered nation it was right to introduce the English tongue (as stated in the Bowles case), cut no ice with Welsh speakers. Bishops, after all, had to confirm Welsh-speaking confirmation candidates, and Welsh was the language of the heart if not of commerce and industry. Sadly, until legislation of 1836, renewed in 1838, the bishops were unable to prevent such appointments, even if they so wished to do.

This position, which the bishops were endeavouring to redress by the Victorian period, if not earlier, allowed the Church's detractors to claim that the Church was alien, English-orientated, and anti-Welsh. It was an unfair criticism. Even a bishop like Copleston of Llandaff, who disliked the Welsh language, accepted that it was his responsibility to provide Welsh-speaking clergy and services for those parishes where they were required. A vast majority of the clergy within the four Welsh dioceses were Welsh speakers, and it was Welsh clergymen who mainly pioneered and supported the Welsh eisteddfod. Nevertheless, there were many within the Church who proclaimed that the problems of the Church of their day had been caused by the Anglo-Welsh bishops and their followers, using this as an argument to obtain Welsh-speaking bishops, whereas others suggested the problem was one of poverty rather than of personalities. Equally, there were many Welsh-speaking clergy who accepted that the language would die out, and amongst them was the notable figure of Archdeacon Griffiths of Llandaff.

The Church needed Welsh-speaking clergy, especially for the newer industrial areas, but in this desire there was a substantial problem. Those who spoke Welsh mainly came from backgrounds where economic circumstances prevented them from receiving anything but an elementary education. Their social manners left much to be desired. Their status as "gentlemen" was more honorary than real. Many came from a background of Nonconformity, simply because the Church alone offered a stipendiary ministry at that time. At times bishops expressed deep anxiety that such men had to be ordained. Yet these men, rough as they were, became the church planters of their day, and did sterling and often unrewarded work in the large and demanding parishes of the industrial areas. Sadly, they were despised by the well-connected and educated English-orientated clergy of the rural areas who generally obtained the better preferment and the posts of dignity. There was thus a real tension within the Church between these two groups, which sometimes manifested itself, especially during the elections to convocation, as we note later.

The bilingual parishes found themselves in an even worse position than similar parishes within the English dioceses. Two languages had to be provided for, which either meant a double set of churches and clergy, or that one language, generally the Welsh, would have to take an inferior place, with services held at the more unfashionable times and in the more lowly of churches.

These are some of the main themes which may be noted in these ten biographical accounts. There are, of course, others, but taken collectively, they reveal with some clarification, that the Victorian Church was not the golden age we might suppose it to be, and the lot of the Victorian clergyman was not an enviable one.

****

I wish to express my appreciation to the large number of people and bodies who have assisted me in my research. These include the Librarians and their staff at the National Library of Wales, Aberystwyth, and Lambeth Palace Library; the archivist and staff at the Glamorgan Record Office; Canon David Griffiths for allowing me to make use of the Gresford Vicar's Book; Canon Glyn Price, Canon D. T. W. Price, and Dr Fred Cowley, for much assistance, and above all to my wife Phyllis who has willingly taken time off from her Hebraic studies in order to assist me at various points and intervals.

I am most grateful to the Provincial Secretary of the Church in Wales for allowing me to use, and quote from, the papers of Queen Anne's Bounty and the Ecclesiastical Commission in the custody of the Representative Body of the Church in Wales; to the dean and chapter of Llandaff Cathedral for similar permission regarding the Copleston letters, and to the marquess of Salisbury for permission to quote from the papers of the third marquess.

ENDNOTES

1 John Williams (ed.), *Digest of Welsh Historical Statistics* (Cardiff, 1985), II 352.
2 Roger Lee Brown (ed.), *The Letters of Edward Copleston, Bishop of Llandaff, 1828-1849* (South Wales Record Society, Cardiff, 2003), p. 19.
3 Ibid., pp. 40-2.
4 J. H. Davies (ed.), *The Life and Opinions of Robert Roberts* (new edition, Cardiff, 1991).
5 The Bowles case was heard in 1773 after the churchwardens of the parish of Trefdraeth in Anglesey took action against the appointment of an English speaker to their almost monoglot Welsh parish. See my "Pastoral Problems and Legal Solutions" in Norman Doe (ed.), *Essays in Canon Law* (Cardiff, 1992), p. 10.

THE REVD THOMAS STACEY
appears on the right of this lithograph by R. Dighton, of the 1830s.
His companions are Edward Priest Richards and John Bird.

I
THOMAS STACEY: PLURALIST

Thomas Stacey may be described as one of those men who typified the Georgian Church at a time when reform was in the air, and when the young Victorian Church was changing its conception of ministry from that of an elegant pursuit to that of a profession. Yet, although he received the odium of the reformers, Stacey, according to the standards of the age in which he was born, was a distinguished clergyman who did much good and gave a notable ministry to those whom he directly served. The term "directly" is deliberate, for Stacey served for the better part of his active ministry as curate of Cardiff, although he was also the absentee rector of Gelligaer, a parish to the north of Cardiff, and in an area that was rapidly developing as a colliery district. In addition, Stacey, an Englishman reaping great rewards for his non-residence in his Welsh-speaking parish, represented the unacceptable face of the Establishment, for most of the Welsh-speaking clergy who served in the industrial parishes of the diocese of Llandaff did so for a poverty-shaped stipend.

As an example of the odium in which the reformers held Stacey, and those like him, we may offer a statement made by Sir Benjamin Hall during his controversy over the Copleston Memorial. Copleston had been bishop of Llandaff, and after his death in 1849 a number of people in the diocese collaborated to establish a fitting memorial to his memory. Hall declined to contribute, on the grounds that Copleston had been inconsistent in his appointments to Welsh-speaking parishes, and equally that he had not been fair to the Welsh-speaking portion of his diocese. The controversy became a little wider than this, however, with the result that Hall could write the following about Stacey, and use it as an attack upon Copleston's episcopate:

> The living of Gelligaer, with Brithdir, value £567, has a population of 5,150 souls, and to show that (even under this present arrangement) this parish is admitted to be Welsh, there is one Welsh service every Sunday in the parish Church, and only

one service in Brithdir, which service is Welsh. In 1827, a former bishop instituted a clergyman to this living, and the bishop afterwards licensed him to the parish of St John's, Cardiff, and he lives at Cardiff, where the incumbent, *also* being non-resident, he acts as English curate, for which service he receives a salary of £150 a year, in addition to the £567 received for not doing anything in his own parish. But he keeps two curates at Gelligaer, whose services he values at precisely half the sum which he himself receives, as instead of paying them £150 each, (which he considers a fair remuneration in his own case) he gives these curates, living in the wilds of Gelligaer, and performing the duties which it does not suit him to undertake for himself only £150 between them! What was the bishop doing all this time? and where has been the '*Oculus Episcopi*?' has he not winked at this unfair appropriation of ecclesiastical revenue? To complete the whole of this case, the non-resident incumbent of Gelligaer, is permitted to be curate in Cardiff, in which there is no Welsh Church service whatever - whilst there are in Cardiff four Welsh dissenting chapels, having congregations amounting to two thousand eight hundred souls ... It is idle to suppose that the bishop has no power to insist upon ample remuneration to curates; and I beg to inform the archdeacon, that by 1st & 2nd Vic. c. 106, it is enacted that in Welsh dioceses, where the bishop shall have reason to believe that ecclesiastical duties are not satisfactorily performed *by the incumbent*, he may appoint curates and cause them to be paid by monition or even *sequestration*.

Another writer, quoted in the local paper, criticised Stacey for paying some Cambrian curate to serve Gelligaer, "whose moderate wants are supplied by a leak and a Welsh rabbit", half the sum he received for serving Cardiff.[1]

The hint was not lost on Bishop Ollivant, as we note later, but it is important to note that Stacey's position was becoming a *cause célèbre* in reforming circles, as well as indicating the friction between the Welsh and the English clergy of the diocese. The Welsh clergy, who generally lacked the educational and family backgrounds of the English clergy, felt that they were the "hewers and drawers" of the diocese rather than those who obtained the diocesan prizes. The friction was to erupt later in the contests for election to Convocation, the Church's parliament, but that is another story which must come later.

Stacey provided another area of comment, and possibly of amusement as well, in his love of the aristocracy. His brother-in-law, Edward Priest Richards, was the solicitor to the Bute Estates as well as Town Clerk of Cardiff, County Treasurer and Clerk to the Magistrates. He virtually controlled the town in the Bute interest, but was certainly an instrumental force in the development of Cardiff as a great port and industrial centre. It is probable that Stacey owed his friendship with the second marquess of Bute to his brother-in-law, and possibly through the same connection he became a chaplain to the earl of Dunraven. These connections were to serve him well over the years, while his brother-in-law's death in 1867 not only provided Stacey with a bequest of £50,000, but his sons also received equally substantial amounts. One of his sons was the third marquess's tutor. But his love of the aristocracy, and his willingness to oblige them, were frequently criticised, writes Jean E. McCann, who adds that Stacey even ensured that the bells of his church played the marchioness of Bute's favourite tune, "Oh Where, tell me where, has my Highland laddie gone"![2]

The sermon Stacey preached on the death of Lord Bute could only add to this impression. The second marquess was a man of great virtue, and the age was an age when there was little reticence about the dead and their achievements, but even then it seems that Stacey went a little beyond the normal bounds of funeral oratory. He stated:

> God had permitted to pass away ... one who, to all human appearances and in the sight of man – endeavoured to live by his faith. One of a long line of honourable ancestry, born of the nobles of the land, nurtured amid all that to our fallen nature too often presents temptations to forget Him who maketh poor and maketh rich; taking his place among the princes and the mighty of this world who are called to the duties of ruling and guiding the people that are under them, he seemed to have remembered that One who is higher than the highest regarded him; and that there was a higher than he. With this sense of Christian responsibility on his soul he was not ashamed of confessing Christ before men; and in the exercise of the multiplied duties with which God had charged him, he seemed to have thought that he was but a steward who must hereafter himself be called to account; and remembered his Lord's charge how to occupy until He came; and had regard unto the recompense of reward. Think of him, ... as you have experienced him to have been; of the highest order of intellect, active and enterprising, hospitable

and generous, just and honourable, bountiful and charitable; and above all, conspicuous, but most unostentatious, in the discharge of the solemn offices of his faith in public and in private, and happy in the full, sound, and grateful acknowledgement of his want of, his belief in, and his humble love of, the Saviour. And what character that can be portrayed to you can more fully represent the *christian in action* than that of this high and distinguished person, the appalling and awful suddenness of whose death in a moment, at midnight, out of hand, has struck us, one and all, far and near, rich and poor, with a grief and consternation as overwhelming as we hope and pray the warning may be profitable and lasting. Oh, who can call to mind the noble acts, and the mighty energy, the benevolent sympathies, and the peacemaking concessions which have proceeded from his heart and hand within the personal knowledge of every individual here; who can dwell now upon the twice-deprived widow, the doubly-bereaved orphans, the impoverished pensioners – the unaided objects of his hitherto pious bounty, and judicious, zealous, and effective support, and not feel all their regret and sorrows for his removal aggravated a thousand-fold?

The sermon, orthodox enough, was used as a means of exhorting his hearers to prepare for their own deaths. Begging them to lay these spiritual truths to heart, and to seek God and his saving knowledge "rightly and faithfully, they would not be troubled with terrible fear, when the master came or summoned them," but rather would be amazed at the "strangeness of His salvation, so far beyond all that they looked for, even through the blood and merits only of a crucified Redeemer."[3]

Various stories were also remembered about Stacey which seem to suggest that this very public figure was regarded at times as being a little absurd. One of these stories concerned Stibbs the barber, who was informed by Stacey that his tithes were much in arrears. "But, Sir," said Stibbs, "I never go to your church." "I can't help that," replied Stacey, "there is a church for you, open every Sunday, if you chose to use it." This conversation having no effect, Stacey sent the barber a written bill for the tithes due, amounting to a considerable sum. A few days later Stacey received an invoice for monies owing to Stibbs for shaving and hairdressing him. In great indignation Stacey went to his shop. "Look here, Stibbs," said he, "what do you mean by sending me this bill; you have never shaved me or dressed my hair." "I can't help that, Sir, indeed," was the reply, "here is my shop open every day of the week for you, if you chose to use it." On another occasion, preaching an effective sermon on the wickedness of pride, Stacey happened to look in the direction of a parishioner by the name of Pride, and shouted at the top of his voice, thumping the pulpit, that pride came from hell. Mr Pride, in all his outraged dignity, rose from his seat, and said, "Thee be-est a liar; I came from Zummerset."[4]

Thomas Stacey was born in 1796, the son of a Carmarthen man and educated at Jesus College, Oxford. He was ordained by the bishop of Bangor by *letters dimissory* in 1822 to serve the parishes of Cowbridge, Welsh St Donat's and Penarth. Probably through his connection with the marquess of Bute via his brother-in-law, Stacey obtained the Bute living of Roath, near Cardiff, in 1824. The population was around 250 people and its value was £96. Just less than half this amount came from a lease of the small tithes, which though worth much more, would have been costly to collect.[5] At the same time he served as curate of the parish of Cardiff for its absentee vicar, John Webb. Here, as was said in his obituary, Stacey "earnestly and effectually discharged ... the whole ecclesiastical duties of the town of Cardiff." In 1827 the same patronage brought him the far wealthier, but perhaps less comfortable, living of Gelligaer, with an income of around £600 and a population of around 2,000, which was to more than double and probably triple during the course of his incumbency, due to the area's development as a colliery district. The living was a rectory, so that the tithe income was considerable, but it was an onerous parish, in so far as it contained an outlying chapelry at Brithdir, normally worked by an assistant curate, and its boundaries stretched from the lower Rhymney valley to present day Pontlottyn and even beyond. Nevertheless, Gelligaer was regarded as one of the ecclesiastical "plums" of the diocese, though Bute probably refused to allow Stacey to hold it in plurality with Roath which he accordingly resigned together with the curacy of Cardiff.

It might be conjectured that Stacey was *sent* to Gelligaer in order to act as a sort of "moral" policeman in the developing industrial areas of the county, which were seen as unruly and disorderly by those in authority. His task was, on the one hand, to preach the Gospel and to seek thereby to establish good behaviour and respect for one's betters, but on the other, as a magistrate, to enforce the discipline and authority of the state when such moral restraints were ignored.[6] It is significant that Stacey was appointed a magistrate and deputy lieutenant of the county almost at the same time as his appointment to Gelligaer, and he was appointed to this office by the same person who nominated him to the living of Gelligaer, namely Lord Bute, who was also lord lieutenant of Glamorgan. As a member of the establishment and also a Welsh speaker Stacey was ideal for his twin roles in the so-called hill country of Glamorgan.

Stacey resided at Gelligaer, maintaining a curate for the Brithdir end of the parish from his own income. Though many poured scorn on his claim that he found the hill country a hazard to his health, and so obtained leave of absence from the bishop, the letters of Bishop Copleston indicate that there was at the time a genuine concern about his health. His obituary stated that "his tender and delicate frame was solely tried by the bleak climate of the inhospitable mountain regions..." An undated letter, which from its context seems to have been written in 1830, notes that Stacey was prepared to preach the visitation sermon at Llandaff even though "his health is now impaired." A letter of July 1833 indicates that "[p]oor Stacey tells me he is advised or rather required by his physicians to leave Gelligaer." Nevertheless Stacey was not looking for a life of idleness, but was willing to take another post in the Church which would allow him both greater ease and also access to medical treatment which might enable him to return to his parish. The same letter states that he was then looking for a curacy at Clifton. One at Stapleton, in that area, was considered, but by early August Copleston was writing that Stacey had given up "the idea of Stapleton", and would continue at Gelligaer, until he could find a curacy "more suitable to his state of health." During October, Copleston wondered if Stacey might take over as curate of St Woolos, Newport, whose incumbent, Isaacson, was in debt, very inefficient and incapable of managing such an important parish. He had been persuaded to employ a curate at Newport at an income of £130, which would release him to care personally for his two other parishes which he held in plurality with Newport, namely Bettws and Malpas. Stacey had been entreated to make a trial of this parish, the bishop wanting "a man of some weight & influence", but Stacey was diffident as the place was "a scene of controversy & discord" due to the animosity of the local Nonconformists to the Established Church. In December Copleston wrote that Stacey was not gaining in health as he first expected, and added that he was under his brother's care. He was going "forewith" to Gelligaer, and felt he could not undertake Newport for a further month at least. At the end of the month he had to state it was out of the question for him to take Newport ("what is to be done, I know not", was Copleston's characteristic comment), for his illness had increased. He felt this had been caused by "weakening medicines". Matters were sufficiently better for Stacey to be in London during January and February 1834, possibly to consult a doctor (one Brodie is mentioned), while he had called on the bishop at his London address, St Paul's Deanery – as Copleston was also a pluralist – but the bishop was out and Stacey left no address.

The next mention of Stacey in this correspondence is in January 1836, when Stacey was appointed rural dean of the Llandaff deanery, which included his own parish as well as much of the Cardiff region. One wonders if this indicates that Stacey had been able to resume residence at Gelligaer, although in the following month Copleston wrote that "[a] very good arrangement has been made for Cardiff". John Webb, the absentee vicar of what was the most important town in the diocese, had appointed Stacey to be his resident curate in the parish, while Henry Lynch Blosse, later dean of Llandaff, was appointed assistant curate of the parish at a stipend of £40. In addition Stacey would allow him the gaol chaplain's salary of the same amount. Presumably Stacey was then already living in Cardiff, possibly acting as the prison chaplain, so that this new arrangement merely gave him a more formal position in the town itself. A letter noted below to Lord Bute suggests that Stacey had removed to Cardiff from Gelligaer in May 1835 and was already caring for the parish in some capacity or another. Writing to Lord Bute in April 1835 Stacey offered him his "respectful and sincere thanks for his honour in acquiescing with his desire to be appointed to the cure of Cardiff." It would never have entered his head to "aspire to it" without his lordship's sanction. It was his "sincere desire and intention" to discharge his duties "in a manner acceptable to your Lordship and to the people of Cardiff – whose welfare your Lordship takes so deep an interest." His stipend, as curate, was eventually arranged at £150 per annum, though the income of the parish was only £240. This sum, however, was the going rate for a person of Stacey's experience and ability. It appears, however, that it had been instigated by Copleston, who wished to retain the services of Stacey in his diocese and was prepared to trust him with some of the most important parishes within it, such as Newport, and now Cardiff. Although he was only the curate of the parish, that title then had a more formal ring about it than we might assume, for short of possessing the freehold of the parish and its total income, Stacey was *de facto* its incumbent.[7] We turn to his Cardiff ministry later.

Another question mark over Stacey's incumbency at Gelligaer was his treatment of his curates, and in particular the contrast between his income from the parish, from which he was an absentee, and the small amount he allowed them for a stipend. According to his own understanding, and the understanding of his generation, Stacey probably thought he was being just and honest, for his curates, mainly Welsh speakers who lacked his educational qualifications and social position, were treated more like domestic servants, or at best, as estate stewards. We need to remember that Stacey would have regarded his living at Gelligaer as a property right, which he held absolutely for so long as he retained the living. No nobleman, he might have argued, would have given his steward a percentage of his income, so why should he, as an incumbent, give his curates a higher rate than they would have obtained elsewhere? A reforming generation saw things in a different light, and felt that responsibility on the one hand, and the growing professionalism of the clergy on the other, merited a higher reward, especially when the giver was simply retaining an income for which he did no work. Sinecure positions, however, were a feature of Georgian life and of Victorian animosity. It may equally be true that Stacey was only willing to continue as curate of Cardiff, a somewhat inferior position to its vicar, on the understanding that he retained his own incumbency, thus retaining a position of authority and consequence within the diocese.

His curates at Gelligaer, however, were often men who found themselves unable to obtain anything better than humble and lowly paid positions within the Church. William Thomas, curate in the 1830s, seems to have preferred to remain at Gelligaer as curate rather than accept the Gwent parish of Llanfihangel Ystern Llewern, then valued at £50, though this was on the bishop's promise that if he remained at Gelligaer instead he would require Stacey to increase his salary to £40. "Mr Stacey," remarked the bishop, "is, I fear, no gainer by his preferment." But Thomas was to be no gainer by Stacey's absence either, for the letter announcing Stacey's removal from the parish also conveyed the information that the bishop feared that Thomas of Brithdir would "feel the want of the only check there was upon his conduct. The first offence must be the signal for removal, - I have desired Stacey to tell him so in the most solemn way." This note was repeated in another letter, but by October Thomas had been dismissed. His problem may have been drunkenness, the besetting sin of lonely clergyman during this time. A further curate, known simply as "Mr Davies", possibly the one appointed to succeed Thomas, used to ride over from Mynyddislwyn to take services at Brithdir, and by his clothing seemed to resemble "an Oriental merchant traveller". Another curate, there until 1851, is noted by his successor, William Evans, later vicar of Rhymney, as being more like a gamekeeper with his red velvet jacket and his dog and gun.

A number of letters from Stacey to Bute suggest that Stacey relied on Bute to find curates for Gelligaer. One of these, written at the time Stacey was leaving for Cardiff in May 1835, takes up Bute's offer of naming "some gentleman" for the senior curacy of Gelligaer. As this was such an "honour" he would take no steps to fill up the curacy himself. This curacy, which required a "superior" person to take the care of the parish church and the oversight of the junior curate, would have a salary of at least £100, together with a good rectory house and a well-stocked garden. He would need a competent knowledge of Welsh, for apart from part of an afternoon service and a sermon, the services and "every intercourse with the parishioners" were conducted in that language. Another, dated in January 1837, notes that L. A. Nicholls, was about to leave the "first" curacy (he had become rector of St Bride's super Ely and St George's) and, because Bute had shown such anxiety for the effectiveness of the Church and so much interest in the welfare of Gelligaer in particular, Stacey entreated him to "consider the nomination, as far as it rests with me, completely at your Lordship's command." His lordship did as requested.

By this time Bishop Ollivant had noted the circumstances of Gelligaer, and considered that Stacey's expenditure of £140 on his two curates, when the income of the parish was said to be £660, was inadequate. Like Copleston, Ollivant seems to have placed his own men in these parishes, and thus "persuaded" Stacey to appoint William Evans to the senior curacy, at a stipend of £120 plus the rectory house and garden, together with an "improved" stipend for the junior curate at Brithdir. At the same time Stacey was given a licence of non-residence from the parish upon the production of a medical certificate. Evans, as curate, performed a notable ministry in the parish, although he was unable to exercise the authority and take the initiative of an incumbent. Nevertheless, Evans restored the parish church, introduced an evening service, and redressed some of the apathy of the previous years.[8] By comparison Stacey's curacy at Cardiff had an income of £150, but he had to rent his own accommodation, probably at a high cost. By this time, therefore, the incomes of Stacey as curate of Cardiff, and that of his senior curate at Gelligaer, were almost identical when an allowance is made for housing.

Stacey remained as curate of Cardiff until 1861, caring for the parish for a period of 25 years. It was another two years before Webb, the actual vicar of Cardiff, was persuaded to resign. By the standards of his own day, though not of a subsequent reforming one, Stacey was a conscientious and successful clergyman. He took a prominent part in the foundation of the National Schools and Royal Infirmary in his parish, and publicly supported such organisations as the evangelical Church Pastoral-Aid Society and the Seamen's Mission. His pastoral ministry and his many acts of kindness were particularly noted during the presentation made to him when he left the parish. As a preacher Stacey was said to be "eloquent and impressive, commanding the attention of crowded congregations, and being gifted with a sonorous voice, he filled the church clearly and easily, so that he was justly held to be one of the most accomplished pulpit orators of his day." However, another writer considered that his preaching style was mistaken, and accused him of over-dramatising the reading of the liturgy.

St John's Church, however, had the reputation of being a society church where "physical comforts were not altogether neglected". The services were choral rather than congregational, and the interior of the church resembled more a preaching auditorium, with the pulpit at the west end of the building, rather than the conventional church we know today. Large congregations were gathered there, and though the church sat 1,000 people it was claimed it was still insufficient for the needs of the town, many of the ratepayers feeling dissatisfied that while they could not be accommodated in a church for whose purposes they paid a church rate, non-parishioners were still able to retain pews within it. Webb's successor, David Howell, was accused by one of Stacey's friends of attracting strangers from the Nonconformist chapels of Cardiff by his preaching, whereas Stacey's ministry should be judged, he claimed, by his ability to retain the same large congregation week by week. Furthermore, he accused Howell of abandoning the observance of fasts and festivals and even of some of the church ceremonies.

In addition Stacey was instrumental in the building of St Mary's Church in Bute Street, which became a new parish soon after its completion. It was built partly to cater for the overflow from St John's (Stacey writing to Lord Bute that he hoped those who lamented the lack of accommodation in that church would rent pews for themselves in the new church), and partly for the poorer population of the docks area, for whom one-third of the seats were allocated free of charge as a condition of obtaining grant-aid for its building. At the time of his leaving the parish another new church, that of St Andrew's, was in course of being built, although a dispute with its architects meant that its building was long delayed and it was finished in a rather perfunctory manner. It was anticipated that this would become a "fashionable" place of worship, being situated in a prestigious suburb.

In 1861 Stacey accepted the earl of Dunraven's offer of the living of Coety, near Bridgend. He had served as the earl's private chaplain for a number of years. This was a parish where Welsh was required, and after Stacey's death there was a noted controversy about the nomination to it of an Englishman. The controversy was so prolonged that the living lapsed into the hands of the bishop, who appointed Frederic Edmondes to it, though his own linguistic competence in Welsh was questioned. Its previous incumbent, John Harding, who was also rector of Coychurch, died in 1861, and had held the living since 1819. It was valued in 1869 at £568, though it had no parsonage, and had a population of 2,300 people. As the laws of plurality were now being rigorously enforced, and it would be unlikely that any bishop, especially Ollivant, would sanction a man holding two large and well endowed livings 20 or so miles apart, Stacey resigned Gelligaer. If we are to believe Stacey's own words we would have to suggest he was hardly able to look after one parish, yet alone two, even if the latter was managed by curates. He replied to the speeches at his presentation on leaving Cardiff that he felt that his feebleness of recent years had meant he had only been able to give an "incompetent supervision" to the "arduous and important requirements of so largely populated a parish as this." He also informed his former parishioners that he had given that parish the years of his youth, "and the strength and energy of my mature life, and such understanding and judgement as I possessed."[9] He was then 63 years of age. As Stacey continued to serve Coety for a further 12 years one must assume he was being modest about his strength.

Little is known about his ministry at Coety, though it is known he served it with the assistance of curates. On his death in April 1872 after some years of infirmity, at his own house, Oldcastle, it was said that the church at Nolton in Bridgend, part of the parish, only drew between 50 and 60 worshippers to its main Sunday service. There is some evidence, therefore, of regression in Stacey's latter years, and it may well have been that he saw Coety as a sort of retirement post, the Church not having any provision for the retirement of its clergy save by providing smaller parishes for them.[10] On the other hand it does appear that he was mourned by many as a benevolent and sympathetic man who had been a friend to all his parishioners.

It is quite clear that Stacey had the confidence and the friendship of his first bishop, some stating that he had been a former pupil of Copleston's at Oxford; the bishop having been provost of Oriel College. This is seen by Stacey's appointment as a rural dean, his selection as a preacher at the bishop's visitations, and his elevation to the post of precentor of the Cathedral, thus making him one of the senior dignitaries of the diocese.[11] There is evidence that Stacey assisted in the earlier restoration work at the cathedral, although Winton D. Wills's assertion that he did most of the administrative work involved in its restoration is unproven. In addition Stacey was also a magistrate and a deputy lieutenant. He had achieved an unshakeable power base in both diocese and local society. Although it appears that Bishop Ollivant, a reforming bishop, found Stacey's ecclesiastical position distasteful, he also found it impossible to dislodge him. Though he insisted on medical evidence that he was unfit to serve at Gelligaer, although perfectly able to perform arduous and laborious work at Cardiff, such evidence was provided, though it does suggest that the bishop was doubtful of Stacey's integrity in this matter.[12]

But if Ollivant found Stacey's position as rector of Gelligaer and curate of Cardiff a compromising one, the Welsh clergy of the diocese found it a source of considerable grievance, as we have noted already. Stacey may have insisted on his property rights as rector of Gelligaer to retain the major part of its income for himself, even though he was an absentee and ministering elsewhere, but his Welsh detractors considered that he was unfaithful to the Gospel adage of stewardship, and was a relic of all that had been bad in the unreformed Church. There was a further conflict. In spite of being able to speak Welsh, Stacey had cast his lot in with the English society of the diocese, and turned away from the native Welsh clergymen, many of whom slaved away in hard parishes with little reward. Besides this, it may have been thought that Stacey, a Tory of Tories, had been sent to Gelligaer to sort out its rebellious inhabitants, but had fled away after a number of years in dismay and perplexity. That was an overstatement, but it was easier to believe than disprove. And so there was some ridicule that the defender of the Tory establishment had been forced to retreat.

The antagonism, which was probably mutual (Stacey probably feeling that some of the Welsh clergy should never have been ordained), displayed its ugly head over the election to the proctorship for the diocesan clergy in 1861. The diocesan clergy elected two of their number as proctors to Convocation, the Church's parliament, which although it had little power, having been revived in 1852, was a useful speaking shop and a means of airing views generally. The Welsh-speaking clergy, led by the redoubtable John Griffith, rector of Merthyr, considered that the whole system of voting in the diocese was unrepresentative, Griffith declaiming that the incumbents of parishes as little as cabbage patches, mainly in the English areas of the Vale and Gwent, had the same vote as those who looked after the large industrial parishes. Curates were ineligible to vote. As a result the diocese tended to elect rural and English-speaking clergy, rather than those Welsh clergy who worked in the large and demanding parishes of the colliery districts. The elections were conducted according to parliamentary rules, with candidates proposed and seconded at a meeting called by the bishop. Some candidates not only canvassed the diocese beforehand, but also produced election manifestos.

John Harding, whom Stacey followed at Coety, had been the previous proctor. At the previous election it seems that the "hill clergy" had been unaware of the election, allowing him to be elected by default, but they had agreed that not only would they be better prepared at the next election, but would have their own candidate. On Harding's death it became known that Thomas Stacey would be proposed as a candidate. As a consequence Griffith came forward as another candidate, and both canvassed the diocese for support. Although Griffith believed that his canvass indicated that he should win the election, his opponents accused him of "a general want of Church conservatism", of equivocation regarding church rates, and a failure to teach the Catechism in his church schools. In reply Griffith suggested that had Stacey been living on his parish of Gelligaer, and attempted to collect a church rate from the colliers and miners who lived in the north of that parish, where there was neither church nor school, "he and his friends would be able to appreciate the fruitlessness of prolonging a contest when the odds were 100 to 1 against the rate."

At the election meeting Stacey was nominated by William Bruce, who mentioned his long and useful labour in the diocese, a matter which the hill clergy might have disputed. Nothing was said about his ability to speak for the Welsh Church which, by contrast, was the main claim for Griffith according to his proposer, Canon Jenkins of Dowlais. In order to do justice to the Welsh Church, he argued, it was necessary to send a Welshman to Convocation: "not only a Welshman well acquainted with the character and spirit – with the wants, all the peculiarities, and all the circumstances of the Welsh Church, but also a Welshman possessing genuine Welsh feeling – genuine Welsh sympathies, and having pure Welsh blood running in his veins." Such a man was Griffith. His seconder, John Griffiths of Neath, later archdeacon of Llandaff, added to these thoughts by stating that it was essential that their proctor was a man who had spent most of his ministry in Welsh-speaking parishes and knew their people. It would be wrong to elect a man who had only officiated in English-speaking parishes for he was not competent to speak on the question of the Welsh Church. Making an even clearer allusion to Stacey he remarked that they had no wish to go back to the old days when two or three churches were under the control of one man whose work was done by subordinate curates. There may have been some unfairness in their statement about Stacey's ability in Welsh. He would have needed it in Gelligaer, though perhaps it was not up to much and he had failed to use it thereafter.[13]

Such speeches would have filled Bishop Ollivant with alarm, for they spoke of a clear division within his diocese and indicated a major confrontation between some of his leading clergy. The Welsh clergy were close to getting their man elected, for the vote was 49 to 45, but in favour of Stacey. That Griffith, the Welsh champion, lost to Stacey, a non-resident and opulent Englishman, left the Welsh clergy with a legacy of distaste and bitterness, if not inferiority, which they never overcame. Stacey served his time in Convocation, making no impression there at all, but declined to stand at the next election of 1868 due to his age. Once again the Welsh candidate lost and an English-speaking cleric was appointed.

As a result of this election Stacey became not only the symbol of English domination in the Welsh Church, but also a symbol of wealth and prestige. By the standards of a reforming age he was wrong in retaining his parish of Gelligaer whilst serving Cardiff, but by the standards of his contemporaries he was simply acting within his rights as a property owner. The ministry he gave to Cardiff as its curate was an outstanding one, and one on which his absentee vicar's successor, the evangelical David Howell, was able to build. But it was a pity he did not retire when he left Cardiff. The reason for this could hardly have been financial. In all probability Thomas Stacey has been more maligned than he deserved, and the abuse poured on him by the Welsh-speaking clergy was more directed to the system he represented than to the ministry he gave or to the person he was.

ENDNOTES

1 CMG, 5 January 1850, p. 3, and 26 January 1850, p. 4. For the background see my article, "The Copleston Memorial", *Morgannwg*, 41 (1997) 38-50.

2 Jean E. McCann, *Thomas Howell and the School at Llandaff* (Cowbridge, 1972), pp. 58, 226-7.

3 CMG, 1 April 1848, p. 3.

4 J. H. Matthews, *Cardiff Records* (Cardiff, 1905), V 331; S. W. Allen, *Reminiscences* (Cardiff, 1918), p. 142.

5 Stacey to Bute, 4 October 1826, NLW, Bute Papers, L78/4; WM, 22 April 1872, p. 3.

6 This emerges in his speech to the National School at Cardiff in which he told its pupils that they were to be dutiful to their master and mistress, loving and obedient to their parents, and to remember that God would require an account of their fidelity to their duties: WM, 12 October 1861, p. 5.

7 Copleston to Bruce Knight, undated but probably June 1830, and 6 February 1834, CL, numbers K134 and K165; Roger L. Brown (ed.), *The Letters of Edward Copleston, Bishop of Llandaff, 1828-1849* (Cardiff, 2003), letters of Copleston to Bruce Knight of 10 July, 4 August 7 October, 18 and 31 December 1833, 28 January 1834, 27 January and 26 February 1836, pp. 130-1, 134, 140, 146, 148, 152, 197, 202; Stacey to Bute, 3 April 1835, Bute Papers, L78/46; WM, 22 April 1872, p. 3.

8 Brown, *Letters of Edward Copleston,* letters of Copleston to Bruce Knight, 13 January 1830, 10 July, 4 August, 7 October 1833, pp. 75, 130-1, 134, 140; and letter to Traherne, 31 January 1837, p. 240; Stacey to Bute, 3 April and 12 May 1835, 23 and 31 January 1837, Bute Papers, L78/46, 71, and L80/13, 18; NLW, Glyn Simon Deposit of December 1968, Box 1: Llandaff Diocesan Memorandum Book 1849-68; T. J. Jones, *William Evans, Rhymney* (Lampeter, n.d.), pp. 13-14; Kathleen Lewis, *In the Steps of St Gwladys* (1959), p. 7. The Ecclesiastical Revenues Report of 1835 gave the cost of the two curates as £140.

9 Roger L. Brown, *David Howell* (Denbigh, 1998), pp. 43-51, 75; CMG, 5 October 1861, p. 5; 12 October 1861, p. 12; WM, 22 April 1872, p. 3; Stacey to Bute, 31 January 1837, Bute Papers, L80/18.

10 See my *Reclaiming the Wilderness* (Welshpool, 2001), pp. 177-8.

11 Copleston to Bruce Knight, undated but probably June 1830, and 18 August 1836, CL, numbers K134 and K283. Copleston did not agree with Stacey's interpretation of "the Rock" being St Peter, ibid., 23 April 1836: ibid., number K267.

12 Stacey to Bute, 31 January 1837, Bute Papers, L80/18: Winton D. Wills, "The Established Church in the Diocese of Llandaff", *Welsh History Review*, 4 (1969) 248-9.

13 See my forthcoming biography of John Griffith of Merthyr Tydfil.

One of Stacey's sons, Cyril, acted as his father's curate for some time in Cardiff and as chaplain of the prison, but appears to have had no clerical post from the 1860s onwards. Another son, Francis Edmund, a barrister, rented Llandough Castle, having inherited much wealth from his uncle, and died there in 1885: H. M. Thomas, "Llandough Castle", *Morgannwg*, 33 (1989) 28-9. A son-in-law of Stacey, Charles R. Knight, a squarson of Tythegston Court, succeeded him as proctor.

2
THE WORSHIPFUL CHANCELLOR
Hugh Williams of Bassaleg and Radyr

Hugh Williams was a pluralist who survived into mid-Victorian times, as well as chancellor of the diocese of Llandaff. This meant that he was an ecclesiastical judge, at a time when these courts were becoming more and more archaic. It may be said that Hugh Williams represented in his person the old regime of the Georgian Church, even though he lived during a period of considerable Church reform.

A Pembrokeshire man, Hugh Williams was the son of George Williams, "gentleman" of Gumfreston and later of East Williamston. Hugh Williams was educated at Jesus College, Oxford, of which he was a scholar and from which he subsequently took his MA degree. East Williamston is four miles from Tenby, and it is possible that his father was a professional man in that town.[1] Hugh Williams was born in 1794 or 1795, but the date and place of his ordination is not known, save that it was not by the bishop of Llandaff. As the records for the diocese of St David's are incomplete for this period, it may be that he was ordained into his native diocese and served his title there, but in 1822 he was licensed as curate of Sully, in 1824 to Radyr, and in 1829 to Roath and Peterstone super Ely. These two livings were in the hands of different incumbents, and one wonders how Williams was physically able to do duty at both churches on a Sunday. In all probability he acted as a resident curate in these parishes, taking sole charge of them for absentee incumbents. This would certainly have been true for Radyr at this time.[2]

By the early 1830s it seems reasonably clear that Williams had become a protégé of Bishop Copleston of Llandaff, his diocesan bishop. The circumstances by which this happened are not known, but clearly Williams's ability as an administrator and as a diligent pastor would have brought him the bishop's favour. Copleston was to write later that Williams "would prove an incomparable secretary", although what organisation the bishop had in mind is not recorded.[3]

In October 1831 Hugh Williams was preferred to the parish of
Llanarth, near Abergavenny. It was linked with the parochial charge
of Bettws Newydd, and in the patronage of the chapter of Llandaff
Cathedral. As Copleston was an active bishop, suggesting to patrons
the names of possible candidates, the appointment would have been
influenced by him. The income was considerable for a Welsh living,
at £285, and the population around 750 in all.

It is quite clear, however, that Williams continued to serve the
Roath curacy after his induction to Llanarth, much to the
disappointment and annoyance of his bishop. This emerges in a letter
of March 1834 from Copleston to Bruce Knight, his vicar-general in
the diocese, as Copleston also served as dean of St Paul's, London,
where he resided for most of the year. In it he wrote that while the
vicar of Roath, Calvert R. Jones (the photographer who was also
rector of Loughor from 1829-36), was not likely to resign the living,
nor could he be compelled to resign it, he would gladly licence a
curate to serve both St John's Church, Cardiff, and Roath. There were
two stipulations to this, however, namely that Hugh Williams was
prepared to quit the Roath curacy, and Knight did not think a Welsh-
speaker was needed at Roath, even though Williams had insisted on
this necessity. Calvert Jones continued as an absentee vicar of Roath
until 1844, though it appears that the patron of the living, the
evangelical marquess of Bute, was anxious to have a resident
incumbent.[4]

It is obvious that Williams preferred to live in the urban setting of
Cardiff, rather than in the rural tranquillity of Gwent, and
consequently he employed a curate, William Price, to serve Llanarth
for him. Copleston had two concerns, however, about Williams's
tenure of Llanarth; namely, his non-residence, and that his
"admirable" curate who was "so able, so meritorious, so assiduous,
should only have a small share of the profits." In all probability Price
had a stipend of about £40 or £50 per annum, and this, thought the
bishop, could only create "discontent". "Do not suppose," he added,
"that I am dissatisfied about Hugh Williams, but I have all the
discredit of it." In the subsequent correspondence between Copleston
and Bruce Knight, Copleston notes how he endeavoured to find
various means of persuading Williams to "dispose" of Llanarth
satisfactorily even to the extent of offering him more valuable
livings. He made clear that he expected Williams to reside as a
condition of appointment. In August 1832 the parish of Newland, in
Gloucestershire, but in the gift of the bishop of Llandaff, become
vacant. At first Copleston had offered it to his friend, J. E. Tyler, who

was rector of the vastly populated parish of St Giles in London, on the assumption he would be "sick ... of London life". He pointed out that its population of 4,000 was much smaller than the 36,000 of his London parish, although its income of £400 significantly less and subject to about £100 outgoings, including £50 for a curate. Tyler had declined the offer, even though the neighbourhood was excellent, the house good, and the people "had a very kind and favourable disposition towards the Church." Copleston wondered, therefore, if Williams would be prepared to take it, in which case he would be able to dispose of Llanarth to a resident incumbent.

Another possibility presented itself that same month, as it seems that either Williams was not interested in Newland or Copleston had second thoughts about offering it to him. Writing once more about his concern regarding the "blemish" of Williams's non-residence at Llanarth, the bishop wished that he could be provided with a living "in which he might reside - for I have a great respect for him and I know he would do his duty conscientiously wherever he may be." Allegations had been made against the junior vicar of Llandaff, Lewis, who was responsible for the pastoral work of the large parish served by the cathedral church, the senior vicar being more concerned with the services at the cathedral itself. These allegations were sufficiently serious to warrant investigation, and the bishop was required to establish a commission to do so. Prichard, the senior vicar, had asked to be excused from serving on the commission "for obvious reasons", but Bruce Knight was an obvious candidate, and Copleston considered that Williams, living in the immediate neighbourhood, ought to be another and, as another letter declared, could hardly refuse after the favours he had received from the chapter. He had written much the same about Williams being offered the post of rural dean. "The discharge of this office," he wrote, "may furnish a strong reason for the indulgence he enjoys of residence at Llandaff." In fact Copleston questioned whether his office as surrogate was sufficient "to justify an irregularity in respect of residence." It was this suggestion about the commission which prompted Copleston to think of Williams in another connection, namely as the obvious candidate for the post of junior vicar, "if, as is probable, we get rid of Lewis." Lewis, however, was "exculpated", and the allegations made against him proved to be false and mischievous.

In December of that year John Llewellin, the vicar of Marcross in the vale of Glamorgan, died, and once again Copleston considered offering it to Hugh Williams, wanting to sound him out "without

committing myself". He did not think the "exchange" would suit
him, although he felt that it was "precisely the sort of living to be
given to a man whose services are valuable, but are ill-paid,
elsewhere." Matters continued until February 1834, when Horatio
James Thomas, who had followed Williams as curate of Radyr as
well as being his brother-in-law, was appointed to Pentyrch as vicar.
"Hugh Williams," wrote Copleston, "will succeed him at Radir."
There is no indication that he did, however, for he appears to have
continued at Roath, unless he served both as curate. The vicar of
Radyr from 1789 until his death in 1837 was Andrews Windsor, who
became the seventh earl of Plymouth in 1833, but in spite of his
elevation and his advanced age, he declined to resign the living as
Copleston had hoped he would.

The bishop persisted in trying to obtain a new living for Williams,
perhaps weighing up the need to have a capable administrator in the
Cardiff area against the offence of non-residence in an outlying but
lucrative parish. By 1836 the bishop determined to act on the latter,
and in February he reported to Bruce Knight that he had written to
Williams on the subject of his non-residence, adding that he "seems
to dread the idea of going to Llanarth." However, the bishop's
suggestion of an exchange with the incumbent of "Bishopstone" had
been rejected "on the ground that it was so much out of the way, so
disagreeable a situation, and inferior in value." This was probably
Bishopston in Gower, in the bishop's patronage, whose value was
£248 and whose incumbent, David Jones, appointed in 1831,
remained in post until 1891. Copleston meant by "exchange" that he
would offer David Jones another living in his gift rather than require
him to take Llanarth, which was in the patronage of the chapter of
Llandaff in any case, although it appears that the chapter was quite
content for the bishop to take over patronage. Dingestow is
mentioned in later correspondence, as was Copleston's desire to offer
Llanarth to Price, the curate of the parish, had the "exchange taken
place". Williams's excuse for non-residence is also recorded in this
correspondence. His excuse that he acted as a surrogate of the
diocese was not considered a sufficient one by Copleston. A
surrogate was a legal official, working under the direction of the
chancellor of the diocese, and mainly involved in the issuing of
marriage licences. In fact Williams was deputy chancellor of the
diocese.

Two days later Copleston wrote again to Bruce Knight, almost in
despair. "Hugh Williams clings to Llandaff," he wrote, perhaps
indicating that he lived in the city itself. "He has written to me at

great length", he continued, "alleging among other things that his conscience is quite easy about Llanarth, because there is so good a curate." Copleston could see the other side of the question, however, and wrote that "I know the curate's merits, & am anxious to reward them. It is not very generous to keep a man in a laborious & important & ill-paid office, because he does his duty well – when others live at their ease – & enjoy the greatest part of the pay." Price, the curate, he added, would have the first claim on his limited patronage over all the Monmouthshire clergy for "[h]e has filled an anxious post ably, & conscientiously, & usefully. The time for his reward is come."

Although in April of that year the bishop was prepared to offer Price the small living of Dingestow, on condition he remained as curate of Llanarth, by June the aged incumbent of Bassaleg was thought to have died. Thomas Leyson, a Wiltshire man, had been appointed to that parish on the insistence of Charles Morgan of Tredegar, the local squire, in 1781. The then bishop, the reforming Shute Barrington, had wished to give the living to a deserving curate, as his patronage was scarce. However, Morgan claimed that the bishops had always honoured his family's recommendations for the living, and contradicted the bishop's opinion that Leyson, a Wiltshire man, was disqualified as he was not Welsh-speaking by persuading his nominee to promise that he would learn the language. He therefore obtained his wish, and his friend and relation came from college to serve the living for the next 57 years. Whether he fulfilled his promise is not known. Upon the rumour of his death Mrs Hall of Llanover, later Lady Llanover, solicited the living for one of her favourites, Evans, but Copleston disliked the thought and replied that as Leyson's death had been so long expected other arrangements had been made which could not be disturbed.

The rumour of his death was in fact untrue, and Leyson lived on for another two years, dying in 1838. Williams applied for and obtained the living of Bassaleg, on condition that he was resident and resigned his living at Llanarth, while Price, his curate, was appointed to succeed him in the living.[5] And yet, as we note later, Williams had obtained the living of Radyr in the previous year. Bassaleg is described in the 1842 *Clergy List* as having an income of £343 and a population of 1,664. Williams appears to have run the parish on his own, without the aid of a curate. Little is known about his ministry in the parish, although one story survived in local memory. In 1861 Williams went to order his meat from the local butcher's shop in the village and was met in the doorway by a local man who said that all

parsons and Baptists ought to be hanged. Although restrained by the
police he still threatened to knock Williams's nose off. We also know
that when a new church was built at Risca, which had at one time
been a chapelry of Bassaleg, Williams collected monies in order to
purchase a stained glass east window. Williams remained as vicar of
Bassaleg and resident there until his death in 1877.[6]

From 1830-45 Williams acted as deputy chancellor of the diocese,
which meant that he assisted the chancellor, Bruce Knight (who has
been already mentioned) as judge of the consistory court. It dealt
with matters relating to probate, clergy discipline, as well as actions
of defamation. The chancellor was also responsible for the issuing of
marriage licences (through his surrogates), faculties for church
buildings and dispensations. Some of these powers were lost as a
result of legislation in 1857, which removed to the secular courts
their matrimonial and testamentary jurisdiction. On the death of
Bruce Knight in 1845 Williams became chancellor, and was entitled
to be described as "His Worshipful".

****

In all probability it was the burden of this office, requiring constant
attendance at Llandaff, which led Williams to apply for the parish of
Radyr, a neighbouring parish to the cathedral, when Andrews
Windsor, its aged, absentee and neglectful incumbent, finally died in
February 1837. Copleston wrote to his friend, John Montgomery
Traherne, that Williams had applied to Mr Clive for the living, and
he hoped he would obtain it. Its value was £59 (together with an
augmentation of £58 from the patron which was probably a voluntary
offering) and its population in 1842 a mere 227 souls, although it was
to grow significantly during Williams's long tenure. It may be that
Copleston disregarded his holding of this parish in plurality when he
appointed him to Bassaleg because it was so small, had no vicarage
house, and also because Williams's duties at the cathedral as deputy
chancellor enabled him to visit it on a fairly frequent basis.[7]

In 1849-50 after the death of Bishop Copleston, a move was set on
foot in the diocese to establish an exhibition in his memory for the
son of a diocesan clergyman at Oriel College, of which Copleston
had been a noteworthy provost. Sir Benjamin Hall, later Lord
Llanover, publicly disagreed with this, alleging that the bishop had
paid scant regard to the needs of his diocese's Welsh inhabitants, and
had permitted non Welsh-speaking incumbents to be instituted to
Welsh-speaking parishes. The controversy soon became one about

the utility and value of the Welsh language. J. C. Conybeare, a London barrister and a son of the then dean of Llandaff, argued that the language was a "deplorable bar to popular education and improvement" and "must die out before the speech of the conquering and more civilised race ..." This may well have aroused the ire of Hugh Williams, an ardent Welshman, but it was suspected by many that he had supplied Hall with much of the information he had used to forward his case against Copleston's patronage, which was in turn rigorously defended by Archdeacon Thomas Williams, Conybeare, and H. A. Bruce, later Lord Aberdare. Bruce, in the course of the controversy, denied that Williams's appointment as chancellor had been occasioned by the fact that he spoke Welsh. Rather it was due to his legal knowledge. The duties of his office, he alleged, were "not performed a whit better or the worse for his knowledge of Welsh." The controversy is recorded elsewhere, suffice to say Hugh Williams discovered that Conybeare was writing both under his own name and that of the *non de plume* "Nemesis", and then quoting his *non de plume* letters in the letters written under his own name. Williams, concurring with the words of another newspaper letter writer that these former letters were "of low invective and personal abuse", commented in a further public letter on this disclosure: "[h]ere we have a person in the position of a gentleman, a member of the bar, and dating his letter from Lincoln's Inn – that nest of learning and special pleading – writing letters of the nature described, in a provincial journal, and screening himself under a fictitious signature; and then writing another letter, subscribed with his own name, in which he applauds those written by himself under the fictitious signature", all the while endeavouring to deceive people into believing that these were two different people. Conybeare, stung into a retaliatory reply, tried to dismiss his imposition as being of little significance, but made some strong personal attacks upon his accuser, writing:

> I shall not seek to learn whether Sir Benjamin Hall derives his *mis*information on ecclesiastical matters connected with the Diocese of Llandaff from its present chancellor. The ties of gratitude which bound that dignitary to the late bishop, would seem to preclude such an assumption ... I have now done with the Chancellor. Should he ever again be treated as a proper person for the episcopal bench, I shall, on public grounds, do my best to save him the pain of a "*nolo episcopari*" by investigating the professional claims of Sir B. Hall's proposed pattern for Cambrian priests. I shall, for instance, ask why the holder of as

important a cure as Bassaleg, not being (to borrow once again his own phraseology) a "duplex personage" should still retain a second and distant vicarage? Also why, if it suits him to be a pluralist, he should not at least employ a whole curate to himself, and so secure two Sunday services for Radyr, which has at present only a fractional interest in the ministrations of the locomotive curate, who is forced to divide his labours between the curacies of Radyr and Cadoxton, and the chaplaincy of the Union Workhouse? As such questions have but little bearing on the statements so rashly impugned, as I wish to have no more than I can help to do with the chancellor, I shall, till he be again backed for a bishopric, leave him to settle the question of Radyr with his one-third share of a curate, and such fractional portion of conscience as may best suit him. And now, cordially thanking him for terminating by his uncourteous tone and coarse style of his Chancellarian epistle, an acquaintance which his ecclesiastical connection with a near relative of my own would otherwise have forbidden me to drop, hoping that he might learn rightly to appreciate the *peculiar estimation* with which he is so generally regarded throughout the diocese, and wishing him, when next he is named as a likely candidate for a bishopric, all the success that the *depth of his scholarship*, his attainments in literature, and the *independence of his character* merit. I take my final leave of him ...

The expression "attainments in literature" alludes to an earlier letter of Conybeare, in which he alleged that Williams's pronunciation of "Crichton Stuart" was proof that "he had not cultivated general literature with sufficient assiduity to eradicate his Celtic fondness for harsh guttural sounds."

David Davies, the incumbent of Risca, came to Williams's defence, his letter appearing in the next edition of the *Cardiff and Merthyr Guardian*. When Williams became vicar of Bassaleg, Davies wrote, he found himself entitled to the vicarial tithes of Risca, which was a small perpetual curacy valued at £90 although serving a population of 2,000 people. Because poverty forced him (Davies) to serve another cure, he was only able to perform one Sunday service at Risca. However, when Williams was appointed as chancellor, instead of resigning Radyr, "which he was conscious he might be expected to do", he proposed to the bishop that he should endow Risca with those vicarial tithes, valued at £54, on condition that an assistant resident curate should be appointed, and a second service established. It was a "sacrifice ... seldom made by men with large families to support and educate," Davies continued, and he claimed that Williams's action had received Copleston's "highest approbation and praise". Although this had little relevance to Conybeare's attack on Williams as a pluralist, Davies went on to state that the living of Radyr was worth £117, of which he gave his curate £60, £10 more than he himself received when he was curate there, and added, "I need not say what is the balance left to the vicar towards subscriptions &c, in Glamorganshire on account of the living of Radyr, nor whether the income he derives from it is not thus applied with greater benefit to the Church and religion than if he had resigned it."

Conybeare, even though he had professed to have taken leave of Williams, could not avoid another stab at him, taking umbrage at Davies's assertions. He queried the actual amount of the vicarial tithes of Radyr, and suggested its income was between £130 and £140 (in this he was correct as the tithes had been commuted for a generous tithe rent charge in 1848). He even disputed Davies's assertion that the remainder of the income, after the "locomotive curate" had been paid, was used for the benefit of that parish or the greater benefit of the Church, while he noted that the income Williams had given up was the smallest of his various enrolments. The greatest "boon" the chancellor could bestow upon that parish, Conybeare quoted from a letter of a person acquainted with it, would be to resign it, "so that it might have a pastor to itself and of its own, who would know his flock, and he known of them." Indeed, he thought there was a legal case to require his resignation. Under the Pluralities Act of 1 & 2 Vic. c. 106, which he claimed was in force when Williams was appointed to Radyr, the various privileges allowed to certain dignitaries under that act only allowed them to hold two livings provided they were within ten statute miles of one another, measured from church to church along the nearest road or pathway. He had no idea what statement the chancellor may have made to the bishop regarding this distance, but while the distance was 9¾ miles as the crow flies, there was no road or footpath that would bring the two churches within ten statute miles of one another. He felt that Williams, as chancellor, was bound "to be well informed and *scrupulous* on such a point as this" and should resign the living of Radyr as it could not be legally held by him. A footnote suggested that the "pious and conscientious chancellor" could not have held these two livings, the chancellorship and the vicarial tithes of Risca, all together at once, and thus his mighty sacrifice was simply making "a virtue of necessity". He ended with a sample from "Simple

Stories, a new Child's Book", which contained a story as to how Hugh Bassaleg, a pupil on Dame Church's school, managed to cheat both Paul Risca and Peter Radyr of their share of cake, and yet convinced Paul Risca (at first) that he was a generous person. Another person is introduced into the story, a boy with the nickname Jelly-jar, who was a great glutton and ate everyone's share of preserves. This person is described as a cousin of Hugh's, and one wonders if it may relate to Thomas Stacey, precentor of the cathedral, and the absentee rector of Gelligaer?

The dispute is interesting as it provides some evidence that Williams was regarded as an undeserving pluralist in the diocese, which occasioned the ridicule and scorn of a well-connected and observant outsider.[8]

Radyr parish was served by a host of curates who, because Radyr at this time did not justify a full-time curate, undoubtedly doubled up by serving another parish, hence Conybeare's cheap jibe about a "locomotive curate". William David, writing in 1895 about the Radyr of his childhood, forty or so years earlier, recalled that the Church "had only the barest foothold in the parish. There was no resident clergyman, no curate even came into the parish to visit the sick, to collect and teach the children the Church catechism, to seek out candidates for Confirmation, to encourage the lukewarm to come to Church, or to instruct any thirsting to be guided into the way of righteousness." He adds that the service was bilingual, either with an English sermon and service and Welsh lessons, or vice versa. The regular congregation consisted of his family, the parish clerk and the sexton. Nevertheless parliamentary enquiries of 1850 reveal that the curate, John Jones, also served as curate of St Fagans, where he resided, and there was one Sunday service, taken alternatively in Welsh and English. The religious census of 1851 presents a better picture. There were now two services each Sunday, the morning one attracting on average 20 people plus the same number of children, with 25 attending in the afternoon. Further evidence suggests that the second service may have been held at Tynant, opposite to the present bridge from the A470 to Radyr, which catered for the workers from the Pentyrch Ironworks at that place, and for which service Mr Booker, the owner, added £10 to the stipend. However, by 1868 the curate of Radyr was also serving as curate of Tongwynlais at the top end of the parish of Whitchurch, for John Parry, the curate, writing that his stipend for serving Tongwynlais and performing an English service there was only £20, requested a grant from the Ecclesiastical Commissioners. He failed to mention, however, that he also served

Radyr, for which he received another £60, and consequently received a polite but negative reply.

Williams continued as vicar of this parish until his death. His successor, Henry James Humphreys, was told by Bishop Ollivant that the parish was in a most unsatisfactory state. There was no parsonage, the parish church was at the wrong end of the parish, and it had grown substantially with the development of industry at the Pentyrch end of the parish and the emergence of a railway depot at its centre. It is hard to refute Conybeare's accusations about Williams's neglect, and it is clear that the parish would then have been in a far more satisfactory state had Williams resigned it in the 1850s. The new incumbent was hard put to find new endowments for the living, to build a vicarage house, a mission hall and a school room, and to lay plans for the building of a new church in the centre of the parish.[9]

****

Williams's work as the chancellor of the diocese, to which he was appointed in 1845, is not well recorded, although two cases did achieve some publicity. One concerned the will of Edward Edmunds, Esq.. His son disputed the will, even though he was an executor, on the grounds of his father's insanity. The proctors (equivalent to barristers) had made their arguments at a previous court, and Williams now had to deliver his judgment. Williams prefaced his remarks by regretting the considerable time the case had taken. This was partly due to the defendant's first proctor giving up the case at a most inconvenient time in its proceedings, and the necessity of finding a substitute, but also due to the large number of witnesses the defendant had called. These cases were always difficult, especially when a brother and a sister, both of the most respectable stations in life, disputed their father's will, and especially so in this case when the son's case rested on proving the insanity of his father. Having heard the evidence Williams declared for the sanity of the father and the validity of the will. A further case, heard at the same time and mentioned in the same report, concerned a will where one witness, a workman, claimed it was not his "mark" which had been affixed to the will. As this raised the whole question of the validity of the will the matter was adjourned for further investigation.[10]

In 1854 there was another case which attracted wider publicity and unfavourable comment, especially because it was seen as another example of the lack of professionalism in these courts and their retention of medieval procedures. This was the case of Charlotte

Jones, of Penydarren, Merthyr Tydfil, who was prosecuted in the consistory court of Llandaff for alleged slander against Louise Roberts, the wife of the agent for the Penydarren Iron Company. Charlotte Jones declined to appear in court on four separate occasions, and at the last court was warned – presumably by letter – about the consequences. However, she had attended the office of the proctor of the "party complainant" and was told, in both English and Welsh, what she should do to oppose the case. She was warned that she risked imprisonment if she did not attend the court, or sign a recantation and pay costs assessed at £6 8s.10d. Upon her eventual refusal to do either she was ordered to be held in custody. The complainants had made it clear that they were disposed to forgo all the costs, save for those they had paid out of their own pocket, provided she submitted to the rules of the court which would have enabled her to be set at liberty. Their offer had been declined.

A letter from one William Simons to the bishop of Llandaff, Alfred Ollivant, dated 22 September 1854, stated that Mrs Jones had been in custody at Cardiff Prison since 10 April, was extremely poor, and had several small children. He pointed out that in order to appear in court she would have had to employ a proctor, and this would have meant her family would have had to go without bread. The consistory court alone, of all courts, could subject a person to such a lengthy imprisonment for this cause. Simons begged the bishop to obtain her discharge and to either abolish or reform these ecclesiastical tribunals. The bishop's reply was not helpful. While he regretted that the woman had not acted upon the advice she had been given to sign a recantation, he pointed out that if people persisted in contemptuously defying the authority of the court, the consequences to them would be very serious. Expressing his sorrow that the woman had been so ill-advised, he pointed out he had no authority to intervene in the matter.

Simons replied. He was not averring in his letter to the rights and wrongs of the case in point, though he understood the woman denied issuing slanderous words, but rather to the cruelty of so long an imprisonment which was due to the delay in hearing the case. He wished not only to expose the barbarous nature of the consistory court's right to force a defendant's appearance before it, but also to challenge the bishop's assumption of the woman's contumacy, whereas her only "offence" was her inability through poverty to employ a proctor to defend her. She had been "incarcerated", he pointed out, because of this inability, and for nothing else. Poverty may be an inconvenience but it was not a crime. The consistory court was supposed to be under the guardianship of the bishop, and he found it impossible to think that anyone could countenance a judicial system which was attended by such practical horrors and undue severity. A note by Ollivant on this letter suggests that a subscription was entered into to enable this woman to pay some of her expenses, but the money had been otherwise spent.

Ollivant's more formal reply of 26 September indicated that he would rejoice to see a reform in the practice of the ecclesiastical courts, now under the consideration of parliament, but meanwhile the courts had to comply with the rules. The chancellor, Hugh Williams, was well known to him and he had every confidence that he would not inflict any sentence but that sanctioned by law and as the circumstances of the case required. Simons was not satisfied, however, and replied that the proceedings had been contrary to the principles of justice and mercy. Hugh Williams, shown this correspondence by Ollivant, replied with gratitude for the bishop's excellent answers to Mr Simons, who, if a lawyer, probably wrote with "not entirely disinterested feelings", though certainly in ignorance of the circumstances of the case. The woman had received the "means" to enable her to appear by a proctor in court, and even if such means was not forthcoming, she could have pleaded poverty in the court had she appeared in obedience to the citation. Warned of the consequences of not appearing, she was ill-advised and had used strong language in bidding defiance to the court. She was sent to gaol by a writ to the sheriff for her wilful obstinacy in refusing to comply with the order of the court when it was within her power to do so without difficulty. Personally, he disliked defamation cases and discouraged them from coming to court. If Mr Simons was a lawyer then he ought to know the procedures which would enable Mrs Jones to purge her contempt.

Simons was a lawyer and was in fact acting for Mrs Jones, so his letters were designed to mislead. It became clear that he was using her case to press forward the passing of an act relating to the ecclesiastical courts then before parliament, as well as to embarrass the Church by what would appear to be a harsh sentence and an unsympathetic attitude. He thus chose to prolong her imprisonment by refusing to take the steps which would lead to her release. He wrote on Charlotte Jones's behalf a petition published in the *Star of Gwent* on 3 March 1855, which noted her circumstances, her ignorance of the law and its procedures, and the length of her imprisonment. An editorial in the same paper called upon parliament to step in and break up "the whole system of our abominable ecclesiastical laws", and described these courts as "tyrannical, merciless, and implacable."

The various papers of the case were sent by Ollivant to Lord Brougham, Dr Phillimore and Mr Bright, all of whom were engaged in the parliamentary review of the ecclesiastical courts, as it appears that this case was as embarrassing to Ollivant and Williams personally as it was in revealing the powers these courts possessed. During the various stages of this review, which led to the Ecclesiastical Courts Act of 1855 (18 & 19 Vict. c. 41) which took away their cognisance of defamation, it was stated that there was no appeal to any higher court from these cases. It was also made clear by Lord Brougham that this particular case had suggested the propriety of the measure, but he fully accepted that the judge of the Llandaff ecclesiastical court had no alternative but to pursue the course which had been taken. His words, quoted by Hansard, are as follows:

> with respect to the case of Charlotte Jones, a woman who has been incarcerated for a long period under such a sentence, he (Lord Brougham) might be allowed to remind their Lordships that in presenting her petition the other day, he made no allusion whatsoever reflecting on the Ecclesiastical Court which had pronounced that sentence, and to which the same remark would apply as he had just used with reference to the chancellor of the Diocese of Carlisle – that they were passive in the matter, and could not act otherwise than as they did. It had gone forth, however, that some remarks were made against the particular court by which she was sentenced, whereas the contrary was the fact; and in the other House of Parliament, when the Bill was brought forward by his learned friend (Dr Phillimore), the case of Charlotte Jones was never mentioned. The chancellor of that diocese, Dr Williams, was, he understood, one of the most respected members of the Church, and had been for 35 years in high ecclesiastical office; and during the whole of that time there had not only been no appeal against, but no exception taken to any of his proceedings.

Charlotte Jones did not sign a recantation until 7 July 1855, when she was released from her imprisonment, a victim as much of the reformers as her own actions. This other case noted in Brougham's speech related to a woman at Carlisle, who, having been found guilty of defamation, and unable to pay the costs awarded against her, was imprisoned "without hope of release." Lord St Leonards, noting both cases, commented that there were some persons who were determined to be made martyrs.

And thus a judicial case heard before Hugh Williams had national repercussions, and helped break down the rights and privileges held by the ecclesiastical courts. Two years later their matrimonial and testamentary jurisdictions were ended by legislation.[11]

Ollivant appointed Hugh Williams as his Welsh examining chaplain. His job was to examine all those candidates for ordination who professed proficiency in the Welsh language, and also, in a wider aspect, to advise the bishop on matters relating to the Welsh language in his diocese, such as the need for a Welsh-speaking cleric in a particular parish. In these cases he might also be required to examine the patron's nominee in his proficiency in the Welsh language, according to the procedures laid down by legislation. As noted before, Williams had advised Bishop Copleston previously in this latter area, insisting that Roath needed a Welsh-speaking incumbent, to the annoyance of its patron, Lord Bute. Although the bishop accepted that Williams, as the curate of the parish, was in a position to assess its need, he was surprised to learn that his then chancellor and vicar-general, Bruce Knight, disagreed with Williams. Copleston concluded that "I am myself inclined to suspect that those who have both languages may set a higher value than is fair on the attainment, & overrate the necessity or the importance of it in particular cases."[12]

Seventeen years later, in December 1851, Williams received the gratitude of Lady Augusta, the wife of Sir Benjamin Hall, later Lady Llanover, a vigorous campaigner for the use of the Welsh language within the Church in Wales. Writing to Thomas James, a Welsh cleric who belonged to the Association of Welsh Clergy in the West Riding of Yorkshire, she complained bitterly about Ollivant's appointments to Welsh-speaking parishes. The inhabitants of Llanfoist had memorialised the bishop requesting he would not appoint an Englishman or any person unable to perform divine service in the Welsh language to their parish. As a result the bishop had appointed a commission to examine the matter. The former incumbent, Lady Llanover declared, was a Welshman and ministered as such to the sick in their homes, but he was "too venial to have Welsh duty to offend the English higher classes". But she claimed that in order to secure "an answer in the *negative*" the bishop had deliberately appointed to the commission the two English incumbents of two Welsh neighbouring parishes, each presented to their livings by the earl of Abergavenny who was the patron of Llanfoist;

Archdeacon Crawley of Monmouth, "an English man totally ignorant of Welsh and detesting all things belonging to it"; "a distant Rector who knew nothing of the language and the Parish", and Hugh Williams, "the only real Welshman out of the five". Hugh Williams, however, had written "a strong remonstrance to the Bishop stating that he had examined the witnesses in Welsh, and that he had not a doubt of the necessity of a Welsh Incumbent; that one man had assured him he went weekly to a Welsh Baptist Chapel in another parish because there was no Welsh in the Church which otherwise he would attend; also that there were many Welsh chapels in the adjoining Parishes attended by many of the Inhabitants of Llanfoist." Only one other member of the commission thought it was desirable that the incumbent should speak Welsh, while another said there was no need whatever for a Welshman. Thus the bishop got his majority, and the earl of Abergavenny's nominee, the English-speaking William Corfield, was appointed.

Soon after this the living of Michaelstone-y-Fedw became vacant, continued her ladyship. The former incumbent, an Englishman, had not "done any thing in Welsh public or private for about thirty years!!" Its patron, Colonel Tynte, "a ruined non-resident proprietor", nominated an Englishman. As the noise about Llanfoist had caused the bishop some unease, the bishop refused Tynte's nominee as he possessed no Welsh qualifications. Tynte then presented another person, "a very illiterate Welshman". The bishop sent him to Williams for examination in Welsh, and he was pronounced incompetent. As a result the bishop refused to institute, and placed an Englishman to do English duty in the vacant parish, with the result that not one word of Welsh had been heard in the church during the time it had been under the bishop's control. In 1852 William Jenkins was instituted to the living, in spite of Williams having declared him incompetent in Welsh. Jenkins had appealed to the archbishop of Canterbury. as the legislation permitted, and the archbishop had appointed Dr Lewellin, principal of St David's College, Lampeter, to examine him. Lewellin declared him competent, and he was thus instituted. The Association of Welsh Clergy in the West Riding of Yorkshire commented on this case in these words: "[h]ere is, therefore, an instance of the deliberate decision of a good Welsh speaking scholar being set aside by that of a person whose knowledge of Welsh is probably small, and the Archbishop reversing the Bishop of Llandaff's refusal to induct on the same unjustifiable ground."[13]

Some years later there was another explosion in the long

controversy between Sir Benjamin Hall and St David's College, Lampeter, which Hall regarded as an English institution training English-orientated clergy for the Church in Wales, instead of providing the Welsh training and environment he thought it should. As the papers relating to this controversy are contained within the papers of Lord John Russell it may be assumed that Hall had brought the matter to the attention of the premier. Comments made by the bishop of Llandaff regarding the quality of the Welsh ordinands produced by Lampeter had reached Hall, and he alleged as a result that there ought to be an enquiry into the management of the college and in particular into the Welsh instruction it provided. In proof of this he alleged that young men who were known to be unable to spell the Welsh language correctly had left the college as "qualified" for Welsh cures. He also suggested that some of these men had been passed for ordination by the bishop of Llandaff's chaplains "for want of a supply of better men". Russell appears to have referred these allegations to Bishop Thirlwall, who was visitor to the college in his capacity as bishop of St David's, and he in turn consulted Ollivant who sent onto him a letter written by Hugh Williams, his examining chaplain. Williams wrote that on hearing the ordinands read Welsh in the Cathedral, he remarked to the bishop, who had been present, that he had been fortunate "in meeting with such a set of thorough *native* Welshmen". However, after a more formal examination he regretted to find that some of the Lampeter students appeared to be deficient in their knowledge of the orthography of the language, writing and spelling it incorrectly. Upon pointing this out to Ollivant the bishop had asked to see some of the worst of their exercises, and Williams had given him two, upon which the bishop thought it advisable to send them to Dr Lewellin, the principal of the college, as this would have a good effect "if the young men knew that such notice was taken of what they did". But Williams did not think then, or now, that this deficiency would interfere with their practical usefulness as pastors, and while there were not Welsh scholars, there was no reason that could justify a refusal to pass them. Hugh Williams also did a useful service for the Welsh-speaking members of the Church by translating into Welsh such works as W. Brooke's *Short Addresses to Children of Sunday Schools* in 1826, Bruce Knight's *A Letter on Infant Baptism* of 1830, and the Prayers, ordered by the King in Council, for deliverance from the cholera during the years 1831-33.[14]

****

The Victorian age was an age of presentations, and it is not surprising that a presentation was planned to mark Williams's 25 years' association with the office of deputy chancellor or chancellor of the diocese, and his 18 years at Bassaleg. The invitation to subscribe read:

> The services so long rendered by the Rev. Hugh Williams in his two-fold capacity of a Christian Minister, and Judge of the Ecclesiastical Court, are of no common order – independent of which there is a strong desire on the part of many persons publicly to testify their feelings towards him on account of the generous manner in which he has always endeavoured to aid his poorer countrymen, by giving them the benefit of his valuable advice, and exerting his influence to bring about amicable adjustments out of court, and so to prevent, instead of encouraging litigation.
>
> As a Welshman, the Rev. Chancellor is also especially entitled to the gratitude and respect of his countrymen; for, although gifted with the literary attainments of an accomplished classical scholar, he has ever been free from that unhappy weakness which induces neglect and indifference to the language of Wales; but has ever been ready to show attachment to his country, by contributing by his own talents and example, to the cultivation of Welsh Literature for the best and highest purposes.

The subscribers included a large number of his Bassaleg parishioners, but also included David Howell, then a student at Abergavenny but later dean of St David's; John Russell, the high sheriff of Monmouth; T. W. Booker, the proprietor of the Pentyrch Works; Richard Prichard and E. P. Thomas, the vicar chorals of Llandaff; Augustus Morgan of Machen; Lodwick Edwards of Rhymney; E. O. Phillips, head of Llandovery College; William Rees of Ton, Llandovery, the publisher, and a large number of others, both clerical and lay.

At the presentation, held at Bassaleg, the chair was taken by John Russell, who indicated the affection in which Williams was held by the large number of parishioners who had subscribed to the testimonial, which consisted of plate worth over £200. His gifts as a preacher, "his general rectitude of character, amiableness of temper, and constant desire to alleviate the suffering of the poorer classes of his parishioners" had commended him to all. Furthermore, he had rendered great service to the county as a magistrate, especially for his knowledge of the Welsh language, and "for his deep sympathetic feeling for those who were unfortunately brought before them." His learning, devotion, and ability were also mentioned, while the inscription on the plate mentioned that he possessed the "piety and patriotism of a true Welsh clergyman".

David Howell spoke in Welsh of Williams's concern for the Welsh language and nation. There was a time, he pointed out, when it was regarded as disgraceful that a dignified cleric should profess patriotism, and one would be mocked for behaving as a Welshman. But better days had come, and he prayed that he might have strength to double his faithfulness to Church and nation. Williams replied that the call of Wales and its language lay heavy on his heart and he was sad that so little had been done for Welsh-speakers by the Church. The people who spoke the language were the most moral, the most religious, the most loyal, and the most hospitable people in Christendom. Clergy needed to speak Welsh easily and naturally, and he hoped that the language would be recognised as a language of the United Kingdom. In his parish there had been many black days and times of discouraging difficulties, doubts, disappointments and trials. But there had also been brighter days – days when he was able to witness the happy death of an aged pilgrim of Zion, and days when he was able to lead "the lambs", the youthful members of his flock, "marked out as early victims of the King of Terrors", to the gate of heaven, and deliver them to the Great Shepherd of the sheep. There was also the help, the support and the encouragement which every faithful minister should receive from his parishioners and his friends. He had lived among them for 18 years in peace and Christian friendship, and he hoped this would continue. Bishop Copleston had entrusted him with the legal work of the diocese, and whether he had put the right man into that office or not it was for the public to determine, but "you have this day kindly given the verdict in my favour". During the days of his deputy chancellorship the "late excellent and ever-to-be-lamented Chancellor" (Bruce Knight) had entrusted him with much of the judicial work of the court, and as chancellor he had had to decide many important wills and other causes involving large amounts of property, which demanded much deep thought and a considerable knowledge of ecclesiastical law. He was thankful that not one of his judgments had been reversed upon appeal, although he was doubtful if any appeal had been prosecuted. A luncheon followed for 50 or so at the Vicarage, with members of the Morgan family of Tredegar House being amongst their number.[15]

Although these testimonials were enthusiastic affairs, and matters were frequently exaggerated, and Williams, true to the form of these events, depreciated himself with a display of humility, it is clear that Williams was regarded as a stalwart and protector of the Welsh language, as a conscientious clergyman in his parish of Bassaleg, and as a distinguished member of the ecclesiastical judiciary. But one wonders what his parishioners at Radyr might have thought had they been invited to contribute. Their names are absent from the testimonial, and that is testimony itself. It is a pity that Williams clung to that parish, for it is a blot upon an otherwise distinguished record.[16]

ENDNOTES

1 Alumni Oxon; Joseph Bradley, *A History of Monmouthshire* (new edn., Cardiff, 1992+), I (2b) 310, and 5 (edited by M. Gray, Cardiff, 1993) 80.

2 NLW, Church in Wales Records, LL/Sc/2131-3; Roger L. Brown, *Llandaff Figures and Places* (Welshpool, 1998), p. 54. *Alumni Oxon* states he was rector of Rhossili, Glamorgan, in the diocese of St David's, in 1820. This seems to be incorrect.

3 Copleston to Bruce Knight, 28 September 1832, CL, number K87.

4 Roger L. Brown (ed.), *The Letters of Edward Copleston, Bishop of Llandaff, 1828-1849* (Cardiff, 2003), Copleston to Bruce Knight, 5 March 1834, p. 161; and 2 April 1836, p. 163, which notes that Hugh Williams was in ill-health and suggests he may have to give up Roath. Calvert Jones's incumbency of Roath is not mentioned in Rollin Buckman's *The Photographic Work of Calvert Richard Jones* (London, 1990).

5 Brown, *Copleston Letters*, Copleston to Bruce Knight, 16, 22, 27 and 31 August, 29 December, 1832, 28 October 1833, 18, 24 and 26 February, 6 and 16 April, 13 June, 1836, pp. 103, 105-7, 115, 142, 199, 202, 208-10, 215; and letters of 22 August (1832?), 11, 27 and 29 August, 3 September, 1832, 5 February 1834, 5 March 1836, CL, numbers K1, 71, 164, 254, 75-6, 78. See also Roger Phillips, *Bassaleg* (Newport, 1991), pp. 111-2.

6 Phillips, *Bassaleg*, p. 88; CMG, 31 December 1853, p. 3.

7 Brown, *Copleston Letters*, Copleston to Traherne, 7 February 1837, p. 241; Brown, *Llandaff Figures and Places*, pp. 54-5. In this, following Joseph Bradley, I indicated that Williams had been a canon of Llandaff Cathedral since 1837. I now find that this is incorrect.

8 Roger L. Brown, "The Copleston Memorial", *Morgannwg*, 41 (1997) 38-50; and in particular: CMG, 26 January 1850, p. 4; 9 February 1850, p. 4; 16 February 1850, p. 3; 23 February 1850, p. 3; 9 March 1850, p. 4. It seems that Williams was regarded as an episcopal candidate during the 1849 Llandaff vacancy. In my *Llandaff Figures and Places*, p. 55, I suggested that Williams had promised upon his appointment to Bassaleg

that he would ensure that there was double duty at Radyr and that a curate
be appointed there. The letter of Davies is ambiguous, but re-reading it
makes clear he was referring to Risca rather than Radyr in this instance.

9 Brown, *Llandaff Figures and Places*, pp. 55-66; I. G. Jones and D.
Williams (eds.), *The Religious Census of 1851: A Calendar of the Returns
Relating to Wales* (Cardiff, 1976), I 141. By contrast in Bassaleg there
were two English services, with average attendances of 130 plus 42
children in the morning, and 70 in the evening, though on the census day
itself the figures were far higher with 150 plus 57 in the morning and 119
in the evening: p. 108.

10 CMG, 16 November 1850, p. 3; Brown, *Copleston Letters,* Copleston to
Traherne, 26 September 1845, pp. 272-3.

11 Glamorgan Record Office, D/D L/DC B1; *Hansard*, cxxxvii (1855) 546,
1373-5; S. M. Waddams, *Sexual Slander in Nineteenth Century England*
(Toronto, 2000), pp. 4-7, 11-13, 67; *Report of the Association of Welsh
Clergy in the West Riding of Yorkshire* (1852), p. 8.

12 Brown, *Copleston Letters*, Copleston to Bruce Knight, 5 March 1834, p.
161.

13 NLW, typescript, *Papers from Llanbadarn Fawr Parish Chest*, pp. 93-5.

14 Public Record Office, London, papers of Lord John Russell,
30/22/9a/144, Bishop Thirlwall to Lord John Russell, 17 January 1857,
enclosing a letter of Hugh Williams. See also D. T. W. Price, *A History of
St David's University College, Lampeter* (Cardiff, 1977), pp. 79n., 96-7.

15 CMG, 7 July 1855, p. 4; 29 November 1856, p. 6; 6 December 1856, p. 5.

16 At least two of his sons were ordained. B. Hall Williams, the eldest son,
died at an early age in 1858 as an "eloquent, impressive, and faithful
preacher of Gospel truth". It was said he had reconciled the two parties of
parishioners at Bampford Speke in the diocese of Exeter, whose vicar, G.
C. Gorham, had had a noted and prolonged dispute with Bishop Phillpotts
about baptismal regeneration. Upon Gorham's death the parishioners had
united in petitioning that their curate, Hall Williams, should succeed to
the living (CMG, 1 May 1858, p. 5). Another son, Basil, died in
November 1929 having served as vicar of Risca for 40 years until his
retirement in 1925. He succeeded an older brother in that parish in 1877.
He had been educated at Marlborough and Wadham College, Oxford:
Monmouth Diocesan Calendar, 1930, p. 108.

ROBERT WICKHAM
Vicar of Gresford and Archdeacon of St Asaph
(from the Gresford Parish Book, by courtesy of Canon David Griffiths)

3
A GOOD ARCHDEACON OR A PARASITE OF EPISCOPAL SLIME?
Robert Wickham: archdeacon of St Asaph

Archdeacon Wickham was one of those Englishmen whom the Welsh patriotic clergy considered had been imposed upon the Welsh Church by the nepotism of its bishops, in his case by Bishop Thomas Vowler Short of St Asaph. Their writings are replete with the iniquity of, and the dire consequences they considered would accompany, such appointments, so that the name of Robert Wickham has became rather sullied over the course of years. Nevertheless, although the circumstances of his appointment lend credibility to this cry of nepotism, and there were certainly areas of his archidiaconal duties which he had to delegate because of his lack of the Welsh tongue, he proved to be a good, wise and reforming archdeacon. It is rather sad that his archdeaconry was a Welsh one rather than one in an English diocese, where he might have received the respect and honour his talents deserved, rather than the uneasy compliance one suspects he received from the Welsh clergy of his archdeaconry.

Born at Winchester in 1802, educated at Magdalen College School at Oxford, and afterwards at Christ Church, Wickham obtained a second class in *Literae Humaniores* at the early age of 21. Needing to find some employment between coming down from Oxford and the minimum age for ordination, 23, Wickham became second master of a preparatory school at Twyford, in the Winchester area. Finding the scholastic profession to his taste, he remained at the school even after his ordination in 1825, taking as his title the curacy of Kingsworthy, which he possibly served in an honorary capacity, a not infrequent occurrence at the time. Becoming headmaster of this school in 1831, it flourished greatly under his supervision, and he remained headmaster until 1847. His teaching was so efficient that when the foundations of Eton and many other public schools were thrown open to competition, his pupils were amongst the first to be elected. It is probable that Wickham became the proprietor of the school, for *Alumni Oxon* records that his eldest son, Latham, was its headmaster from 1862-87 (when he became vicar of Is-y-coed, near Gresford), and he was succeeded in turn by his son, Charles Townshend Wickham.

In 1847 Wickham's brother in law, Thomas Vowler Short, appointed him vicar of Gresford and as one of his examining chaplains. Short had been rector of the parish in which Wickham had served his curacy, Kingsworthy, from 1826-34 (when he had been appointed rector of the vast parish of St George's Bloomsbury), and it is probable that he met his wife, Short's sister, through this association.[1]

The living of Gresford, near Wrexham, was in the bishop's patronage, and was one of the most valuable ones in the diocese, valued in 1859 at £714, with a population of 2,500 people, many of whom worked in the local collieries. Its previous vicar was Hensley Horsley, son of a previous bishop of the diocese, who was also rector of the equally valuable living of Castle Caereinion in Montgomeryshire. Falling into debt in 1805-6, with his extension to Gresford Vicarage half completed, Horsley fled to Scotland, residing in Dundee and then Edinburgh, where he served the episcopal chapels in that capital city. His Welsh livings were sequestrated in order to pay for curates to serve them, and this disgraceful situation continued until Horsley's death in 1846. Thus the protest which followed Wickham's appointment not only related to what was seen as yet another piece of episcopal nepotism, but must be seen also in the light of this lengthy non-residence by the previous incumbent of the parish, as well as the feeling that Gresford was a Welsh-speaking community and needed a Welsh speaker.

The protest was loud, long and ineffective. Once Wickham had been instituted there was little that could be done to remove him. And there he stayed to the end of his ministerial days.

The shrillest of the attacks came from Richard Williams Morgan, perpetual curate of Tregynon in Montgomeryshire, and a most bitter critic of Bishop Short and his appointment to the see of St Asaph. Morgan, a nephew of Archdeacon John Williams of Cardigan (who had been the first rector of the Edinburgh Academy and in Sir Walter Scott's words, "the first schoolmaster in Europe"), took up his uncle's theme that Wales needed Welsh-speaking bishops. He argued with his uncle that the so-called Anglo-Welsh bishops had accepted their elevation for purely financial considerations in direct and wilful violation of the canons of the Church and the tenets of Scripture, knowing full well that they could not speak the language of most of their flock. Morgan, however, had been effectively and tragically marginalised by a rumour, which Short cruelly accepted as fact, that he had fathered an illegitimate child. As a result Morgan's allegations – which were generally sound in fact if a little spurious on interpretation – were regarded as the outpourings of a frustrated, revengeful and angry man. And as such their credibility was questioned. Besides this his extravagant and impassioned language did not help his cause.[2]

Morgan alleged that Short's appointment as bishop had been a political one and that his task was to "Whiggify" the Church in his diocese, Morgan being a Tory and as such representative of most of the Welsh clergy. Playing on Short's policy of counteracting Nonconformity by the building of church schools as proselytising agencies, Morgan alleged that he wished to make all his clergy "state schoolmasters". Their task, he claimed, was to introduce the English language into Welsh-speaking areas, eliminate dissent, and presumably introduce them to the doctrines of Whig imperialism. We continue with his own words, which if the circumstances were true, are extremely poignant:

> Dr Vowler Short being such a Bishop summons into his presence a Welsh Curate whose only means are his £100 per annum, whose only prospects, preferment in his profession, whose only Establishment, the numerous one of his own family. His offence consists in having applied for a vacant Living to which he thinks twenty years' service in the Church gives him some claim. Instead of the Living he receives a Lecture – pointedly severe and personal – on the dreadful Sin of worldly-mindedness in a Christian minister. The Palace preached to the Cot; the Annual thousands to the Annual tens; Dives to Lazarus, the Bishop that cannot discharge one duty, to the Curate that has for twenty years discharged every duty, on the heinous crime of not being content with his £100 per Annum for his wife and family. The Curate is the silent and patient back, the Bishop the stringing scourge in this sanctimonious castigation. The poor wretch quits the presence of his Superior cut to the heart by words delivered with all the security of Despotism, and driven home with all the unctuousness of self-satisfied and prosperous Hypocrisy.
>
> The ensuing week, he observes the Living given away to one, who has never done a minute's work in the Diocese – the Brother-in-law of his heavenly minded Censor. Whatever his

sensations are, he must bury them in the solitude of his own bosom, for his next clerical neighbour may be "in the Bishop's confidence" – in other words a Diocesan spy and informer. He gazes on his children and resigns himself in the stagnancy of despair to the system.

Morgan estimated the value of the living to be £800, and asserted that Wickham before his appointment "had lived the life and discharged the duties of an Advertising Schoolmaster in Hampshire – compatible doubtless with his responsibilities to his pupils and their parents, but not clearly so to the Church and his Parishioners." There were some people, Morgan claimed, who attributed this appointment more to the fact that Wickham was a successful schoolmaster than the bishop's brother-in-law, but these people, he continued, were those who would "never permit themselves to suppose the existence of a virtue in poverty, or of a vice in rich and successful chicanery." In Sidney Smith's words the whole matter stunk of the "breed and the Parasites of Episcopal Slime". Compare, Morgan suggested, the £4,000 earned by Bishop Short "for duties infinitesimally small, and depravation incalculably injurious", or the £1,000 received by his brother-in-law from "the resources of the same abused and wasted Church", with the £600 per annum granted by the same Whig establishment to Bishop Selwyn of New Zealand. Selwyn had "just returned from laying the foundation of a new Kingdom of Light and Life in the inhuman regions of the Savage East, master of its language, familiar with every idiom, a Teacher and Preacher in every hamlet of his Diocese, conversant by face and speech with every Chief and influential Native of the Zealand converts." But Bishop Short and his brother-in-law, in receipt of far greater income, could neither preach, read or converse with the people committed to their charge in Wales, and were in the same position as if they had "found themselves commissioned and settled amongst our Maori Antipodes of New Zealand."[3]

Another more stringent though restrained comment came from the Association of the Welsh Clergy in the East Riding of the County of York. Founded in the 1820s, the association was mainly comprised of a number of Welsh clerics attracted into the area by Lewis Jones, vicar of Almondbury, near Huddersfield. During the 1850s, claiming that as outsiders they could speak without fear of reprisal, they stated the facts, as they saw them, about their native land and Church, and published their proceedings in an annual report. In their first published report, of 1852, the members claimed that Bishop Short "was very anxious to introduce Saxon blood into the diocese, that the clergy should henceforth be a mixed race, and with that view had already preferred several Englishmen to Welsh parishes." This intermixture of races, akin to that of Israel of old, would "be a snare to effect the entire extermination of Welsh congregations in the churches of those parishes, to which the aliens will be appointed." While they might laugh at the absurdity of his lordship's scheme, yet

> His Lordship's plan of introducing aliens into the diocese would operate most unjustly upon the native clergy, who ought to be appointed to those benefices, to which persons unacquainted with the vernacular can have no qualification, nor particle of claim. This system appeared still more oppressive when the value of preferments given to Englishmen was considered. For to what kind of benefices had his lordship inducted his English relatives and friends? Was it to such as possessed scanty stipends? No. He never heard of Englishmen being introduced into Wales in order to take charge of small incumbencies. It was to the most valuable livings in the diocese that Dr Short made the appointments of which he complained. His lordship had given the vicarage of Gresford, in Denbighshire, which was worth above £700 per annum, to his brother-in-law, another Englishman.

Other examples were given of Short's abuse of his patronage, such as his nomination of his wife's relation, William Bruce, to the rectory of Llanfechain worth £530, and the parish of Chirk to Joseph Maude, a former curate of his when he was rector of Bloomsbury. Bruce, however, declined the appointment, accepting that he was totally unfit for the duties of a Welsh parish. Was such a system to be tolerated? asked the speaker, Thomas James, incumbent of Netherthong, as he presented a projected address to the archbishop of Canterbury for the approval of the association. The address protested against the appointment of non-Welsh speakers to Welsh-speaking parishes, and gave as illustrations the appointments at Gresford and Chirk together with examples drawn from other dioceses.[4]

Yet another protest came from "A Pauper Clergyman", who wrote a pamphlet addressed to the bishop of St Asaph regarding a better provision for the cure of souls. Writing about Short's appointment of his brother-in-law to Gresford, he asked; "[o]ut of the whole body of poor incumbents and curates of that diocese, was there not one that needed such a preferment and was suitable for it? Was there not one of pressing family wants, of long standing, of proved efficiency, of personal merit, or just claim, to entitle him to that preferment? or was there not one who could, and would, declare to the people, *in their own tongue*, the wonderful works of God?" There were many such, he concluded, but the bishop "could not see the fitness or the claims of such; he could not recollect that his patronage was a trust *for his own clergy and his own people*; he could not perceive that the 'cure of souls' requires a knowledge of the people's tongue ..." And this was because he had a brother-in-law, and consequently the bishop was prepared to abuse his "patronage for the pecuniary benefit of a *kinsman* and a *favourite*."[5]

How widespread was this feeling? When John Griffith, then vicar of Aberdare, who was to become the firebrand of the Welsh Church, wrote a series of published letters to Lord John Russell about the iniquities of the Church in 1847-8 under the pseudonym "Ordovicis", he received a number of replies to the allegations he made in these articles. In one of these articles Griffith, writing with heavy sarcasm, suggested that when Prebendary Horsley had died the previous summer,

> The Bishop, of course, followed the example of his predecessor, and gave it to some worthy who had toiled years and years on the Welsh mountains. He did, my Lord, but he did not follow the good Dr Carey; he followed the Luxmoores, the Cleavers, and the Horsleys, *he gave it to his own brother*. His brother is, I believe, a Clergyman with a London living, and, therefore, he civilly declined it, as he could not, under your Lordship's Act, do as the Luxmoores did, and *keep both*. But he has *kept* the Canonry. Well, here is another chance for a man of St Asaph. Not so, my Lord, he must go to the *diocese of Winchester* and give it to a *schoolmaster*. I pray your Lordship to remember this. The valuable, the important, the *neglected* living of Gresford is given to a teacher of nouns and substantives. My Lord, are we *again* returning to the days of the Luxmoores? God forbid. For if we are, I for one will not answer for the consequences. Destruction, utter, inevitable destruction must be the fate of our venerable, our much-wronged, still our holy Church in the principality of Wales.

W. D. Conybeare, then dean of Llandaff, replied to Griffith, detailing the virtues of Short, his brother, and Wickham ("I have never conversed with a more cultivated or Christian mind") and reproving "Ordovicis" for despising the office of a schoolmaster. Conybeare continued:

> in every diocese and some situation will exist which requires a superior refinement of education to that which the local circumstances of the Church can render common among her provincial ministers. Far be it from me to speak with the shadow of a shade of disparagement of the Welsh Church, on account of the difficulties under which it labours, and the poverty which is the source of those difficulties. Among the Curates of Wales I have numbered friends whose Christian singleness of heart and faithfulness of exertion I should be happy could I in any degree reflect. Yet with these high and essential virtues, other comparatively inferior points might have been wanting to confer an exact fitness for some official and social position. Is it not natural and just, then, to believe ... that a Bishop may be influenced by such conscientious motives.

It was not difficult to reply to this argument that the situation would hardly have applied if the living of Gresford had been a poor one, but then it could hardly be expected that Wickham would have been tempted to give up a prosperous school for such a living.

"A Native Presbyter of the Diocese of St Asaph" also wrote a letter of protest which was printed in *John Bull*, a radical magazine. Sympathising with the bishop in the difficulties of his office and his desire for the best interest of his diocese, he could understand his desire to have "in his Diocese a Clergyman who, in addition to the pastoral qualifications possessed by others already in the diocese, presented the comfort and advantage of near relationship; especially as the Bishop has, in addition to his episcopal labours, to endure domestic affliction by the long projected illness of his lady." Mrs Short in fact died not long afterwards. Under these circumstances he could see no objection to Wickham's appointment, "as a solitary instance", though he would be opposed as strongly as anyone could be to episcopal nepotism. He denied that the parish of Gresford was in a worst state than many other parishes in the diocese, and was in some cases superior to them, while he added there was no Welsh service in the church at Gresford. This writer seems to have forgotten that Wickham's appointment was linked with other instances of Short's nepotism and was not "a solitary instance".

A further writer, replying to the secretary of the Association of Welsh Clergy in the West Riding, maintained that his assertion that the parish of Gresford was Welsh-speaking, and that Wickham's appointment would deprive the Welsh speakers of that parish "of that godly instruction and consolation to which they are justly entitled" was incorrect. The church service in Welsh at the parish church had been discontinued about a century before, while the inhabitants, apart from those living at Gwersyllt, were anglicised in language and habits. Even in that hamlet there were probably no people unacquainted with English, although they might prefer Welsh at their own fireside. However, he pointed out that a new church had been built in that district and served by a Welsh curate, courtesy of Bishop Short and the vicar of the parish, Wickham. Yet in the 1851 religious census the Welsh-speaking Calvinistic Methodist chapel at Gresford had an average Welsh-speaking congregation of 260 in the morning and 360 in the evening, together with 210 scholars in the afternoon. By comparison the English-speaking parish church had a morning congregation of 200 with 136 scholars, and an afternoon one of 120 plus 100 scholars. It seems clear that the parish of Gresford had a Welsh-speaking population that was not provided for at its parish church.[6]

****

Little can be found about Wickham's ministry at Gresford, although the Vicar's Book, commenced by Wickham in obedience to a request from Bishop Short, indicates his affection and care for Gresford Church. It is probably the only Vicar's Book which has continued in use to the present time. He built a new boys' school and master's house for the National Schools in 1874 at a cost of £2,000, in memory of Bishop Short, who had ended his days two years earlier, in retirement, at the home of his sister at Gresford Vicarage. The money was derived from a legacy of the bishop to Wickham, which he declined to use for his own benefit. The parish of Gwersyllt was partly formed from the parish of Gresford in 1851, and endowed with £81 of the vicarial tithes by Wickham, who later transferred five acres of his glebe to this parish. His daughter Laura married its first vicar, Robert Wynne Edwards. A church-school was built at Burton in 1862 and later licensed for Holy Communion, thus fulfilling Wickham's hopes that the population of this area should be brought under "the influence of the religious ordinances of the Church" and supplied with the means of education "and proper pastoral superintendence". During his vicariate the church at Gresford was restored, a new organ placed in it and its bells recast, at a cost of

£4,000. Wickham also rebuilt a new vicarage house in 1850 on a more convenient location, obtaining towards its cost the massive sum of £1,000 in dilapidations from the estate of his predecessor. His obituary states that the inhabitants of the parish "will preserve the recollection of their Vicar who laboured so long and so earnestly to promote the spiritual and temporal happiness of his people."[7] But according to a successor of his as archdeacon, David Evans, he had an even greater reputation as an improver of a breed of pigs, bringing with him into the parish his Berkshire pigs. Significantly new pigsties were added to the vicarage in 1854.[8] His parishioners placed a stained-glass window in Gresford Church to his memory, while the surplus from the public subscription was used to establish an annual prize in his memory at the Gresford National Schools.[9]

In 1854 Bishop Short appointed Wickham as archdeacon of St Asaph, and to a canonry in the cathedral. It was hardly to be expected that the critics of his appointment to Gresford would remain silent over what they would have considered a second and still more significant piece of family nepotism, especially as the canonry was valued at £350 per annum and required three months' residence each year or, as one writer later put it, enforced idleness.[10] R. W. Morgan thus wrote in protest:

> The principal functions of this Archdeacon are first to visit Welsh Parishes and charge Welsh Churchwardens, and secondly to examine the candidates for Holy Orders in the Welsh Church, whether they be "apt and meet" to exercise the ministry of the Gospel. He has to present them at the altar to the Bishop, saying, "Reverend Father in God, I present unto you these persons present, to be admitted to the order of Priesthood." The Bishop, the brother-in-law, who has appointed him, thus warns him, thus, – "Take heed that the persons whom ye present unto us, be apt and meet for their *learning* and godly conversation, to exercise their ministry duly, to the honour of God and the edifying of his Church." The Archdeacon answers, – "I have inquired of them and *also examined them*, and think them so to be." ... Archdeacon Wickham knows not a word of Welsh. When therefore he addresses Welsh Churchwardens in English, they, as a matter of course, rise and leave the Church. To be pronounced "apt and meet" for the ministry of a Welsh Parish, the candidate for Holy Orders must, as the service implies, be examined previously as to his "learning", on this point, by the Archdeacon: this the Archdeacon cannot do. If he assures his

brother-in-law at the altar that he has done so, he will be guilty of an impious untruth. If he does not examine or attend, but some Kymric Clergyman be appointed in his stead, we come to the usual practice - one man does the work, while another man receives the dignity and emoluments of office.

At his first visitation it was alleged that the majority of the churchwardens left the church immediately after they had signed the declaration and adjourned to a neighbouring hostelry. Only three churchwardens remained to hear the charge.

The Association of the Welsh Clergy in the West Riding almost repeated Morgan's argument word by word, adding that they could not see how he could say that he had examined the Welsh candidates and found them fit for the work of ministry, "when he knows not whether they are competent to preach in the language of the people."[11]

These arguments may seem like special pleading, for most bishops and archdeacons had to delegate some aspect of their work to others, though it could be argued that the delegator needed to be able to check on the efficiency of those undertaking the work for him. As late as 1869 there was still criticism, when *Cambro-Catholic* in a letter to the *Church Times* hoped that Short would take advantage of the new episcopal resignation act, for the sake of the diocese, as he was physically incapable of performing the duty, although his "courageous self-confidence had never failed." He went on to suggest that Short had given church patronage in his diocese to the value of £4,000 to a number of relatives and to one personal adherent, all of whom, with one exception, were entire strangers to it. "I venture to think," he continued, "that it would have been more praiseworthy to have enriched these relatives out of the Episcopal income (which was in every sense his own) than to have bestowed upon them the revenues of a diocese in which they had never laboured."[12]

As canon of the cathedral it is known that Wickham took umbrage at a number of changes introduced by Dean Bonnor, a man with some evangelical sympathies who was instrumental in restoring the cathedral fabric and in promoting a number of changes within its services. Complaining that the dean had introduced changes within the "usages" of the cathedral without the sanction of the chapter, Wickham alleged that Bonnor had even denied its right to interfere. The changes Wickham complained about were the commencement of a Wednesday Lenten service in the Welsh language; invitations to clergymen unconnected with the cathedral requesting them to preach at this service and at another one on Friday evenings "contrary to all precedents"; the dean's desire to establish a choral celebration of Holy Communion on Christmas Day; introducing *Hymns Ancient and Modern* into the cathedral's services; and placing a credence table and proposing to place a reredos at its east end. It seems to us a little pedantic, but such liturgical changes were bitterly resented by many in that day, although it is not known whether the real protest was about this or the status of the cathedral chapter. One imagines that the new bishop, Joshua Hughes, would have given Wickham short shift on some of these points, which would have enabled the cathedral to be more "user friendly" in today's jargon, although it is interesting to note that these changes were introduced only after Short's departure as bishop.[13]

****

The office of archdeacon had been revived in the diocese by Bishop Carey in 1844, having lapsed for many centuries by being held *in commendam* with the bishopric. At the same time a new archdeaconry, that of Montgomery, was created. Nevertheless, it is said that the two archdeacons did not enter upon their duties until the death of Dean Luxmoore in 1854, so that when Wickham was appointed to his archdeaconry "the position was still a novel one." His obituary writer speaks of his "assiduous zeal" in which he carried out the duties of his office, which made him well known and widely respected throughout the diocese. He continued:

> But it was his personal qualifications for the post which were [the] chief reason for his authority. At once a scholar and a gentleman, he had a natural dignity of character which gained him the respect of those who acted with or differed from him. He was sincerely anxious to promote the real interests of the Church; and he always displayed the greatest honesty of purpose; while his business ability was excellent, and his diligence and energy untiring. His annual visitation of the several rural deaneries of his extensive district was only a small portion of his work as Archdeacon, but it was necessarily that portion which the public was best acquainted with. And the numerous charges which he delivered, discussing the various subjects which from time to time appeared to be of importance in the Church, were always thoughtfully written and served to

elicit usefully the opinions of the assembled clergy.

Perhaps we might add that as a former schoolmaster he was probably ideally placed to serve as an archdeacon!

After 23 years' service as archdeacon Wickham resigned on the grounds of poor health, and also because of the death of his wife. She had given him much encouragement in his work. Three years later he died and was buried in his wife's grave at Gresford.[14]

****

We may judge Wickham's concern for the Church and its reform by studying his visitation charges and his other miscellaneous writings. Fourteen charges (or at least those which were published) were delivered between 1855 and 1876. In addition he published a letter to the churchwardens of the archdeaconry on the act for the abolition of compulsory church rates in 1868, and an address on the duties of churchwardens in regard to pews, based on his 1863 charge. His concerns are carefully expressed, his advice clearly stated, and his desire for reform and the extension of the Church obvious.[15]

His first visitation, of 1855, was as much a novel experience for him as it was for his auditors, as hitherto, because of the circumstances mentioned above, they had been exempted from visitation. Although churchwardens needed to be cited in order to make their oaths and render up a faithful account of the condition of their various parishes, Wickham felt it would be expedient if the clergy were cited as well. Not only would their attendance give greater effect to these requirements but he could also bring various matters relating to the well-being of the Church to their attention and for their counsel, so that the Church at large might be strengthened and edified. These visitations, Wickham felt, would enable the Church in the diocese to be a united body rather than a collection of separate parishes, and also to "dissipate the error which has prevailed so widely and so mischievously – that of separating the Clergy from the Laity, and forgetting that the Church is constituted – not of one of these bodies, but of both together." For himself, he offered his first auditors the assurance that it was "his heart's desire to discharge my office in no suspicious or exacting spirit – but as a fellow-helper with you in all that can advance the glory of God, and the salvation of men," while he pledged his time and his labour to their service, both corporately and individually, in their several parishes.[16]

The office of churchwarden, he pointed out, was an honourable if exacting one. Not only were churchwardens required to watch over the fabric and property of the Church, they were also required to witness the faithful performance of ministerial duties and to guard the morality of the clergy. Furthermore, it was their duty to remonstrate against evil practices and to reprove open vice in their parishioners. As such, parishioners needed to be careful to choose as their wardens men who were regular attenders and communicants at their church and of blameless life and conversation. No one could estimate the amount of good such men could do "by the discreet and prudent exercise" of their office. Wickham expressed in 1860 his gratitude that many deaneries had adopted the plan of one Mr H. Hoare, and approved by the Bishop, whereby the deanery clerical chapters invited laymen to attend some of their meetings. This had not only sorted out some difficulties about church rates, but was also a step towards realising the true idea of the Church "as a body consisting of many members". However, in 1864 he had to remonstrate that some wardens had been negligent by not attending visitations, and some parishes had even neglected to appoint wardens. Until those elected had been sworn in they could not act as wardens, and this might affect their position as *ex-officio* overseers of the poor, charitable trustees, and guardians of the church and its contents. Wickham was still pursuing this theme at his last visitation in 1876. In 1867 wardens were reminded that they could not interfere directly with the mode of conducting the services of the Church, and in 1869 Wickham noted that some parishes still elected a Nonconformist as warden, not any longer in order to obstruct the setting of a church rate, but in order to ensure that the parochial charities were given with equal partiality to church people and Nonconformists. This he depreciated, suggesting that the distribution should be committed to other trustees who could be more representative of religious feeling in the parish, for only men "who can heartily enter into the objects for which the Church exists" should be chosen as wardens.[17]

A question being much discussed in the early 1870s was the formation of Parochial Councils, for which a bill had been brought into parliament. Wickham sympathised with the feeling. More "constant and systematic communication" was needed between clergy and laity regarding the religious, moral and social welfare of their parishes. The bill could have consequences that might not be beneficial, but Wickham held that the revival of the office of sidesmen, and forming a committee comprising them with the churchwardens and clergy, might have a good effect. For though changes might occur more slowly, they were less likely to be motivated by sudden impulse or caprice, and so might be more acceptable in the end.[18]

It is not surprising that the usual archidiaconal reflections were given in these visitation charges. The usual concerns about "the want of very trifling repairs" which gradually produced serious mischief, and the delay in commencing work which produced "a needless waste of money", were frequently noted. Furthermore, churches which were dirty, shabby and showed obvious signs of neglect, both in their building and their interior fittings, indicated "that 'Holiness to the Lord' was not the watchword of their worshippers." But he accepted that in some parishes, where there were disputes about the church rates, there was a reluctance to spend money on such matters for fear of causing agitation.[19]

Most of the Charges indicated the progress of the Church in the Archdeaconry and diocese. The number of churches built or restored, additional services introduced, and schools established, was given in many charges, together with notes about the various diocesan boards and charities, and appeals requested for their financial support from the parishes. The establishment of two Sunday School unions to assist the work of individual schools and teachers was noted in the 1873 Charge.

Another item frequently mentioned was that of dilapidations. This was a matter of great concern to the clergy who were required to keep their parsonages in good repair, and to pay those dilapidation charges required to put these houses back in good order for their successors when they left their parishes. In many cases these charges proved to be a heavy burden upon the estate of a deceased cleric. As such Wickham reminded the clergy in that charge of 1873 of the availability of mortgages which would permit them to put their houses in good repair during their lifetime, rather than impose a burden upon their executors.

In addition, matters of concern or interest to his hearers were mentioned in his charges. In 1857 Wickham reminded his hearers of Lord Blandford's Act which made arrangements for new district churches, although there was only one in his archdeaconry. He also suggested, in reference to recent legislation relating to marriage and registration, that clergy could accept a superintendent registrar's certificate in lieu of banns, knowing the unwillingness of many people to have their banns published in their parish churches. This would encourage people to be married with a Church ceremony rather than by a registrar, and so maintain "one of the few remaining bonds of union among us". However, he pointed out, that while the act allowed those married in a registry office to have the Church service of marriage read over them and entered into the marriage register of the church, on production of their certificate, the clergy should nevertheless point out "to the parties the undoubted sin of which, as members of a religious body, they are guilty, in setting at nought the appointed ordinances of the Church to which they belong." They should not proceed any further unless they accepted that the "Marriage so previously contracted is no Marriage at all."[20]

In 1858 Wickham spoke about the act which permitted divorce, noting that it merely allowed this without the intervention of parliament, so placing "the relief" which was previously attainable only by the wealthy within the reach of all. But the necessity for such a law was a shame and reproach to Christian people. While it allowed clergymen a discretion about whether they should officiate at the marriages of divorced people, Wickham considered that its proviso of allowing another licensed cleric of the diocese to do so in their place would be destructive of the Church's order. He hoped that in practice no clergyman *"'entitled to officiate within the same diocese'* will be found capable of intruding himself into the Church of an unwilling Brother." At the same time he also expressed concern about the bill for legalising marriage with a deceased wife's sister, though he accepted there was room for argument over the various passages of Scripture on which this prohibition had been founded. The tendency, he noted, was to relax all ancient restraints on any question which might admit of an argument.[21]

The question whether suicides, or those who had been excommunicated, should be buried with a Christian service, which had come before the Church's Convocation or Parliament in 1864, was discussed at length in his charge of that year. In a lengthy historical section Wickham argued that the Church had once had a disciplinary power, but that to enforce such a discipline in the present time would mean that the Church "must abdicate her position as a National Church, and become a narrow sect, vainly aiming to be what never was, and never will be in this world – a field in which there are no tares visible, a flock in which there are none but the true sheep, a net in which none of the fish taken shall be found worthless at the last." It would be better, he concluded, to make some alterations in the service to accommodate such cases, than to force conscientious clergymen to break the law in respect of these burials for the sake of charity.[22]

The 1867 charge noted that many parishes had accepted his

suggestion, at the previous visitation, of an offertory at the Holy Communion service, though it seems that this was devoted to charitable causes rather than for the upkeep of the church. Nine years later he remarked with some concern that ruridecanal reports requested by the bishop had indicated that hymns sung at church services were being chosen by lay people rather than the minister. This to Wickham seemed to be a relic of the days "of slovenliness" when the choir was left to make its own choice. He claimed that the choir often chose the hymns during the service itself and did so with more reference to the tune than to the sense of the words, "as if the purpose of the singing were merely relaxation and relief from the monotony of prayer." But well-selected hymns reinforced the teaching of the Church and the theme of the sermon, and the best judge of these matters was the minister himself. [23]

In 1858 Wickham spoke at length on the subjects of intemperance and unchastity. The first could be checked by strengthening people's characters rather than taking away their liberty to choose between right and wrong. Nevertheless, he argued that a change in public opinion was needed about unchastity, for this sin was gaining ground. It equally needed a change in the way the poor lived, especially in the crowding together of a family into a single sleeping room. As clergy they needed to remind landlords and masters and the heads of families about their duties, and also warn the latter that if they did not make provision for the Sabbath day, and the moral and spiritual care of their charges, "nothing less than practical heathenism can be looked for as the result of their neglect." This led him to speak about the need for education, and in particular Church education, as Bishop Short was one of the most zealous promoters of National schools in the kingdom, believing that they offered a means of bringing back Nonconformists to the Church. Wickham, however, saw education more as a means of bringing children into "contact with religion and morality from their earliest days." It was a question of following the Scriptural maxim, to "train them up in the way they should go." He was equally concerned for the provision of "innocent amusement" for the populace, which would help to bring the various sections of society together and help end "that class isolation so greatly to be deplored in these days". [24]

Matters of education were noted from time to time, although not as often as one might have supposed. In 1866 Wickham expressed his concern that the conscience clause was made a condition of a building grant from the government, by which Nonconformist children could be exempted from "Church" teaching in these Church schools. As a result, he believed, some managers dispensed with Church teaching entirely, especially if there was a predominance of Nonconformist children within the school. In any case, the existence of the conscience clause in a trust deed could entirely destroy the character of a Church school. Consequently, Wickham felt that they had to refuse the conditions and risk the consequences. These consequences, he added, " can never surely be so serious, as would be the evil of educating the children of our Parochial Schools as if for this world only, and leaving them to the chance crumbs of religious knowledge which they may pick up elsewhere."

His following Charge noted that many parishes, in view of these difficulties, had decided not to apply for government grant-aid for their schools, with the result that "[w]here education is most wanted and least attainable, there it remains almost utterly neglected", or was conducted with an unwise economy. He accepted, however, that the religious teaching in the schools should teach the grounds of "our own faith, without directly impugning that of others", though in so doing they should set forth the belief "that there is no form of religion so pure as that which is set forth in our Articles; that there are no services so edifying as those prescribed by our Book of Common Prayer; no form of government so scriptural as that of our own Church." Yet Wickham entered a caveat. Perhaps this kind of teaching could only be carried out effectually in the Sunday schools. No child should be permitted to attend the Sunday school whose parents did not desire it to be taught definite Church teaching. He even suggested there should be some agreement between the incumbent and the parents regarding this. Far better to have a small Sunday school on this model, than a large one where no definite teaching was given, and where sometimes secular subjects such as reading were taught. This would be better for the Church, as such children were more likely to become faithful and attached members, " and better for our own peace, when we look, as we naturally must do, for some fruit from our labours." Those who argued that compulsory education would help remove crime and immorality were informed that those who perpetrated the "atrocities" of Trade Unions, of the Fenian outrages, or the "monstrous frauds in the commercial world" were not uneducated men. Rather, their system of secular education had ignored Christian truth and consequently had failed to promote love and charity. Only a religious education could produce this. But, on the other hand, a system of compulsory education was incompatible with *one* religious system of education. Those who had to pay for it would demand a voice in management and would resist assisting any education which was against their own religious principles.

Wickham's 1873 Charge noted the appointment of a full-time Diocesan Inspector of Church Schools. Wickham thought his appointment would enable improvements to be made, especially in the annual testing of the pupil teachers in religious education. Though he accepted the existence of School Boards in his 1875 Charge, and allowed that education paid for by compulsory rates had to be unsectarian in character, however imperfect and unsatisfactory it might be, Wickham was concerned that a number of Church schools were transferring to these boards, even two from his own archdeaconry. He did not know the reason, but it was certainly not because of the conscience clause, for not more than half a dozen children, mainly Roman Catholic, had taken advantage of this clause. A year later it seems clear that financial considerations were causing these transfers, but Wickham begged his hearers to realise that even though it might be said that there was some form of religious instruction allowed in the board schools, specific "Church" teaching was not permitted, and what teaching was given was discretionary rather than mandatory. A child could still pass through such a school "without ever hearing the name of Jesus, or learning to 'give an answer to him that asketh a reason of the hope that is in him.'" The Public Elementary Education Act had limited religious education in Church schools to one hour a day (generally the first hour of the school day, so allowing those pupils who had opted out to come later), and consequently Wickham requested the clergy in 1876 to personally superintend this teaching, as it was impossible for the ordinary teachers to effectually undertake this work during the time allowed. Although it had been suggested that the Sunday schools could substitute for this loss, this was difficult to implement in Wales where many of these schools were all-age schools, and attended by children "seeking instruction independent of our Church system".[25]

The 1859 revival prompted Wickham to suggest in his 1860 charge that there was much in it which was spiritual, and which could not be "accounted for on merely physical grounds, or attributed wholly to human motives, or human agency." Here he could recognise the hand of God and the work of the Holy Spirit, even though, as he declared later, he could not recognise "Enthusiasm". Though "the leaven of the flesh and of the world" had been mixed up in it, there had been an *"extraordinary effusion of ordinary grace* upon those who heard the Word." They themselves should not depreciate the work by referring to its "extravagances", but rather hail with delight a movement which would modify those influences which were neutralising so much of their labour. Yet they needed to remember that God works by human agency, rather than encourage an expectation that "the operation of the Holy Spirit, in these days, will be attended with miraculous signs." Those who would charge the Church with a "cold formalism and want of spirituality" should remember that there was "not a single phrase of spiritual life which is not anticipated, and its wants supplied in our Book of Common Prayer." If people were craving after "other systems", it was because "from the fault of their early education, and the unhealthy religious atmosphere in which they have lived, they have never fairly been placed under the influence of the Church." As such they knew neither its principles nor its privileges. Those who suggested that the practices of Nonconformist bodies were more conducive to producing a revival of religion were informed that this was untrue, but in order to "indulge the preference which may shew itself for unusual religious practices", Wickham reluctantly allowed Bible classes, prayer meetings, and communicant meetings. Such meetings, he argued, should be held under the superintendence of the clergyman of the parish, and he trusted that they would not "depart from the sober practices of our Church." Though some clergymen had taken part in joint services with Nonconformists, Wickham did not see how this was possible in good faith. This was because the Church of England stood as a witness to "the Truth", and those with whom "we are invited to unite in this movement" had grounded their separation on some denial or perversion of this truth. So how could they join together "in full assurance of faith"? There could be no reunion until error had been removed, though he hoped that the Spirit of Truth in the revival might hasten that day – though Wickham clearly meant this sentiment to apply to Nonconformity rather than to the Church![26]

If any one subject stands out in Wickham's visitation charges, it is the national character of the Church of England. This is shown in a number of ways, many of them reflective of contemporary events and concerns. A vital part of the national character of the Church concerned the rights of parishioners in their own parish churches, and the need to accommodate all, especially the poor, at its services. Those to whom "especially the Gospel of Christ was to be preached, are in many instances practically shut out from hearing it", Wickham claimed, arguing that the Church, through the use of appropriated and so-called private pews, was regarded as the prerogative of the wealthy. This was to suggest that the Church was the Church of the propertied classes rather than the Established Church whose basic concern was for all. It was also the reason for the estrangement of the poor from "the services of the Church of their Fathers" and meant that many of them "were perishing for lack of knowledge". Pointing out that the distribution of seats lay with the wardens, Wickham urged them to ensure that those who claimed proprietary seating rights should be required to produce evidence of these rights. Equally the wardens should decline to allow individuals to repair their pews, as this could mean they could claim them for their exclusive use, nor should they allow the free seats to be converted into private pews. In addition, Wickham added his own strictures against the "traffic in pews" by which pews were let or sold, generally illegally. At his next charge Wickham noted that his remarks about the "traffic in pews on the part of those who have ceased to use the sittings once assigned to their houses, has not been without its benefit in more than one populous parish." Further advice was offered in his 1863 Charge, which included an appendix entitled "A Few Words on Pews". Though many churches had been rearranged the same system of allocating pews had continued. Consequently in 1866 Wickham urged wardens contemplating the reordering of the interior of churches to require those who claimed rights to make good their claim, and to allow the remaining seats to be "open and free". Nevertheless he hoped that most parishioners would decline to press any claims, "since all who themselves value the privilege of public worship will surely rejoice to have such arrangements made, as will enable the largest possible number of their fellow Parishioners to share that privilege with them."[27]

Wickham's concern about the accommodation available in churches was because of his fervent belief that the Church of England was the Established Church to which all belonged. It is not surprising that one of his charges, that of 1861, should be entitled *The Importance of Maintaining the National Character of the Church*. In this charge Wickham expressed great concern about political Dissent, which he distinguished from religious Nonconformity, and whose adherents had introduced a number of bills into Parliament, such as allowing Nonconformists to be appointed as trustees of endowed schools, and to permit Nonconformist services in churchyards. With respect to the latter, Wickham opined that most Nonconformists had no objection to the burial service of the Church, even though this was the only permitted service which could be used in a churchyard and only an ordained clergyman could officiate. Though Nonconformists were now able to make use of their own cemeteries or those provided by Burial Boards, where they could make use of their own forms of service and have their own ministers to officiate, Wickham accepted that many parishes only possessed a churchyard. Not only did restrictions apply here, but clergymen were forbidden to bury those who were unbaptised in consecrated ground, so that the burial of the unbaptised children of Baptist families had become an emotional concern. Wickham felt however that these cases were few and far between, and that once Nonconformists had gained access to the churchyard they would wish to use the church itself for their own ceremonies.[28]

Wickham continued with a similar theme in his 1863 Charge, entitled *The National Church: Its Nature and Duties*. In this he maintained that by necessity the Established Church had a flexibility about "defining the terms of communion with her", and a certain liberty of interpretation, though this did not allow the denial of the fundamental doctrines of the Gospel. Though it could never be a National Church in the truest sense of that word, yet it was the duty of the State to ensure that the spiritual benefits of the Church should be placed within the reach of the whole nation. As such he believed that the State should provide church buildings for this purpose. Though Wickham noted earlier precedents for such provision, he now had to accept that the task of church extension depended on church people, and thus he commended the work of the Diocesan Church Building Society and the various national societies devoted to that same end. Equally, clergymen were needed for these churches, and so he called the attention of his hearers to the work of the Church Pastoral-Aid Society and the Additional Curates Society, who gave grants for curates, and of the Ecclesiastical Commissioners who offered endowments to populous parishes. Similarly, in 1866, he stressed the importance of school-churches in the work of church extension.[29]

One of the principal concerns of Wickham's time was the question of church rates. Wickham saw this as a matter relating to the viability of the Established Church as a national body. Church rates had been paid since time immemorial by every householder in each parish, and the rate was used for the upkeep of the church fabric and the maintenance of its services. By the early nineteenth century Nonconformists were becoming increasingly opposed to paying this rate, on the grounds that they did not attend the church or that conscience forbade them to support an Established Church. Others regarded their abolition as the first step towards the confiscation of the Church's revenues and as a means towards its disestablishment. In some instances, as the vestry meetings were open to all ratepayers, they either opposed the setting of a rate, or elected one of their own number as a churchwarden in order to control matters themselves. As a result vestry meetings often became bitter encounters between rival groups. In 1855 Wickham considered that the church rate was still the law of the land, and that it had been "the means of maintaining for centuries the poor man's Church." Without such a rate he could not see how many churches could be maintained. Nevertheless he asked the wardens to act in such a way "as to give no reasonable offence to those who think and feel differently from yourselves." In former days many items had been paid for by the church rate which were not strictly within its province, and this had not been questioned. But now the wardens should be careful to include only the necessary items and leave the remainder to be paid by voluntary subscriptions. He probably meant in this category such items as the expenses of a choir and organ, or the provision of items of furniture.

Nevertheless, Wickham argued two years later that " [t]he right which everyone possesses to the use of the Parish Church of necessity implies an obligation for the maintenance of its services." He feared that if the rates were abolished, or the burden of the expenses put on pew-holders in order to avoid controversy, then the churches would cease to be parish churches, the clergy would no longer regard themselves as parish priests, the doors of the parish church would be shut against all those who did not contribute to its support, the dissenter would be unable to return to the Church of his Fathers, and the Established Church would become a congregational church or a sect. It would mean, in turn, that the Church would no longer be able to become "the rallying point for all that is really religious in Wales." Nor could it become the nucleus of a uniting church, embracing dissent within its system. On the one hand Wickham had to accept that the opponents of the Church would not be satisfied with the removal of the church rates, but rather wished to end the principle of an Established Church. The object was political, rather than religious, as Wickham argued in his 1860 charge. But by then the Braintree Judgment had been declared, and a select committee of the House of Lords had recommended, as a result of that judgment, that the church rate should be a voluntary one. This, felt Wickham, abandoned all the principles for which he and others had been contending, and would make the Church into little more than a voluntary association. He hoped this recommendation would not be carried into law, and that instead the owner, rather than the occupier, should be required to pay the rate, as many others were suggesting. In 1864 Wickham argued that if vestries did not impose a rate, then it would be more difficult to impose a charge in future, especially on new property or on property which had changed hands. He believed that the feeling of the country in favour of the ancient system had been clearly demonstrated, while the adoption of other expedients in other places had not had the desired effect. Rates made under the new legally prescribed rules could be enforced with little expense, and no false delicacy to the few who opposed them should prevent the making and enforcing of a rate.

It was an interim measure, and a new bill, following the suggestion of the House of Lords on a previous occasion, proposing to make the rate a voluntary one, and to exclude those who did not pay these voluntary rates from voting at vestry on church matters, filled Wickham with horror. He would prefer abolition instead, for that would leave the Church as the Church of the nation, a Church in which every one born in the land might claim an interest if they chose, which he assumed the proposed measure did not allow. This bill was subsequently modified, so that in 1868 Wickham wrote a letter to the churchwardens of his archdeaconry to explain the act which modified, rather than abolished, the church rate. He asked wardens to make a fair trial of this act which allowed a voluntary rate, but to make it a matter of moral rather than legal compulsion. If the rate failed to produce what was required then recourse could be made to a subscription list, which had the disadvantage that it was difficult to keep going for any length of time, or of an offertory. Though many had found the latter successful, Wickham objected to its use as a substitute for Church rates, as it drew a line between the regular church goer and the rest of the parishioners, and so destroyed the concept of a national Church. Equally, it might deflect from offertories devoted to other charitable work. In 1871 Wickham expressed his displeasure that some churches had introduced a "pew rate" or pew rents in order to compensate for the loss of the church rate. Considering these rents would be as difficult to collect as the former charge, he felt it was "attaching a money object to the enjoyment of an unjust privilege." They needed to look instead to the liberality of church members, and to a due sense of the duty of all Churchmen "to bear their proper share of the burden of maintaining" their parish church. We may note here some slight change in Wickham's position over the years as he changed from a theoretical to a more pragmatic approach.[30]

By 1869 the controversy had become wider, with the question of the Church's disestablishment being openly discussed. Wickham felt, however, that the principle of Irish disestablishment, passed in that year, could not be applied to Wales, for in Wales all were Protestants, and the articles of religion were the basis of the authorised teaching of most of the religious bodies in Wales. There was now an effort, he reported, to ensure the separation of the Church from the State in England. There were some people, Wickham alleged, even a number of Churchmen, who felt that this result "might be conductive to increased spiritual life in the Church", while others held that a Church enjoying exclusive principles was inconsistent "with the principles of Toleration" introduced by successive governments. But, if this were so, replied Wickham, then this country would "have ceased to confess Christ before the world" as a people, and as a nation would be religionless. Those who felt disestablishment would be conductive to spiritual life had truth on their side. There were still abuses to be rectified and reforms needing to be introduced which had been prevented by "jealous obstructions of the Legislature". But would the good which could be done in this way compensate for the evil which would inevitably follow the separation of Church and State? The different parties in the Church would be at strife over a new constitution and doctrinal formulation; the clergy instead of facing the restraints of the Church's connection with the State would be placed under the yoke of dependence upon their congregation, while the parochial system would collapse and the masses of the people, whom the Church cared for, would be left without a shepherd. While they should not enter into the political struggles of the day, nevertheless it was for them "to insist more earnestly upon those principles of our holy religion upon which all political wisdom is founded."[31]

The Victorian additions to the liturgical pattern of the Church's services were mentioned from time to time. In 1866 Wickham regretted that there had been difficulties in ensuring that a service for Harvest Thanksgiving would be added to the Prayer Book.[32]

By 1866 the issues of ritualism had surfaced, and as such Wickham mentioned them in his Charge of that year. While he would not discuss the finer points of the rubrics on which learned and good men had failed to agree, he would yet point out the important principle of uniformity within the Prayer Book. He could understand the offence caused to lay people by the introduction of ritual and ceremonies in their churches upon the arbitrary fancy of their minister, and he was equally concerned that those who wished to introduce ritual did so in order to teach doctrines "which cannot be read upon the bare face and letter of the statements and formularies of the Church, and which most of us believe to have been thoughtfully and purposefully excluded from the written doctrine of the Church of England." He accepted that such people were "truly zealous for the honour of God and for the best interests of His Church", but he was concerned that the peace and unity of the Church would be at risk if individual taste was not restrained. Returning to the same subject in the following year, Wickham lamented that if there was ambiguity in the existing doctrine of the Church, " as would leave it doubtful whether our Martyrs did not really die in vain", and if there was no power to remedy these disorders, then there was a sad and dreary prospect before them, even possibly schism, and the only comfort was their belief that "The Lord reigneth". Speaking to his "younger brethren", possibly those most disposed to ritualism, he addressed their argument that the proponents of ritualism were often men of learning and earnest minded. Warning that learning could be misdirected, Wickham pointed out that the claim that Scripture should be interpreted by the consent of Catholic antiquity, as Keble had suggested, was a false one. Rather, the Church "has adopted from the '*traditions and ceremonies*' of the Ancient Church whatever she found not repugnant to the Word of God; and she has rejected, or at least passed by, those which she considered either mischievous in their tendencies, or not conductive to edification." All had to be tested by Scripture. Although the Church allowed a variety of interpretations on non-essential doctrines, it was wrong for a clergyman to force his own interpretation upon his congregation. It was his prayer that they should keep constantly in mind the great principles which made "our beloved Church, not only the purest, but also the most charitable, and therefore the most comprehensive Church in Christendom."

The Charge of 1875 was devoted to the Public Worship Regulation Act, in which Wickham repeated many of these arguments, and expressed concern at the Lower House of Convocation's decision to permit some liturgical diversity but to attach no doctrinal significance to it. Only once, in a ministry of 50 years, and that within the last five years, had he seen the eastward position used, and he, with others, not only felt distracted by it, but could not help suspecting that those who introduced this innovation meant something by adopting it.[33]

Wickham frequently remarked that they were living in difficult days, but this was to remind his hearers that they must never pursue ends by means which the Almighty could not bless. Rather they should follow the apostolic exhortation and "walk in love". They should also remember that while order and decency in the churches, outward propriety and correction in its officers, were important, these matters could exist without true and vital religion. They should beware lest the pressing concerns of the day should distract them "from the great duties of watching over the moral and religious training of the young, the building up of the middle aged in a sound faith, and the preparation of all the members of our flock for a better world."[34] The Church would increase both numerically and spiritually through the humble and faithful discharge of the clergy's ordination vows. Yet, in speaking to the clergy, Wickham depreciated what was called "pulpit eloquence", which often encouraged an appetite for excitement, "without ever reaching the heart, or helping forward the work of its conversion to God." The effect of popular preaching might be compared to that of stimulating drinks, giving an energy at first but then leaving the body more listless and feeble than before. The preaching of the Established Church was characterised by a "sobriety of mind and manner", and the life-giving power was not in the preacher but in the Word itself. If the preacher is taught by God himself, then he cannot be a weak or inefficient preacher of the Gospel. Advising his clergy to follow Bishop Burnett's recommendation of reading the Ordination Service four times a year, he reminded them that their labour was in the Lord, and they may not always see the fruit of it. But the Lord required them to have (in Burnett's words) " a passionate desire to save souls, and an unwearied diligence in the pursuit of that noble design."[35]

It is obvious that Wickham gave clear directions to the clergy of his archdeaconry, and offered them useful advice and encouragement to adapt their churches, services, and methods, to the tune of a new and reforming age. By bringing them together he encouraged the clergy and the leading laity to consider themselves as belonging to something greater than their parish structures, and instead to work together as a diocese. As Arthur Burns points out in his study of the diocesan revival in the Church of England, it was the revival of the office of archdeacon, and the work of such archdeacons as Wickham, that helped counteract Bishop Short's complaint, given in his 1850 charge, that "[w]e regard the Diocese as a combination of so many single parishes, and ourselves as so many single priests, and not as a Diocese."[36]

In a similar way Wickham's concern that the Church should remain a national one, open to all who wished to resort to it, had ramifications not only regarding the unity of the Church, but also a practical outworking in the issues of church rates and in the provision of church accommodation. His desire that clergy and laity should enter into a partnership together for the good of the Church was far in advance of his day. His desire for a spiritual dimension in life to be available for all was the basis for his concern for the independence of Church schools from state interference, and for the need for new forms of services. His concern for the unity of the Church possibly helped stem some of the more unattractive features of ritualism from the diocese in which he served, unlike – for example – the diocese of Llandaff. Nevertheless, Wickham found it difficult to accept that people could differ and depart from the spiritual treasure house of the Church, and his views of society were very much of his age. His dislike and fear of enthusiasm made him wary of the 1859 revival, and perhaps indicated that at heart he was still an Englishman exiled in Wales incapable of understanding the temper and ethos of the Welsh people. Furthermore, it may be suggested he lived in a state of siege mentality. He remarked in 1864 that this was the first time for ten years in which there had not been a measure of direct hostility to the Church in Parliament (though he added it had not ceased to exist), while in 1873 he warned that they should not suppose that "the attacks of our adversaries will not be again and again renewed."[37] Yet, all said and done, Wickham gave a clear leadership to his Church at a vital stage of its development, and this must counteract the criticism, and it was a just criticism, of his appointments. We might well echo the remark of an anonymous newspaper correspondent, "Celt", who pointed out in 1857 that while he had been one "of the greatest opponents of Archdeacon Wickham's appointment", he, with many others, now confessed that "he has grown upon their esteem."[38]

ENDNOTES

1 Wickham's obituary is found in a cutting contained in the Church in Wales papers at the National Library of Wales, SA/DR/51, fol. 107; *Bye-Gones*, December 1880, p. 172.

2 for R. W. Morgan see my *Parochial Lives* (Llanwrst, 2002), pp. 131-64.

3 R. W. Morgan, *The Church and its Episcopal Corruption in Wales* (2nd edn., London, 1855), pp. 12, 66, 77-9 and the quotation on pp. 36-7.

4 *Report of the Proceedings of the Association of Welsh Clergy in the West Riding of Yorkshire*, 1852, p. 7 (which noted that the parish was Welsh-speaking), and pp. 39-43. These assertions were drawn upon by a letter published in *Baner ac Anserau Cymru*, 29 January 1870, p. 7. Described as a letter translated from the *Daily Telegraph*, its constant refrain was

that "the good of the place" (alluding to one of Short's expressions) required the appointment of one of the bishop's relatives.

5 "A Pauper Clergyman", *How to Make Better Provision for the Cure of Souls* (London 1857), pp. 38-40.

6 *John Bull*, 5 February 1848, pp. 86-7; 12 February 1848, p. 103; 19 February 1848, p. 119; *Cardiff and Merthyr Guardian*, 8 May 1852, p. 3; I. G. Jones (ed.), *The Religious Census of 1851: A Calendar of Returns relating to Wales* (Cardiff, 1981), II 139-140. Conybeare had ended his letter by asserting that the bishop had appointed a Welsh speaker to Horsley's other parish of Castle Caereinion. There exists a manuscript reply to this which asserts that Short would have stood far higher in the estimate of the public had he done the same for Gresford: National Library of Wales, MS 7942D, fol. 101.

7 A. N. Palmer, *A History of the Old Parish of Gresford* (new edn., Wrexham, 1987), pp. 82, 148; D. R. Thomas, *A History of the Diocese of St Asaph* (2nd edn., Oswestry, 1913), III 256; obituary in SA/DR/51, fol. 107.

8 David Evans, *Adgofion* (Lampeter, 1904), pp. 148f.

9 SA/DR/51, fol. 108.

10 The printed letter of Townshend Mainwaring dated 2 September 1878, in SA/DR/52, fol. 25. He stated that although Wickham had resigned as archdeacon he had retained some portion of his canonical income, which meant that Bishop Hughes's desire to reform the "system" had been frustrated. Another protest was noted by the *Carnarvon and Denbigh Herald*. Wickham, it claimed, had insisted on the Ecclesiastical Commission building a canonry at St Asaph for his three-month residence there, though the money was needed elsewhere: 1 August 1857, p. 5.

11 R. W. Morgan, *Scheme for the Reconstruction of the Church Episcopate and its Patronage in Wales* (London, n.d.), pp. 4-5; and his *The Church and its Episcopal Corruptions*, pp. 77-8; *Carnarvon and Denbigh* Herald, 18 July 1857, supplement p. 2; *Report of the Association of Welsh Clergy*, 1855, p. 18.

12 *Church Times*, 12 November 1869, p. 439.

13 Archdeacon Wickham to Bishop Hughes, 15 December 1870, SA/LET/811.

14 Obituary in SA/DR/51, fol. 107, and *Bye-Gones*, December 1880, p. 172. One son, Thomas Vowler Wickham, was vicar of Rossett and a diocesan inspector of schools and died in 1892: Palmer, *Gresford*, p. 148. Another son, Latham, was master of the Grammar School at Twyford, Winchester, in 1862-87, and later vicar of Is-y-coed, Denbighshire, 1887-94 (a Charles Townshend Wickham replaced him at Twyford, possibly a son of another son, Townshend, who was not ordained). A further son, Henry, was probably a master at Winchester College. Canon Wynne Edwards, rector of Llanrhaeadr, in Denbighshire, was a son-in-law, having been curate at Gresford 1849-52. He died in 1885: SA/DR/46, fol. 442. Edward Charles Wickham, dean of Lincoln until his death in 1910, who married a daughter of W. E. Gladstone, may have been a cousin: *Bye Gones*, 31

August 1910, p. 255.

15 His other writings, according to *Bye Gones* of December 1880, p. 172, were *Sermons on the Lord's Prayer, The Sacraments of the Church of England, The Offertory,* and *The Rubrics of the Communion Service.*

16 Robert Wickham, *A Charge delivered to the Clergy and Churchwardens of the Archdeaconry of St Asaph,* 1855, pp. 2-5; 1873, pp. 3-4.

17 Wickham, *Charges,* 1855, pp. 12-15; 1858, pp. 4-8; 1860, pp. 9-10; 1864, pp. 3-7; 1867, pp. 4-5; 1869, pp. 6-7; 1871 (entitled *The Duty of Churchwardens*), p. 11; 1873, pp. 5-7; 1876, pp. 14-15. He expressed concern in his latter charges that churchwardens were resisting paying the lawful visitation fees to the registrar, and in 1867, fearful that parish clerks were exposed to a "hardening ... familiarity with holy things", he requested that wardens should assist them on the right path: pp. 5-7.

18 Wickham, *Charge,* 1871, pp. 11-12.

19 Ibid., 1855, pp. 5-6; 1857, pp. 11-12.

20 Ibid., 1857, pp. 5-11; 1866, pp. 10f.; 1873, pp. 14-15.

21 Ibid., 1858, pp. 2-3, 19-20, 23-24.

22 Ibid., 1864, pp. 21-32: on Convocation see ibid., 1866, pp. 17-18.

23 Ibid., 1867, pp. 8-9; 1876, pp. 15-16.

24 Ibid., 1858, pp. 10-18, and appendix on the same subject therein, pp. 27-30.

25 Ibid., 1866, pp. 19, 23-4; 1867, pp. 10-21; 1869, pp. 10-12; 1873, pp. 9-12; 1875, pp. 12-15; 1876, pp. 5-12.

26 Ibid., 1860, pp. 11-24.

27 Ibid., 1855, pp. 6-9; 1857, p. 13; 1863, pp. 6-21, 31-6; 1866, pp. 4-7; 1871, pp. 6-7. His pamphlet, *The Duties of Churchwardens in regard to Pews* (London, n.d.) is based on his 1863 Charge. See also my *Pews, Benches and Seats: being a History of the church pew in Wales* (Welshpool, 1998) for a discussion on this whole subject, in which I make considerable use of Wickham's *Charges.*

28 See also Wickham *Charges,* 1861, *in passim*; 1875, pp. 16-18; 1876, pp. 3-5. He felt that concessions ought to be made in the interests of charity and peace, though without denying the rightful position of the Church.

29 Wickham, *Charges,* 1861, pp. 4-12, 20-1; 1863, pp. 9-15, 21-3; 1866, pp. 7-9. In his 1864 Charge Wickham castigated those who wished for a change in the form of subscription and declaration required of all those holding ordained office in the Church. While he accepted that the wording needed some revision, any more radical change would permit false teaching to enter: pp. 11-20. In the same Charge he had expressed concern about the book *Essays and Reviews*: pp. 32-5.

30 Wickham, *Charges,* 1855, pp. 9-12; 1857, pp. 3-5, 11-18; 1858, p. 23; 1860, pp. 4-9; 1861, pp. 12-19; 1864, pp. 7-9; 1866, pp. 19-21; 1867, pp. 8-9; 1869, pp. 1-7; 1871, pp. 9-10. He also wrote a letter, published in 1868, *The Act for the Abolition of Compulsory Church Rates,* in order to assist wardens to understand the new position. He noted a just complaint in his 1857 Charge, by which the combined church rate of four parishes in his archdeaconry amounted to £633, but of this sum only £77 was used

for church repairs, though the rate was primarily meant for the maintenance of the church fabric: p. 5.

31 Wickham, *Charges,* 1869, pp. 7-10, 13-17.
32 Ibid., 1866, p. 12.
33 Ibid., 1866, pp. 12-17; 1867, pp. 22-6; 1873, pp. 15-17; 1878, *in passim,* but note p. 9.
34 Ibid., 1855, pp. 14-15; 1861, p. 22; 1863, p. 27.
35 Ibid., 1857, pp. 19-22.
36 Arthur Burns, *The Diocesan Revival in the Church of England* (Oxford, 1999), p. 260.
37 Wickham, *Charges*, 1864, p. 7; 1873, p. 15.
38 *Carnarvon and Denbigh Herald*, 20 June 1857, p. 6.

4
PASTOR AND PREACHER:
WILLIAM LEIGH MORGAN OF CARDIFF

Writing in his Diocesan Memoranda Book during November 1876, Bishop Ollivant of Llandaff recorded that the Revd. W, Leigh Morgan had "entered into rest".[1] Though the deaths of other diocesan clergy are recorded in these books the normal expression used by Ollivant is that they had died. It seems that Leigh Morgan was on terms of close friendship with his bishop, apart from being a canon of the cathedral and for a period rural dean of Cardiff. It may be that the bishop valued his honesty and impartiality. E. Turberville Williams, in a letter to Ollivant, recalled an incident of November 1871, when Leigh Morgan, "evidently under the greatest possible emotion, uttered in the presence of your Lordship, two archdeacons and the rural deans, 'My Lord, you are living in an inner circle."'[2] Bishops need such men around them, and Ollivant was wise enough to know it. They shared the same evangelical faith and both had a pastoral heart, and if Ollivant's task was the building up of a diocese whose population was expanding at an enormous rate, Morgan had the task of building up a church in the docklands area of Cardiff.

Little is known about Leigh Morgan's background. Sir Joseph Bradney states that he was the son of David Morgan by Anne, daughter to Edmund Leigh, vicar of ... [sic]. The Leigh family formed a clerical dynasty, and included William Leigh, vicar of Eglwysilan, who died in 1860 and is known to have been an uncle of Leigh Morgan, and his son in turn, another Edmund, who followed Leigh Morgan as incumbent of Bedwellty and later presented himself to Tredegar.[3] Another, but a more junior member of the family was Daniel Leigh, who was vicar of Llanfabon until 1901. All of these men were well known as evangelical Welsh-speaking clergy during their lifetime.

We know nothing about Leigh Morgan's education. He was not a university graduate, and as he was not included in a list of the more celebrated men who had attended Abergavenny Divinity School it is possible he was trained at the Cowbridge School, whose divinity department also prepared men for orders. Bishop Copleston closed it down, amidst protests, in 1847, as it catered especially for the Welsh-speaking ordinands. A letter of Bishop Copleston of 1840 indicates that "Leigh Morgan of Coychurch" had been offered the parish of Bedwellty,[4] suggesting that he was then curate of this vale parish. His uncle William had been curate of Llangan before his appointment to Eglwysilan in 1833. This may suggest that there were some family connections with that area in which David Jones, rector of Llangan until 1810, had exercised a powerful and decisive evangelical ministry, and which had been continued by Henry Philips who served as curate of Coychurch until the early 1820s. It was Philips who managed to retain for the Church the church people of the area after the 1811 Methodist secession.

By 1844 Morgan had left Bedwellty to become vicar of Roath, then a village of a few hundred people on the outskirts of Cardiff, although at the same time his name was mentioned for the new parish of St Mary's, Cardiff. There were still problems about this appointment, however, for the dean and chapter of Gloucester needed to find a Welsh-speaking vicar for the parish of Llantrisant in their patronage. Accordingly they had suggested to the bishop that perhaps he could appoint someone from his own diocese to that parish and in return allow them to present to the vacancy thus caused by this move, provided it was not a Welsh-speaking parish. Copleston wondered if he should present Morgan or Edward Knight to Llantrisant, so allowing Roath to be filled by the dean and chapter (if Morgan was appointed), provided its patron, the marquess of Bute, agreed.[5] Eventually another candidate was found, Evan Morgan, vicar of Llantwit Major. Leigh Morgan was thus available to serve as the first "official" vicar of the newly constituted St Mary's Church, which he held in plurality with the parish of Roath.

****

The town of Cardiff had within it two historic parishes. St John's cared for the upper part of the town and St Mary's the lower. But in 1607 the church of St Mary was badly affected by flooding and, although it continued in use for some years thereafter, eventually fell into decay. Nevertheless baptisms took place within its ruins until the eighteenth century. The bereft parishioners of St Mary's thereafter attended St John's Church, where they built a gallery for themselves, but continued to elect their own churchwardens until 1808. In that year the two parishes were formally united, though they had been served by the same incumbents for almost two centuries. By the 1830s it was all too clear that the growing seaport and town of Cardiff needed additional church accommodation: in 1839 it was argued that St John's Church held only 1,200 people out of a population of 9,000, and the 4,000 people living in the Docks area, excluded from the earlier figure, were destitute of church accommodation.

A church was needed to hold at least 2,000 people, and it was thought necessary that half of the seats should be free. Thus the 2nd marquess of Bute, an evangelical who may well have been concerned at the rather docile and certainly socially oriented ministry given at St John's Church (apart from the long-standing non-residence of its incumbent), determined not only to erect a new church to serve the lower end of the parish, but also to ensure that it was served by an evangelical minister. The procedures for creating a new parish were rendered much easier by the union of the two benefices; apparently it was far easier to separate the two in ecclesiastical law than to create an entirely new parish. Nevertheless, section 5 of the Act 8 & 9 Victoria c. 70 was specifically framed to meet the needs of this particular case.

The dean and chapter of Gloucester, as patrons of both livings, were persuaded to transfer their patronage to the marquess on the condition that he endowed the living, thus ensuring the new incumbent had a permanent stipend. This was done by transferring to Queen Anne's Bounty the reversion of a number of ground leases of property in Bute Street, valued at £60 per annum, which sum formed the endowment. To this benefaction Bounty governors added a grant of £400 capital. This property (on an 80-year lease), which at one time included a Gospel Hall as well as houses and 14 shops, caused considerable problems in the years ahead. In May 1850 Morgan noted that the new South Wales Railway was causing permanent injury to the value of this property (it later purchased part of this property for £200). Morgan was equally disturbed to find that contrary to the conditions of the leases two new public houses had been opened in the street and more were being planned.

The living also benefited from some commuted vicarial tithe income of about £45, which came through an accommodation with St John's parish (Bute compensated the vicar of St John's for his loss with a £40 endowment, while the dean and chapter of Gloucester gave a similar gift). Pew rents, linked to the stipend, were estimated to be worth £60 per annum; surplice fees in 1846 brought in £30 and the Easter offerings (collected by custom from every male person in the parish – an almost impossible task) £15. The total income, when fully augmented, was about £210 net. But no parsonage house was provided. Instead Morgan had to rent accommodation which was said in 1846 to be a quarter of a mile from the church. Lord Bute, it appears, also expected the new incumbent to be given the chaplaincy of the workhouse in order to increase his income. But the guardians elected another cleric instead. Bishop Copleston felt their action "must be a mortifying thing to Lord Bute, and will be felt also by Leigh Morgan as a serious diminution of his expected income." The bishop was also annoyed that the person chosen, one Jonah Jones, lived at some distance from Cardiff. It was also thought that the magistrates would give the part-time chaplaincy of the prison to the new incumbent in order to increase his income, but once again this did not materialise. By 1861 the income had swelled to £427, although even that figure was lower than that of five years previously at £489. This was because of the opening of a new municipal cemetery which had significantly reduced the burial fees. The pew rents had increased to £167, clearly the sign of a prosperous church. But if St Mary's, Cardiff, was one of the best livings in the diocese, it was also one of the most difficult to manage.

The site of the new church was given by Lord Bute, and in 1842 John Webb, still vicar of the united parish, and his curate, J. C. Campbell, later bishop of Bangor, appealed for funds to build it. The Commissioners for Building New Churches gave a magnificent sum of £1,500, and by 1839 the promised subscriptions amounted to £2,400, which Thomas Stacey, then curate of Cardiff, considered to be the maximum amount achievable. A great bazaar was held, and poets, including Wordsworth and Montgomery, wrote poems in support of the building fund. John Foster of Bristol, as architect, built a huge Romanesque edifice, allegedly based on the south transept of Norwich Cathedral, though his original brief, from Stacey, was to make it as plain and undecorated as possible, as funds did not allow an expensive building. By 1841 the original plan of a cruciform church, with two wide transepts, had to be abandoned for lack of funding (thus reducing the total accommodation). There was fear too that the two belfries would have to be omitted as well, saving £650, though the completion of the railway enabled a much superior stone for the walls to be obtained at a more economic cost. Additional costs were incurred when in July 1842 part of the south wall fell in causing the collapse of two piers, indicating all too clearly the hasty, cost-cutting and defective workmanship of the builders. This was further confirmed by Leigh Morgan's complaint in January 1845 that the western end was so saturated with damp that it was letting in rain "most desperately". Morgan insisted that this and other defects should be rectified before he signed the completion certificate, even though the architect claimed he would have to pay some of the cost from his own pocket.

The new church was opened with much ceremonial on 16 December 1843. This was much later than arranged because two weeks before the original date in August it had been discovered that no conveyance had been made of the site to the Church Building Commissioners, and this had to be rectified. By this time the cost of the building had soared to £5,724, though there was thankfully a deficiency of only £250 in the funds. St Mary's was consecrated on 8 November 1845 after this debt had been paid. The interior was more akin to a preaching auditorium than a traditional church building. There were five blocks of pews on the ground floor and no central aisle, three galleries above (the west one set apart for choir and organ), and in the centre, almost concealing the communion table and its semi-circular communion rails, was the three-decker pulpit, which served as the focal point of the church's interior. Seats for 1,800 were intended and, although the numbers do not add up to this figure, they were originally categorised as 400 rented sittings (fixed into three classes, of 10s., 7s.6d., and 5s. per annum), and 1,300 free seats, including 269 sittings for children. Between 1855-6 Leigh Morgan wrote to the Ecclesiastical Commissioners, as the successors to the Church Building Commissioners, pointing out that the wardens were being overwhelmed with applications for rented seats. Pointing out that there were 12 to 14 benches in the centre aisle (on either side of the pulpit and facing its sides), which had remained unoccupied since the church had opened as the poor refused to make use of them, Morgan asked if these could be converted into rentable pews. Furthermore, he suggested that some of the pews in the galleries, which could not be rented because they were too close to that part of the organ gallery which was occupied by the children of the union workhouse, could become free seats. This alteration would give 609 rented seats and 1,200 free seats, the number stipulated by the Incorporated Church Building Society, and would provide for those who had hitherto been driven out of the Church by a lack of suitable accommodation. The request was allowed.[6]

****

We need to return to Morgan. He was appointed to the new parish by Lord Bute in order to further the evangelical interest in Cardiff. That Morgan was of this school is quite clear from his public statements and by the ministry he conducted at St Mary's. At a meeting of the Bible Society in Cardiff Morgan argued that while there were those who believed that the safety of the nation lay in the "old wooden walls", he himself thought that "our best bulwark and safest protection is the Word of God, faithfully preached from house to house throughout the length and breadth of our country." On another occasion he begged the SPCK to print a new edition of the Welsh Bible. On a fast day appointed for the Crimean War Morgan begged his congregation, in "the commanding style of the preacher", to fast and repent, while, on a happier note, in 1860, he promoted the visit of John Venn to Cardiff in order to speak on the Irish Revival.[7] Such societies as the Church Pastoral-Aid Society, a home missionary society, were commended because of their evangelical nature and their concern for the conversion of people.[8] The Irish Church Mission was equally dear to him, partly because of the large number of Irish in his parish, and also because of its desire to lead those living in superstition towards "the light shed by the Gospel".[9] He also called upon people to contribute liberally to the work of the evangelical Church Missionary Society.[10]

The services at St Mary's were congregational in tone and evangelical in witness. When the militia attended a morning service in 1853, during which a new or improved organ was used for the first time, a newspaper correspondent, although he noted that the choir performed its part with great taste, eulogised the use of the old psalm tunes. He contrasted these unfavourably with the modern tunes and hymns which did not allow hearty congregational participation. Morgan, he noted, spoke plainly to the congregation, many of whom had never been in a place of worship before, and though the church was crowded "breathless silence prevailed." By the end of his ministry the evangelical collection of hymns known as *Harlands Collection* was in use at St Mary's.[11] It seems, however, that the congregation was not too enamoured of the organ and choir, for there was often an embarrassing and substantial deficit in the specific fund out of which the organist was paid and the costs of the choir defrayed.

The matter was only resolved when an offertory collection for church purposes was introduced at each service with much success during 1861.[12]

The church building was established as a preaching auditorium, and to get to the communion table one had to pass around the huge pulpit. Within it the preacher was always arrayed in his black preaching gown. Time and time again it is recorded that the church was crowded for the services, of which there were generally three each Sunday, morning, afternoon and evening. An obituary on Leigh Morgan recalled his powers of oratory, especially "his ability to send home to the hearts of his hearers the riches of the Gospel expressed in polished and vigorous Saxon", which would be long remembered by Cardiff churchmen. In addition Morgan taught his congregation to pray in an extempore fashion at the weekly prayer meetings, although his successor found their language uncouth, undignified and "not conductive to devotion".[13] But Morgan believed this prayer meeting was the power house of his ministry and the Church's life.

The ministry which Leigh Morgan and his curates gave to the parish was not simply a Sunday preaching ministry; rather it was lived out day by day. This was no easy task. The parish had grown from a population of about 4,000, when the church was first planned, to a population of 24,288 in 1863. Though the building of All Saints, Tyndale Street, as the Welsh Church (it later received its own parochial district) relieved Morgan of a population of 6,000, the building of an iron hut in the dockland area of the parish in 1855 increased his responsibilities. Writing to the Ecclesiastical Commissioners during January 1868 Morgan said he was quite unable to provide for the wants and necessities of this very populous parish, containing one of the greatest seaports in the kingdom, and requested their assistance in the provision of a third curate or lay worker (one curate was grant-aided by the Church Pastoral-Aid Society and another was supported by the Assistant Curates' Society). However the commissioners felt unable to assist as his case came outside their regulations, mainly because St Mary's was not an industrial or mining parish in the strict sense of that term, even though as Morgan had rightly pointed out, it was a parish totally dependent on the coal trade.[14] To assist him, Morgan also had a Scripture reader, and a district visiting association comprising lay people who visited a given number of homes on a regular basis and distributed tracts.

The parish, being a part of the dockland area, soon became

notorious as an area of social deprivation. Public houses abounded, houses of ill-fame were not uncommon, and disorder was frequent. The then senior curate, J. Timpson Wrenford, writing in 1852, complained that many would-be worshippers at the Sunday evening service at St Mary's felt unable to attend because they lacked the courage to push themselves through the crowds lining the streets, with prostitutes "unblushingly" calling out their services, and having to hear foul language and expressions of the "vilest descriptions". Those who did attend found themselves forced to walk in the middle of the road however dirty it might be. At times policemen had to be summoned to attend the church services in order to prevent disturbances, particularly in the galleries.[15]

It was against this background that Morgan conducted his pastoral ministry. Speaking to a CPAS meeting in Cardiff, Morgan stated:

> It was a lamentable fact that there were scores of persons who lived close to the means of grace, who never darkened the doors of God's house. They were visited and asked to attend, and it was with the greatest difficulty any were prevailed upon to come in. Certainly, so far as he, himself, individually was concerned, he could not complain of a want of attendance at Church - the attendance was very large, and he could not complain, but although there were perhaps fourteen or fifteen hundred persons in St Mary's Church every Sunday evening, still there were thousands of persons close to the Church, visited by the Scripture Reader and Tract Distributors, who still continued to disregard the things which belonged to their everlasting peace. What was to be done? Great responsibility rested upon all, but a very great responsibility devolved upon the people themselves. What should be done was to carry out the maxim that there should be a fold for every sheep, and a shepherd for every fold. Unless that was done he did not know what could be done. If they were to multiply their ministers so that every pastor should have the charge of one thousand people then they would have to multiply them in Cardiff ten-fold, and this was the state of things in all our large towns. Notwithstanding all the agents at work, there were many who were never visited at all - many could neither read nor write, and many were totally ignorant how they were to be saved - there were thousands of professed infidels who did nothing but scorn and scoff. If persons in the towns were ignorant that there was an Infirmary, or a Savings' Bank, or a

Clothing Club, or a Poor Law Union, or other charitable institutions, they would say "it is a pity"; but when they remembered there were thousands passing into eternity who did not know, or who did not care, what became of their souls after death, it was a terrible thing to think of ... Instead of having only two or three churches in a town like this, they ought to have ten or twelve, and they would soon see a very different state of things.[16]

On another occasion, Morgan read from the report of his Scripture reader, who was grant-aided by a £40 grant by CPAS. Within the course of one year, in a parish whose population was then about 17,000, his Scripture reader had visited 2,912 houses and 3,220 families. Furthermore, "[h]e read and explained portions of Scripture, in a simple manner, to 2,127 families", and spent 38 days in urging parents to send their children to the Sunday Schools. As a result he had started a Sunday School in Newtown, where there was no means of grace whatsoever, and this was now attended by 72 children, though Morgan regretted that the only place where it could be held was in the yard of a public house. The reader had also held 12 juvenile missionary meetings, 62 cottage lectures "in the most destitute places in the parish", and eight meetings with Sunday School teachers, while he had encouraged a number of children to attend the morning service at St Mary's. He had also sold 273 Bibles, 87 Testaments and 123 Prayer Books to sailors. Morgan also quoted from his reader's case book as follows:

In this house I met with a man who was so grossly ignorant that he could not tell me who Jesus Christ was. To use his own words, he supposed him to be some 'Nice man'; and it was with astonishment that he listened to my remarks on the Saviour, when speaking of his person, character, and mission. He had never read the Bible, and but two or three times in his life attended any place of worship; but he promised me that if he would be in Cardiff on Sunday next, he would attend Church.

... a man who has not been in Church or chapel for years; and he seemed to be very ignorant. I said to him – "Do you know you have a soul to be saved?" "No, I do not. What is a soul? I don't understand you." I told him what I meant by a soul, and proved that it must exist for ever, and that also either in everlasting torment or happiness. I told him also of a Saviour who died to save that soul, and the condition by which it may be saved.

Last night, at half-past eleven o'clock, a messenger came for me to go and see --- , as she was in a dying state, and it was her earnest wish to see me. I went and found it was but too true that she was dying. I knelt by her bedside, and said, "Do you know me?" She answered, "Yes." "Have you been praying to Jesus to pardon your sins, as I before exhorted you to do?" "Yes." "And now seeing that you have not long to live, let me ask you one question more, – Are you happy?" "Yes," she replied; and was then too weak to answer me any further questions. I still knelt down, and read the 39th and 90th Psalms, and earnestly prayed that God would take her to himself, and prepare her for heaven. I think I may hope that she had made her peace with God. After I had finished prayer, one of her family (who is a Mormonite and also a preacher with them) seemed very desirous to argue with me, on the fitness of men to be priests, according to the order of Moses and Aeron, and other such views as they hold. But I said – "Sir, this is not a fitting place for such controversy. My duties are with the dying, and the only priesthood I can now talk of is after the order of Melchizedek, He who is our great High Priest; and if you are a Christian man, you will be more anxious to pray to that great High Priest to hear our prayers, and save the soul of this poor dying woman." This put an end to the wished for controversy, and in a few moments after, the poor woman died.[17]

If this depicts the more spiritual aspect of mission, there was also a deep concern in two other areas, these being the pastoral care of the seamen passing through the port, and the social care of the population at large.

Speaking to a meeting of the Cardiff Mission to Seamen in 1870, Morgan spoke of the difficulties of seamen in that port:

In the first place he was withdrawn from the moral, social, and religious restraint, which those feel on shore. He had no father nor mother to instruct him, and when he arrived in port no sister or brother to speak a kind word to him; generally mixing with a godless crew, and if he had any spark of religious feeling in him, he was unable to show it from the fear of meeting with the gibes and jeers of his companions in the forecastle. Before the vessel arrived in port she was boarded by crimps, and he engaged himself to some low lodging-house, where he spent his money in drunkenness and debauchery, and when he attempted to go to sea again, he had to obtain an advance note to procure the means of getting a suit of clothes to enable him again to proceed on the voyage; and thus he went on year after year, and there appeared nothing left for him but to spend his money in this way, and then go to sea again.[18]

This work amongst the sailors had started through the initiative of Dr Ashley, who had founded the Bristol Channel Seamen's Mission. It later developed into the Missions to Seaman, an international Anglican organisation. The explorer Sir John Franklin was deeply interested in its work. In 1852 a church was opened for seamen in the Bute Docks. Morgan preached at the opening service, noting the number of sailors who were men of God and the number of ships which were places of prayer. During the previous 18 months he and his curates had never lacked a congregation on any ship which they had visited and to whom they had preached "the glad tidings of redemption". Morgan finished by telling the assembled seamen never to go to sea without a copy of the Bible. His message so struck home that within nine years it was common to find daily prayers held on board many ships, while many captains asked where they could obtain copies of the Bible in the language of the countries they were visiting in order to distribute them.[19] Later an old wooden-walled ship, *HMS Thisbe*, was utilised as a centre for seamen, with a chapel on deck together with other facilities. A lay reader, and later a curate, was made responsible for this mission work, and in 1864 it was reported that in four months over 2,455 seamen had come to services on this ship, averaging 120 at the afternoon service and 70 during the evening, while 928 had come to read periodicals provided in a reading room. Seeing a seaman with smallpox driven from door to door with no one willing to take him in, Morgan obtained a hospital ship for seamen, the *Hamadryad*, and in 1870 opened a seaman's hostel which could accommodate between 60 and 70 men. He also provided a banking service for their money.[20] It was not only sailors who benefited from his activity. The militia, billeted in Cardiff during 1853 whilst on a training camp, were each presented with a Bible by Morgan at a service in St Mary's, during which he congratulated them on their behaviour, especially as many of them had been billeted in public houses.[21]

Morgan's social concern within the community was as substantial as it was varied. The provision of schools was one. By 1848 St Mary's National Schools had been founded. In that year Morgan announced that the Queen Dowager had given a £10 subscription to the schools and Lady Mary Cole £20, though he berated those men of property in his parish who had not subscribed a single shilling. Property, he commented, had its duties as well as its privileges.[22] As we have noted already, in the reports of the Scripture reader, there were large Sunday Schools, although these appear to have been for children, rather than for adults. Mothers' meetings were held on a regular basis, and a Clothing Club was started in 1845 by Leigh Morgan's wife. It was hoped that this club would assist poor families, who might "otherwise suffer from the results of improvidence," to save on a weekly basis towards a Christmas distribution of flannel and blankets. Private subscriptions enabled the committee to offer a bonus of about four shillings in the pound. The average amount saved was £3. Morgan's hope of establishing a Savings Bank was never realised, though at one stage it appears that the parish ran a lending library.[23] The promotion of temperance was also part of this social remit. Not only did Morgan advocate teetotalism from the pulpit, he also chaired a public meeting in 1860 requesting the magistrates not to license any new public houses in the town.[24] During the cholera epidemic both Morgan and Thomas Stacey, the curate of St John's, endeavoured, with others, to improve the sanitary condition of the town through their membership of the health committee of the Board of Guardians. And in 1855, during a period of considerable hardship, Morgan was asked to act as the relieving officer of the Cardiff Poor Law Union for the docks area, during which time he was responsible for the distribution of £400 worth of relief.[25]

"Valuable hints to the working classes" was the title of a talk Morgan gave as his contribution to a series of lectures for the working classes at the St Mary's National Schoolroom. This, or a similar lecture, appears to have been given on a number of occasions between 1854-62 to the Young Men's Christian Association, an organisation which was one of Morgan's many interests. The value of good ventilation in houses was stressed, particularly in sleeping rooms, where many spend one third of their time, and "sentimental young ladies ... about one half of their time". He also spoke of the need for good, wholesome food, well prepared and ready for the husband when he returned from work. Public wash-houses were required, for when a working man came home to find the kitchen taken up with damp washing, he was inclined to flee to the hospitality of the local hostelry. Other lectures stressed the need for model lodging houses, savings banks to be open during the evening hours, and the necessity of ragged schools for the extremely poor. The need for temperance was also stressed in these lectures. In his 1854 lecture he calculated there was one beer shop for every 13 houses in his parish.[26]

****

Throughout these years at St Mary's Leigh Morgan also continued as vicar of Roath, holding this parish in plurality, keeping a curate there, and taking the services once a month. The old parish church of Roath was a survivor of an earlier age, with its whitewashed interior and old-fashioned box pews. An old man came from Cardiff each Sunday to lead the worship with a piccolo and to conduct a small children's choir. The clerk and minister (who used the black gown in the pulpit) said the psalms alternatively in "the good old English style", the congregation possibly repeating them after the clerk.

Although the population on his appointment was in the hundreds, by 1863 it had reached 3,044, and was to double again within ten years. In that year the value of the living was £137, and from this sum he paid a curate £100 for his services. Although in his earlier days at St Mary's this additional income might have been very necessary to Morgan, and was probably the reason why the plurality was allowed, it is hard to understand why he retained the living of Roath throughout his Cardiff incumbency, unless he feared that the Bute trustees would appoint a non-evangelical or even ritualist as his successor. In 1869 he applied to the Ecclesiastical Commissioners for an augmentation of this living as it was over 3,000 in population (according to the terms of the Commission's advertised offer) and for assistance towards the building of a new daughter church in the Splott area of the parish. This assistance was based on a local claim, for a large part of the rectorial tithes belonged to the dean and chapter of Gloucester, but was now in the custody of the commissioners, who were prepared to act as "good landlords" in such parishes. Lord Tredegar (he wrote) had fitted up a chapel from an old barn in Splott, a place with a rapidly increasing population, and he was prepared to allow this building to become a school and to offer half an acre of land for a church and parsonage house, plus a sum of £200 for building of a church. This was the nucleus of St German's Church. His lordship was already providing £40 per annum towards the cost of a curate for this district. Lord Bute, the other major landowner in the parish, was at that present moment rebuilding the parish church of St Margaret's as a memorial to his father and could not assist in any further work. A commission was appointed to investigate. It noted that the income of the parish had risen dramatically since 1862. By 1866 it was £184 gross and in 1868 £212. This increase was because glebe land had been sold for building purposes and the money invested, while a lease had been given of the minerals under lands belonging to the vicarage in the parish of Bedwas. But it also noted, as it had to, that Leigh Morgan was incumbent of St Mary's with a net income of £353 and a population of over 26,000, and the patron of the Roath living was the trustees of the Marquess of Bute. It was thus in private rather than public patronage, a matter much disliked by the commissioners. Consequently they laid down their terms. They would augment the living by £57, to bring it up to a value of £300, on condition it was no longer held in plurality. And they would give an equivalent benefaction for the proposed parsonage house of up to £1,400 provided an equal sum was obtained from private individuals and subscribers (though the value of land could be taken into account), subject to the same stipulation.

Morgan's work in persuading the marquess to rebuild the parish church, starting a mission in another part of the parish, and ensuring that his successor had an augmented income and possibly a home in which to live, were solid achievements. But Morgan was never appreciated in Roath, and his later resignation was greeted with delight as it meant a full-time incumbent would be appointed. Furthermore there had been complaints that he had neglected the parish, leaving its work in the hands of a curate, and appointing wardens without holding a vestry meeting. His answer to the latter complaint was abrupt. He had always appointed his wardens in this way and he felt legally obliged to continue this practice. If his parishioners felt grieved then they could apply to the courts for redress. Not surprisingly Morgan was accused of flinging the law at his parishioners. Another dispute concerned his curate, Thomas Clapp, who accused Morgan of making him shoulder the costs and problems of the National School, and when he had resigned, of declining to reimburse him the £50 he had spent on this account.[27]

By this time Morgan had spent over 25 hard years at St Mary's, starting as priest in charge and ending as vicar. In fact at the 1847 vestry meeting he was asked to clarify his position, was he rector, vicar or curate? He could only reply that as he was in receipt of the ground rents he understood he was the rector, although he was not formally instituted to the cure of the parish until 24 July of that year.[28] The initial years were years of promise, due to the patronage of the second marquess, but his death in 1848 destroyed the anticipated hopes of substantial sums being made available for parochial use, as well as depriving Morgan of the moral support of an evangelically minded peer, who had been (in the words of Morgan's funeral sermon) "the friend and patron of true religion".[29] By 1871 Morgan was probably old and weary (as indicated by the Roath disputes), and possibly welcomed the offer by the Bute patronage trustees of the country parish of Llanmaes in the vale of Glamorgan. Nevertheless, this offer probably caused him a dilemma. He was well aware that the marquess was using his patronage trustees as a means of avoiding the legal requirement that his patronage, as a papist, should be exercised by the university of Cambridge, thus allowing himself some say, behind the scenes, in choosing men for the parishes of which he was patron. He must have been equally aware that the new trustees had been chosen for their sympathy with the Tractarian movement; Bute possibly considering that this was the next best thing to membership of the Roman Church. Morgan's fear that his successors in his two parishes would be Tractarians must have been real, even though he might have felt that the trustees would not dare to appoint a Tractarian to succeed him at St Mary's, knowing the evangelical tone of the church and the "weight" of the congregation. Morgan was much mistaken if this was the case. Advanced ritualists were appointed to both parishes.

A presentation was made to Morgan by his St Mary's parishioners which stated:

Rev. and Dear Sir, – We, the undersigned, on behalf of the congregation of St Mary's Church and subscribers generally, desire to express our heartfelt regret at the severance of the tie which has so long existed between us; and in doing so wish to bear our testimony to the faithfulness with which you have exercised the duties of your pastoral office during the 28 years you have been amongst us.

We feel that the Gospel of Christ has been preached by you in all its purity and simplicity, with an earnestness which showed your extreme anxiety for the souls of your people, and you have exemplified the same by the consistency of your daily life.

We appreciate most highly the patient perseverance and energy which you have exhibited in the management of the various institutions and charities which owe to you their origin. You found us destitute of many appliances for the advancement of the religious and moral welfare of the poorer inhabitants of the parish, and you leave us with large, flourishing, and efficient day and Sunday schools, Bible classes, clothing clubs and many other kindred societies.

The framed address went on to to speak of his wife's "invaluable and untiring assistance". In his reply Morgan noted how the parish had changed over the years of his ministry:

You have assisted me liberally in maintaining the church, parish, and other charities, and enabled me to deliver them into the hands of my successor unburdened with debt. The schools, which were the heaviest charge, have a large balance in their favour. Upon my part, I know of many deficiencies, faults and failings in duty. I can honestly say, however, that I tried to do my best, but, oh, how far was that from which I could have wished it had been! ... As to the all-important matter of preaching the truth of the everlasting Gospel, I have not shunned to declare unto you all the counsel of God, but have warned everyone night and day. As far as I have known the truth, I have conveyed it sincerely to each of you without respect of persons. In this portion of my ministerial labours I have always felt my constant need of Divine grace and of your earnest prayers. I have no doubt but that both have been freely given. If I have felt my infirmities and failing in my parochial ministrations, how much more have I felt them in my labours among the great congregations? To give those up was a great trial to me, as to perform them was my great pleasure.[30]

Similar sentiments were generally recorded on these occasions in most parishes, but they were none the less real for that. Morgan was a typical evangelical clergyman of his period, sincere, earnest, and pastorally and spiritually concerned for the edification of his parishioners. Perhaps we could say no less for his successors; they too were earnest and spiritually minded men, but of a very different tradition.

At Roath the Bute patronage trustees appointed Frederick Puller to succeed Morgan, and Puller started a noteworthy ministry along Tractarian lines in that busy and growing parish. The trustees originally offered the living of St Mary's to the equally high church vicar of St Mary's, Shrewsbury, T. M. B. Bulkeley-Owen, but he declined the offer,[31] and they eventually settled upon Griffith Arthur Jones, who had been vicar of Llanegryn in Merionethshire since 1857. The congregation protested at the appointment of an advanced ritualist, having petitioned for the appointment of a former curate, D. Parker Morgan, then vicar of Aberafan and Baglan, who was regarded as a powerful preacher.[32] What they feared occurred. Although the Tractarian rituals were not immediately introduced, the teachings which lay behind them were, and the congregation, well instructed by Morgan, were aware of their significance. Protests poured into the bishop's office, but he could do little, although a consistory court was held to decide whether Jones had made unauthorised alterations and additions to the church furnishings. Many of the congregation left, a fact admitted by Jones's biographers. A number of the congregation memorialised the bishop for the formation of a new district out of the lower part of the parish, which was to become St Stephen's district, and made it clear that this was because of the introduction of certain forms and ceremonies at St Mary's which they regarded as ritualistic. Bishop Ollivant tried to remain neutral but, in a letter of 17 November 1873 to the Ecclesiastical Commissioners requesting a grant for an incumbent for this new district, he made it clear that the congregation would make up all the necessary monies required for a new district, "as it is to escape from what they deem his [Jones's] religious opinions that they have been acting all along." Another group became the nucleus of St Paul's Free Church of England which remained in Cardiff for a number of years. Although Father Jones managed to obtain another congregation, it took many years, and a church which had had a powerful voice and ministry to Cardiff was marginalised and it never recovered its wider impact on the life of the town.[33]

The parish of Llanmaes was small, a population of 452, with an income of £430, together with a parsonage house. In many respects it was a semi-retirement post, for at that time there was no system of retirement pensions for clergy unless they could afford to obtain an annuity on the private market. Little is known of Leigh Morgan's ministry here, although he continued as a canon of Llandaff Cathedral till his death in November 1876. Equally little is known of his family life or personal characteristics, but it is clear that his was a faithful ministry which gave in spite of his paternalism (that Victorian virtue!) encouragement, spiritual hope and practical assistance to people of all classes in society, especially to the poor. A modest man, he would not have asked for any further tribute.

ENDNOTES

1 NLW, Church in Wales Records, Glyn Simon Deposit, Box 1: Llandaff
   Diocesan Memorandum Books, Vol. II, for 5 November 1876.
2 Letter of E. Turberville Williams to Ollivant, 9 January 1872, NLW, John
   Morgan Papers, Box 10.
3 Joseph Bradney (ed. M. Gray), *A History of Monmouthshire* (Cardiff,
   1993), V 151; CMG, 3 March 1860, p. 5.
4 Copleston to J. M. Traherne, 15 April 1840, CL, number T83. In
   Copleston's correspondence with Bruce Knight he suggested to Copleston
   that Morgan might be replaced at Bedwellty on a temporary basis by his
   cousin Edmund: 11 December 1843, CL, number K342.
5 Roger L. Brown (ed.,) *The Letters of Edward Copleston, Bishop of
   Llandaff, 1828-1849* (Cardiff, 2003): Copleston to Traherne, 17 July
   1845, p. 270.
6 See generally, John Guy, *St Mary's Church, Cardiff* (Cardiff, 1971); the
   papers of the Church Building Commissioners, EC and QAB are held by
   the Representative Body of the Church in Wales; Brown, *Copleston
   Letters*: Copleston to Traherne, 28 August 1843, p. 262, and ibid., 6 April
   1844, CL, number T118; Letter of Thomas Stacey to Lord Bute, 31
   January 1837, NLW, Bute Papers, L80/18 (it noted the need for the new
   church and expressed the hope that the Gloucester chapter would pay for
   it). The lease of the ground rents was renewed in 1878 for 46 years at an
   annual charge of £498, on a valuation of £3,330. By 1877 the value of the
   living had substantially declined. Morgan's successor, Arthur Griffith
   Jones, found that his Tractarian policies had caused a diminution in the
   pew rentals, while the erosion of the middle classes from his parish for
   "more healthy and genial localities" also had its effect. The surplice fees
   also diminished, due to the erection of a public cemetery and the lack of
   space in the joint St Mary's and St John's churchyard given them by the
   2nd Marquess. Jones, in letters to the Ecclesiastical Commissioners,
   claimed he had an income of only £140 and no parsonage house, with
   three curates, possibly four, to support. Noting that All Saints' Church,
   taken from his parish, had a population of under 1,000 and yet an income
   of over £200 plus house, he asked if he could substantiate a local claim
   against the estate of the dean and chapter of Gloucester, administered by
   the commissioners, who held the tithes of his parish. Though he was not a
   grumbler he yet felt that if other and smaller parishes could receive
   assistance his should as well. But as only £26 of this income arising from
   these tithes remained inappropriated (most having gone to All Saints
   Church) and his parish was in private and not public patronage, his
   application failed, even though Ollivant supported him by writing "if you

can get an addition to your miserable income it will give me great pleasure." A grant of £500 offered him for a parsonage house had to be turned down as there was no land available on which it could be legally built.

7 CMG, 16 June 1849, p. 4; 16 March 1850, p. 3; 31 March 1855, Supplement p. 2; 6 January 1860, p. 6. For his concern for the Sabbath see CMG, 8 January 1853, p. 3.

8 CMG, 9 December 1848, p. 4; 29 December 1854, p. 3; 3 November 1855, p. 6.

9 CMG, 22 May 1852, p. 2.

10 CMG, 31 May 1851, p. 4; 12 May 1854, p. 4.

11 CMG, 4 June 1853, p. 3; 1 January 1870, p. 5.

12 CMG, 5 April 1862, p. 5; CMG, 24 April 1847, p. 3, suggests this was because of Nonconformist opposition to such payments from the church rates. On this occasion the redoubtable John Batchelor asked the vestry not to press for a church rate. The introduction of the Sunday offertory enabled the church rate to be suspended. The congregation were generous: in 1861 over £2,155 was subscribed for church expenses and 29 other causes, including the Assistant Curates' Society, Llandaff Church Extension Society, the Scripture Readers Association, and other mission organisations: CMG, 5 April 1862, p. 5.

13 J. W. Ward and H. A. Coe, *Father Jones of Cardiff* (London, 1907), p. 33.

14 EC file, 13 January 1872. Lady Bute had assisted Morgan by a grant of £40 as a moiety of a stipend for a curate to work "in the docks": Lady Bute to E. P. Richards, 1 October 1850, Glamorgan Record Office, D/DA/34A/61. Arthur Jones as Morgan's successor also applied to the Ecclesiastical Commissioners for a grant stating that the two curates he could afford were totally inadequate for the needs of the parish – at least 11 curates were needed – and though there were many company offices in his parish, few of them contributed to his funds. Although he pleaded the importance of Cardiff as a place with considerable influence, he too was unsuccessful for the same reason.

15 CMG, 21 August 1852, p. 3, and 14 January 1865, p. 8; cf. *Cardiff Times*, 12 June 1869, p. 8.

16 CMG, 26 November 1859, p. 6; 6 December 1862, p. 6.

17 CMG, 8 October 1853, p. 4.

18 CMG, 26 March 1870, p. 6.

19 CMG, 4 September 1852, p. 4; 14 August 1852, p. 4; 20 April 1861, p. 8.

20 CMG, 5 March 1864, p. 6; 21 March 1868, p. 6. John Mayberry in *I Saw Three Ships* (Cardiff, 1988) suggests that the founder of this work was Dr H. J. Paine, the medical officer of health for Cardiff. He makes no mention of Morgan's name in the booklet though Lady Bute, in the letter mentioned above in reference 14, wrote that several captains had agreed that services could be held on board their vessels whilst in harbour.

21 Bryn Owen, *The History of the Welsh Militia and Volunteer Corps, II,*

The Glamorgan Regiments of Militia (Caernarfon, 1990), p. 75. The Bibles were obtained by public subscription.

22 CMG, 20 May 1848, p. 2. R. M. Goyne, the schoolmaster, was later ordained and served as vicar of All Saints' Church: CMG, 21 June 1856, p. 5.

23 CMG, 3 January 1852, p. 2. The lending library is noted in a letter of 13 January 1868 in the Ecclesiastical Commissioners' file for the parish.

24 W. R. Lambert, *Drink and Sobriety in Victorian Wales* (Cardiff, 1983), pp. 136-7.

25 CMG, 16 June 1849, p. 3; 10 March 1855, p. 10.

26 CMG, 26 May 1862, p. 6; 21 January 1854, p. 3; 28 January 1854, p. 1; 9 February 1855, p. 3. 1,500 people were present at one of these lectures: CMG, 31 October 1857, p. 6.

27 The 1832 parliamentary return (in the EC file for Roath) said it had a population of 272 and an income of £92 gross, of which £50 was paid to the curate. The mineral lease was dated 1853. See also M. Warner and A. C. Hooper, *The History of Roath St German's* (Cardiff, 1934), pp. 14-15; CMG, 10 February 1865, p. 8; 22 April 1871, p. 5; 29 April 1871, p. 5; 8 September 1865, p. 5.

28 CMG, 24 April 1847, p. 3.

29 CMG, 1 April 1848, p. 3. Morgan served as a domestic chaplain to the second marquess's widow.

30 CMG, 13 January 1872, p. 6.

31 F. D. How, *Memoir of the Revd T. M. B. Bulkeley-Owen* (London, 1914), p. 15.

32 CMG, 16 September 1871, p. 5.

33 See Ward and Coe, *Fr Jones*, pp. 30-6; Roger L. Brown, *David Howell* (Denbigh, 1998), pp. 56-61.

5
ÉMINENCE GRISE: JOHN GRIFFITHS, ARCHDEACON OF LLANDAFF

Archdeacon Griffiths did much, and might have done more. He was one of the best natural speakers Wales has ever produced; under more favourable auspices he might have developed into a great orator. Had he entered the Nonconformist ministry, his name might have been linked with the great preachers of the century; had he entered Parliament he could not have failed to become a conspicuous figure in its debates. It was the Archdeacon's misfortune that he was born a Churchman. He was a man whose popular sympathies stood against his promotion in an alien and anti-national church. He was no bitter sectarian; he refused to treat Nonconformists as social pariahs or schismatical heretics. He was a Welsh Nationalist at a time when it was not fashionable for every Tory candidate or ecclesiastical fledgling to assume the title. He was an ardent Eisteddfodwr, when *The Times* still poured the vials of its hatred and contempt on the old institution. He believed in Welsh utilisation when the *Western Mail* was yet unconverted, and was content to voice the grumblings of the Philistines and the boors. The highest offices of the Church were denied to him, for they are reserved for men of the type of Bishop Edwards: but his throne was a greater and more sacred one than lies in the gift of an Erastian Premier. He was enthroned in his nation's heart, and in days to come, when the Welsh Church is awakened to her real mission and responsibility, many a pilgrim will turn his steps to the lonely grave by the Atlantic's surge where lie the relics of him who in dark and troublous times taught his church that love is more than wealth, that charity is more than prestige, and that the weapons of religion are not carnal, but powerful through God for the casting down of strongholds.[1]

With these words the editor of *Young Wales* announced the death of John Griffiths, Archdeacon of Llandaff. But was Griffith simply "a might have been" as implied here, for bearing in mind his background, his lack of a university education, and his openness to Nonconformity, he still rose high in the ranks of the Church. And if pilgrims no longer wander to his grave in Aberaeron his name is still remembered by historians of nineteenth-century Wales, even if that name is sometimes relegated to a footnote. During his lifetime he was popular and well known, becoming almost an icon for the Nonconformist press as to what a good Churchman should be. But popularity has a transient value, and it is time to make some assessment of Griffiths's contribution to the Church and society of his own day.

Born at a humble farmhouse, Parcyneuadd, in the vale of Aeron, in 1820, the son of a much-respected cattle drover, his parents moved to a small mansion, Dolau Gwartheg, near Aberaeron, soon after his birth, his father having been appointed agent to two estates in that area. The family had Pembrokeshire and Carmarthenshire connections. Two of his brothers were also ordained; a not untypical position in Cardiganshire families of that day. The area Griffiths was brought up in was within range of Llangeitho, then still a centre of Methodist pilgrimage. The local clergy after the Methodist secession of 1811 kept their parishes loyal to the Church by adopting or continuing methodist activities such as prayer meetings, preaching meetings, *seiats* and Sunday schools. This was especially true of David Herbert of Llanrhystud. It is likely, therefore, that Griffiths was brought up in an atmosphere of evangelical life amongst those who had experienced spiritual revival.

Griffiths shared in the education provided for his landlord's son by John Lewis, vicar of Llanrhystud, and at 16 he entered Cardigan Grammar School, then under the distinguished mastership of W. Grey Hughes. Fellow pupils were Dr David James, vicar of Panteg and a later warden of Llandovery College, who sympathised with many of Griffiths's own interests, and Dean E. O. Phillips of St David's. This private-venture school had attained a notable reputation as a place of classical scholarship, and in the year after Griffiths's birth its pupils had enacted Euripides' *Medea* in the original Greek. This might account for Peter Williams's assertion that when Griffiths entered St David's College, Lampeter, "he possessed a knowledge of the classics far above the average of his fellow pupils." He was later to win the senior prize in classics. Alfred Ollivant, who was later bishop of

Llandaff and who appointed Griffiths to his archdeaconry, was then vice-principal. At that time, however, the college was not a degree-giving body, and possibly the expense of studying at one of the older universities was beyond Griffiths's means. Instead, as he had a few years to wait between finishing this course and reaching the minimum age for ordination, Griffiths was appointed by the Mayor and Corporation of Cardigan to the headmastership of his old school. It could hardly be described as a prestigious appointment. The number of pupils was small, the school looked like a prison with high walls surrounding it, and the expectations of parents were limited.

John Morgan, in an obituary article in the *Geninen* recalled those days. In appearance Griffiths was taller than most, of a strong build, with wide shoulders, the red cheeks of healthy living, and dark brown hair slightly curling. To his pupils he appeared like the god Jove as described by the classical writers. As a teacher he was a strict disciplinarian but was ready to approve good work. He taught his pupils to enjoy good books, to use their memories, and he established a public-speaking competition for his scholars. One morning, Morgan relates, Griffiths was missing from school, and was away for the whole week. On his return he informed his pupils that he had been to Margam in order to be examined by Bruce Knight, the bishop of Llandaff's chaplain, and after passing that examination he had proceeded to London to be ordained by the bishop. In a few days time, having sorted out the school for his successor, he left, an occasion which Morgan described as "painful to most of us in the school".[2]

Like many Cardiganshire men, Griffiths was ordained into the diocese of Llandaff. He was appointed to the curacy of Blaenau or Blaenavon, which had been recently formed from the parish of Llanover. One wonders if he was drawn to Blaenavon by some connection with the Hall family, the local magnates, for Lady Llanover, as Mrs Hall became, knew Griffiths well enough to write on a later occasion some extremely derogatory remarks about him. He did not remain there for long, for in 1845, when he was ordained priest, Bishop Copleston appointed him to the new Peel district of Nantyglo. For a man used to the countryside these harsh industrial parishes must have been as emotionally difficult as they were physically taxing. This would have been especially true of Nantyglo, situated as it was in a barren wilderness ravaged by industrial waste. Its iron furnaces were constantly aglow and the cinder tips provided an even further note of depression. His sense of desolation emerges in words he uttered nearly 50 years later when he described to a meeting of the Church Pastoral-Aid Society, an evangelical home missionary society, the effect of receiving one of their first grants for a curate's stipend: "The good news" of the Society came "as cold water to a thirsty soul" to men in his position, "the solitary representatives of the Church in their thinly-populated parishes. The society supplied what was urgently needed – more men for the Church's work. It did more, it required that the best men that could be found, the men best qualified in head and heart, should be engaged as assistant clergy." Consequently the "well-nigh dying embers of the Church on the hills and in the crowded valleys of the southern portion of the Principality" were fanned into flames by the men brought there by this Society, and by others who received encouragement through its work. Such men, continued Griffiths, "inspired the country parson with new desires; [and] they rescued the old Church from the disrepute which had long lain on her, of having no men who could exercise the weapon of preaching to any credible extent."[3] This reads like the personal testimony of a man who, having been discouraged by the sheer immensity of the task entrusted to him, found himself revitalised by such support and encouragement.

The lords of this area were the Crawshay Bailey family, who exercised a lordship which many a medieval magnate might have envied. The family attended Nantyglo Church, and often brought with them some of their guests, who after a substantial dinner were not always in a state of sobriety. On one occasion a guest woke during the service, struck the pew with his fist, and in a voice which rang throughout the congregation called for "Another bottle of that '16 port, please. It is rare good stuff!". But there was a credit side. A friendship developed between Griffiths and the family, so that he became a trustee of the family estate, and was able to use his position, on at least one occasion, to benefit the Church in his diocese. Mrs Crawshay Bailey, junior, later erected a tablet to his memory in Llandaff Cathedral.[4]

Griffiths's time at Nantyglo was short, less than two years in duration; possibly he overtaxed his strength or found himself totally unsuited to that kind of ministry. As a result Sir Joseph Bailey, brother of Crawshay Bailey, offered him the vale living of Llansannor in 1846, with its population of 204 and income of £105 (Nantyglo was £150). This was informally linked with the curacy of Llangan, where he acted for Richard Prichard, rector since 1821, but whose main ecclesiastical function was senior priest-vicar at Llandaff

Cathedral. The following year saw his nomination to the adjacent parish of St Mary Hill by its patron, Sir Digby Aubrey, with its income of £90 and population of 258. One of the main problems of this grouping was the lack of a benefice house. In February 1848 Griffiths was permitted to occupy the rectory house of Llancarfan and Llanilid parish during the vacancy there, but Bishop Ollivant, who came into the diocese as a reforming bishop, gave Griffiths notice in May 1850 that he was to quit the curacy of Llangan, reside in and take the duty of his own parishes, and build a rectory house. A note is appended to the diocesan memorandum book that Griffiths had promised Sir John Aubrey that he would build this house. But build he did not, at least not at St Mary Hill, for when he left the parish in 1855 it was still without a parsonage house.[5] These must have been quiet years for Griffiths. Little is known of them. As his daughter placed a bust of him in St Mary Hill Church they must have been happy years, or at least for her in her childhood. But Griffiths's growing reputation as a preacher and as an evangelical leader prompted the trustees of the second marquess of Bute to offer him the parish of Neath in 1855. The late marquess was an evangelical, and his trustees at that time pursued his concern of appointing like-minded men into the parishes of his patronage. The parish in fact was a consolidated one, linking together the ancient parish of Llantwit with the more modern parish of Neath.

The parish of Neath must have seemed a huge contrast to the rural life of his previous years. As Griffiths put it in 1861, the change was "of no ordinary character. He felt his own weakness when entering upon the work, but he was supported by a strong determination, which he ever had, God willing, of doing his utmost to carry out faithfully the duties which developed upon him." But Neath was no frontier town like Nantyglo, rather it was an old established market town with an expanding industrial belt around it. There was still, we might say, a civilising influence within it. Neath was also a growing town. In 1863 the population was returned by Griffiths as 8,063, but 13 years later he estimated it had reached 13,000. A previous rector had estimated his income as £454 gross, but in Griffiths's time the income declined due to the fall in value of the tithe-rent-charge as a result of agricultural depression. By the 1890s he returned his income as £397 gross and £308 net, for from it he had to pay taxes based on the full value of the tithe, and also make a significant contribution to the stipends of his curates.[6] Griffiths was to remain in this parish until he retired, although in 1861 he was offered the parish of Llanbadarn

Fawr by Bishop Thirlwall. Griffiths wanted the existing plurality of Llanbadarn with Aberystwyth to remain, but Lord Blandford's recent act against pluralism had made this impossible, and so he withdrew his acceptance. It caused a little embarrassment, especially at Neath, where a presentation had been organised. The organisers, with a charm equal to the occasion turned the matter to good account, making the occasion an opportunity to mark the esteem in which Griffiths was held in the parish and of their thanksgiving that he was now to remain amongst them.[7]

"A very indifferent clergyman," wrote H. A. Bruce, first Lord Aberdare, of Griffiths to the premier, Gladstone, in 1870, while Lady Llanover, 13 years later during another episcopal vacancy when Griffiths's claims were again being pressed, threw out the rather derisory question, "What is he like in his parish?" Laicus, writing a letter in the *Western Mail* was even more pointed, describing him at the time of another episcopal vacancy as intolerant and hasty, no manager of his own or of parochial affairs.[8] What was the truth, so far as it can be ascertained?

His predecessor at Neath was Henry Hey Knight, rector from 1826-55, a man of scholarly attainments and a scion of an old and recognised county family. "He would have done credit to any English parish, but he was out of place as rector of such a parish as Neath," wrote Peter Williams, while Griffiths, in a letter to the Ecclesiastical Commissioners, alleged that there had been no Welsh language services in his churches which "the people could properly understand and appreciate" for 50 years prior to his appointment. Though Griffiths wrote in 1886 that Neath was by then an anglicised town (with people attending Welsh chapels even though they were not habitual speakers of the language), the situation was clearly different at the start of his ministry, when he claimed that one half of his parish was Welsh-speaking. He accordingly introduced Welsh language services and endeavoured to obtain an additional curate to serve this part of the community. The results were dramatic, as he himself reported to the 1856 annual meeting of the Llandaff Church Extension Society, which had given him a grant for this Welsh-speaking curate. Two hundred or so people attended the evening service in a newly provided chapel, and he had about 50 Welsh communicants, 45 of whom had been recently received into the Church. A Welsh day school with 110 children and an all-age Sunday school of about 120 had been started. All this, he continued, had been bitterly opposed by those who ought to have rejoiced in this work.

There had been a great deal of unpleasantness which had given Neath "quite an insatiable reputation", and sentiments had been expressed and actions performed by some "which, perhaps, in more sober moments they wished had never taken place." After the building of St David's Church as an English church in 1866, the old parish church of St Thomas became the Welsh Church. This decision had met with "general approbation" in the town, while the funding for the new church had been provided through the "great liberality" of the church people.[9]

When Griffiths came to the parish in 1855 it possessed two churches, those of St Thomas in Neath and Llantwit. St David's Church was build in the centre of the town with a seating capacity of 1,200, and much of the money required for its building came through grants and subscriptions. At one time it was thought it might become the parish church of a new district. St Catherine's Church was also built with a similar aim though this too did not materialise. This was unfortunate for the additional requirements imposed by the Ecclesiastical Commissioners for the building of a contemplated parish church could be extremely costly. Although the site for St Catherine's had been given free of charge, its estimated cost of £3,000 seemed prohibitive at a time when money was tight and much concern was expressed by Griffiths about these financial liabilities. Both parish churches were restored, a church built at Tonna, and mission churches established. In 1891 Griffiths claimed that when he came to the parish there were only three English services each Sunday, a congregation of about 150 and 60 communicants, but by that date he had five churches instead of two, ten Sunday services, 1,300 in his congregations and 800 communicants. In addition there were over 1,000 people in the Sunday schools, of whom roughly a third were adults. Much of the credit for this increase was attributed by Griffiths to the work of the Church Pastoral-Aid Society which provided grants for his four curates. "I know the value of the Society, and therefore speak strongly. I owe to it more than I can tell you, and mainly by its aid has the Church become what it is in my parish," he wrote in 1878. On another occasion he wrote more graphically:

Thirty years ago I commenced my ministerial work at Neath, an important town on the Glamorgan seaboard. I entered on the work alone. I was surrounded by a large population, most of them strangers to the Church and to her services. I required help. The emoluments derived from the Church by the incumbents of Wales are, as a rule, very small; they afford no margin for the maintenance of curates. I looked to Falcon Court, a name not strange to me. [With its assistance] ... I was thus enabled to increase the number of services, and to enlarge the field of pastoral superintendence, and to make more adequate provision for my parishioners. Especially was I able to provide for the Welsh-speaking portion of my people, who constituted at the time more than half the population of the place, and who for more than half a century had been left destitute of means of worshipping God in the language understood and appreciated by them. For these means they had to look to others – they had, in fact, to look to themselves. The work prospered, and soon I mustered courage to send forth another appeal, and this time again to the same quarter. Another grant was made to me, and from that time to the present, they have continued.

Some of the curates who served under Griffiths were outstanding men and all testified to the value of the training they received from him. David Howell, later dean of St David's, a man he had discovered following the plough and persuaded to be ordained, was the first; and Howell was to preach his funeral sermon. Pritchard Hughes, bishop of Llandaff, and Archdeacon Buckley, vicar of Llandaff (who wrote that their relationship was like father to son), as well as Peter Williams of Troedyrhiw, all served as his curates, and all followed him onto the temperance platform. A cutting in one of John Griffith of Merthyr Tydfil's scrapbooks states that Griffiths was "adept at drilling his subordinates to something like efficiency in parish work". It may offer a somewhat intimidating picture of him, but at least it is a contrast to the accusations made against him.[10]

Griffiths's own example of pastoral care in his early days at Neath was impressive. Speaking to the Llandaff Church Extension Society, after one year in his new parish, he clearly inferred that until he came the people had not been visited in their homes, and were thus unaware that their clergy took an interest in their spiritual and temporal welfare. In part this was due to a lack of clerical assistance which that society had now remedied. As a result his parishioners had much appreciated the clergy's visits as an act of kindness, and he was aware from experience that it was producing an effect. A picture is given by Rhys Phillips of the rector being nicknamed *Shôn Trefan* by the rather happy-go-lucky Mera community, for this was his watchword as he emphasised to them the importance of economy and system in household matters. As George Eaton remarks, Griffiths was well known for visiting his parishioners.[11]

Within his parish Griffiths co-operated with every effort made to improve the spiritual and social good of his parishioners. When the Joshua brothers, "Happy" Frank and "Hallelujah" Seth commenced their work of evangelism in Neath during 1882, although they did so as members of the Welsh Methodist Church, they received every encouragement from the rector. He frequently preached in their tent, so that Frank was able to comment: "[h]e never preached in St David's Church, like he did in the tent. In the tent he was a living force. And under his tent ministry many professed conversion." On Sunday mornings many of these converts marched from the tent to St David's Church to receive communion at his hands, until some busybody complained to the bishop that not all were confirmed, after which this practice had to stop. In 1884 when the tent was replaced by a mission hall Griffiths arranged a bazaar for its building fund at Alderman Davies' school, and he also became a trustee of the hall.[12] Another example is even more telling of the respect which the Nonconformist community had for Griffiths. A division took place within the membership of the Orchard Place Particular Baptist Chapel, with one group supporting the minister, and another group, the majority, supporting the deacons. When it seemed that the matter might go to a court of law, both sides agreed to ask Griffiths to act as arbitrator. His decision was that the minister and his party should leave the church even though they had materially assisted in the cost of its building, and do so without compensation, but the group remaining should be responsible for the various costs of the case. Although he understood his decision was to be final, the occupying party, which as a result of the decision was left in undisputed occupation of the chapel, refused to pay the costs, thus creating much bitterness as well as hardship to one of the lawyers concerned.[13]

Griffiths's early days at Neath convinced him of the need for temperance work. The results of heavy drinking were all too obvious to him. At first he endeavoured to counteract Saturday night drinking by holding popular entertainments in the town, but when he complained to an old Quaker that he was not making as many temperance converts as he wished, he was told: "[t]hou hast tried what speaking will do: try now what thy example will do." As a result he became a total abstainer and later journeyed throughout Wales advocating this cause with all the energy he possessed. It was not an easy position to adopt, for many whom he respected were opposed to the principles of total abstinence, and he felt his stand would be misunderstood within the parish. But for Griffiths it was not simply a social campaign, although he recognised, and made clear, its domestic and national implications. Rather it was a spiritual campaign, for alcohol abuse "hindered ... the progress of all good, tied the wheels of the Gospel chariot ... and produced in fact a physical incapacity for the reception of religious truth, kept men fools and made thousands brutes ..." It was all part of that "most important work under heaven" in which he was engaged, namely that of winning "souls to Christ and to prepare them for another world." The temperance cause became for Griffiths yet another way in which the various Christian traditions could co-operate together. This was a theme he powerfully argued to the Neath Total Abstinence Society in 1859 during a meeting to commemorate the late Evan Evans, a Quaker, and one of its leading members. This organisation had only come into being in the spring of that year, Griffiths being its leading organiser along with James Kenway, a local business man, with whom he had had a controversy over the church rates issue. Archdeacon Buckley told an amusing story of Griffiths continuing his temperance activities when he came into residence at Llandaff Cathedral. Coming out of the chapter house with the ordination candidates, Griffiths spied the organ-blower, a well-known character by the name of Preece, and asked him "in his breezy way" if he was still a teetotaler. Replying in the affirmative he said it was 11 years since he had signed the pledge. To this Griffiths answered, "I was a teetotaller for twenty years", and Preece immediately replied, with a twinkle in his eye and within hearing of the candidates Griffiths had just examined, "Oh Sir, but you broke it!"[14]

There was much involvement too in the life of the town, although the principle on which he worked might not be found acceptable in our more egalitarian society. Speaking to the Neath Mechanics' Institution Griffiths argued that the difference between the classes was in the natural order of things and it had pleased the Almighty to so ordain society, though there was no harm to let them mix in discussion classes and other similar events! Nor was there any harm in letting them read the same books, for he was one of the leaders of the campaign to establish a public library in Neath. It was unsuccessful. He was also involved in the Young Men's Institute, the Benevolent Society and a Building Society during the 1860s.[15]

Griffiths's main social concern was undoubtedly the education of children and young people, and this too had a spiritual dimension. Schools had been started at Melincryddan and Tonna, but Griffiths's main activity was with the Alderman Davies School in the town itself. This school had been re-established in 1813 with the money left for that purpose by Alderman Davies in his will of nearly a century before, but Griffiths revamped the charity and erected a new school in 1857-8. This was at a time when the British School had been established in the town "and was conducted with very great ability and under exclusive and influential patronage." Yet in spite of this strong competition within two years of opening the new "church" schools over 1,200 children had passed through them, 400 having been entered within the first half year of its opening.

Griffiths made it plain that Nonconformist children were welcome in these schools and that there would be no discrimination or attempt at proselytising. The new trust deed of the school stated that "the religious instruction shall comprise the Bible and bible history, and (subject to the provisions hereinafter contained) the Church Catechism shall be taught in each school, and the religious instruction shall be consonant with the principles and doctrine of the Church of England." These provisions permitted the parents of Nonconformist children to withdraw them from such religious instruction. Writing to Bishop Thirlwall of St David's, then engaged in a debate with John Bowstead, one of the inspectors for education, Griffiths proudly stated that in no instance had this privilege ever been claimed or objection made to these principles. While they invited the children to attend the Sunday worship, it was not compulsory, although he endeavoured to find out from those who were absent what amount of religious instruction they had received elsewhere. He continued:

> I am not able at this moment to state the exact proportion of children of Dissenters that attend the schools, but it is large. I take pains to keep out of sight these distinctions; I regard them as the children of my *parishioners*, as such I give them what I believe to be sound religious instruction on defined and recognised principles. I endeavour to do so without doing injury to the expressed feelings and convictions of the parents of any who do not conform to the Church. ... My experience tells me that Church of England Schools, properly conducted, command the confidence of the country generally.[16]

The confidence of Nonconformists in Griffiths's impartiality was such that they resolved not to form a school board during his lifetime. These boards were established by Foster's Education Act of 1870, and allowed local authorities to build and maintain schools using, in part, income from the rates. It also allowed the various boards to work out their own policy regarding religious education. In Wales many boards only allowed the Bible to be read in their schools, if that, and prohibited any doctrinal or denominational teaching. As a result the elections to the various boards became bitter struggles between Nonconformity and the Church, with frequent displays of sectarian temper. However, by the time Griffiths came to retire matters had changed. It may have been his realisation that the Bute trustees, as patrons of his parish, acting through a dubious legal loophole on behalf of the Roman Catholic marquess of Bute, would not appoint an evangelical, or even a man sympathetic to that viewpoint, to succeed him, but would prefer a high churchman who would promote anglo-catholic teaching and ritualistic practices within the parish. In fact the spread of Anglo-Catholicism in Glamorgan was primarily due to the way in which these trustees exercised their power of appointment. It may even be that the Nonconformists anticipated this event by forming a School Board. But there may have been other reasons, possibly financial, for the schools were dependent on voluntary effort.

A series of letters about the Alderman Davies School may be found in the correspondence of Archbishop Benson at Lambeth Palace Library. During January and February of 1896 the attention of the archbishop was drawn to the circumstances of these schools. David Davies, a Neath man, petitioned the archbishop to prevent them from being handed over to the newly formed Neath School Board. The Alderman Davies school was one of the largest schools in Wales, he wrote, with 1,200 children on its books. The church people had worked hard to raise the money for its building, over £6,000, by bazaars and subscriptions, and as such it was felt that the building belonged to the church and was used for church meetings. The church people felt that to hand over this school to the board was an act of gross injustice. The secretary of the National Society, J. G. Brownrigg, shown this letter, responded by agreeing that the matter was a scandal, but both the society and the bishop had had to agree that nothing could be done to prevent the school from being handed over. While it was termed a National School it had never received any grants from their society, and thus they could not interfere, while the trust deeds permitted this transfer to take place. "I know

Archdeacon Griffiths, and I am afraid he will not listen to me," he added, but as he was always friendly he would ask him to delay the matter. A letter from the archbishop might possibly change his mind, for there seemed to be no reason for this transfer.

What the archbishop wrote is not known. What Griffiths replied *is*. He expressed thankfulness for the archbishop's interest in the school. He would send on to him a statement about its position, but it was not a National School, merely a charity school. It was a polite letter, but in reality it told the archbishop to mind his own business.[17] It was not the end of the story. For after his retirement, when (as he feared) he was followed by a Anglo-Catholic man, the *Church Times*, in congratulating the parish of Neath on its new progressive and theologically correct vicar, cast aspersions upon Griffiths. One of these aspersions was that he had handed over these schools to the local School Board. To this allegation Griffiths replied: "I shared with others the management of three sets of schools, which afforded accommodation for more than two thousand children, two of these sets of schools being private property. Their owners handed them over to the newly established School Boards. I had no voice in the matter. The great town schools continue to be worked under a scheme sanctioned by the Charity Commissioners forty years ago, the trustees of which are the rector, the churchwardens, and the overseers of the parish of Neath." Griffiths was being less than honest, though it does appear that he had temporarily withdrawn the offer of these schools to the local Board after substantial pressure had been put on him by the National Society. Possibly he thought that in the hands of a secular authority the children of these schools would receive religious teaching based on the Bible rather than upon spurious tradition and dogma.[18]

It must be clear from this last episode that Griffiths was an autocrat in his parish. He did not consider parochial church councils particularly useful,[19] and refused to delegate any of his parochial responsibilities. It is perhaps significant that although St David's and St Catherine's were built as district churches, that is, as churches around which a new parish would be formed, they never achieved that status. When Griffiths was appointed a residentiary canon of Llandaff in 1878 (insisting the house be put into decent repair before he resided)[20] it meant that he had to spend three months of the year in residence. Although he used part of the £350 income of the canonry in employing another curate in the parish to make up for his absence, this time, together with the month or so he spent on holiday at his birthplace (though it is said to have given him a new lease of life[21]), and the duties involved in being archdeacon of Llandaff – a responsibility which covered the whole of the Glamorgan area of the diocese – meant that he was away from the parish for a substantial part of each year. Perhaps authoritarian by nature, his absences and his dependence on curates possibly made Griffiths rather defensive about his parochial responsibilities during his latter years.

This scenario emerges in a correspondence which related to an incident at St Catherine's Church during September 1895. It ostensibly concerned the harvest services but the actual incident widened into a full-scale confrontation as the real issues were revealed. This church, it appeared, had over many years arranged the harvest services, dates, times and preachers as well as the recipients of the offertory, on condition that Griffiths approved of these arrangements. But on this occasion Griffiths went ahead and had the posters printed without consultation. As a result the church members felt that they were being treated in a derogatory way, and the curate argued that his authority had been questioned as curate-in-charge (especially as he had been addressed by letter as the assistant curate of Neath). There was equal hurt that the offertories were being devoted to another and outside cause when they, as a congregation of working men whose earnings did not exceed 30s. a week, had an average liability of £25 each for the cost of the boundary wall.

As a result the curate, J. R. Hosbons, was suspended by Griffiths, and having broken down during the last service at which he officiated he found himself with a even greater degree of support from the members St Catherine's Church than he might otherwise have had. In various letters the congregation claimed that Griffiths, by refusing to sign the deeds of the church requiring the building of the boundary wall, had placed the liability upon working men instead, adding for good measure that whenever a good man was appointed curate Griffiths became so jealous of his success that obstacles were thrown in his way and he was forced to leave. If Hosbons was forced to leave the offertories would decrease and they would be unable to pay even the interest on the remaining debt. Griffiths's choice of the Revd Henry Williams as the Harvest preacher was also criticised as a snub, for as one anonymous writer wrote to Williams, "I assure you, Sir, and this is the general feeling, we have heard and saw enough of you." As these letters were being written the situation deteriorated even further. Many of the congregation absented themselves on the following Sunday, and others walked out together with the choir, who were received with cheers by "a crowd of toughs" (to quote the archdeacon's words) and a "riot" resulted. The sidesmen who were expecting trouble had failed to turn up with the result that the building had been left in the hands of the "malcontents", although nothing more serious had happened than the throwing of stones. Hosbons had moved to Cadoxton but, claimed Griffiths, was not unaware of the situation, and had a large following of people from the church and wider community.

Griffiths in his letter to the bishop of 25 September probably touched upon the root of the trouble. St Catherine's wished to be an independent chapel, and he had had continual problems with its committee, even though it had done good work in helping to build the church. Had the committee approached him through the curate, as had been customary during the previous 30 years, he would have listened to any representation they cared to make. But the curate knew the dates fixed by him several days before the bills were issued and had made no complaint. The real question now was that of his authority in the parish. Griffiths had been urged by his leading churchmen not to solve the problem by any "act of cowardice" but rather to assert his authority, and certainly not to be dictated to by the public press. Unfortunately both he and his wife's health had been sorely tried by this episode, and his wife wrote privately to the bishop expressing her concern about him: "this ... matter affects him terribly", she claimed, but the Neath people would not allow him to give way.

Hosbons, whom the church members of St Catherine's regarded as a born leader, having built up a crowded and appreciative congregation and a well-attended Sunday school as well as a recently commenced devotional meeting in English and Welsh, was regarded by Griffiths as a man sorely deficient in certain qualities. Griffiths had refused his offer of an apology on the grounds that the whole position was now in the bishop's hands. The scandal and public notoriety Hosbons had caused made his position impossible in the parish. Griffiths therefore hoped that the bishop would find another post for him, for he was doing more harm in the parish than he could possibly tell. Somehow matters were patched up for Hosbons remained at Neath until 1897, although as he remained an assistant curate for most of his life Griffiths's comments about him may have been an accurate assessment of his personality. But the situation had to end in the re-assertion of authority by Griffiths, although the total story is really one of a church feeling its way to independence and being resentful of the restraints of a distant authority.[22]

An obituary note on Griffiths indicated that he had made the Church in his parish a power felt for good,[23] and it is hard to dispute this judgment. Despite his autocratic ways - in which he was typical of his age - the parish was run efficiently, the Gospel commended, and all good works endorsed. It may be that in his last years, for he was in his late 70s when he resigned, things had slipped a little, but there had been clear and solid achievements in his earlier days and progress even in the latter. A correspondent's outburst against him in the *Church Times* of 12 February 1897, announcing the appointment by the Bute Trustees of the Revd Arnold Frederick Evans, curate of Aberdare and a Tractarian, as the new rector, was greeting with anger by his friends. The late rector "was not much in the parish", and had handed the church schools to the school board, and from an income of £221 had taken a pension of one third (Griffiths wrote a polite letter denying both allegations). It went on to state that the new rector had much work to do, but believed that many in the parish would welcome the changes in teaching and practice his appointment now allowed. There would be opposition, of course, for many of the congregation were nominal churchmen and really dissenters, but drastic changes would soon ensure the support of the real church people who were longing for better things after 42 years "of Protestant gloom". The anonymous writer went on to assert that since hearing a local lecture on the Oxford Movement many of the church leaders had said it was badly needed at Neath. But others made clear that these assertions were not true, including the churchwardens, one of his former curates, and even one of the trustees who held the patronage. The Welsh Church newspaper, *Y Llan*, expressed indignation, stating that those who held such views as those expressed in the *Church Times* article were a distinct hindrance to the Church's real progress.[24]

****

Appointed rural dean of the Groneath deanery in 1877, Griffiths became archdeacon of Llandaff in the same year. It was a post he relished, and it is said that the white hair he now possessed enabled him to fit the part admirably. The archdeaconry was combined with a residentiary canonry at the cathedral and, to give him added distinction, Griffiths was awarded a Lambeth BD by Archbishop

Tait. Bishop Ollivant had appointed him to the archdeaconry, but Ollivant's successor, Richard Lewis, said that Griffiths had been a tried friend, a loyal official and a helpful counsellor to him personally, as well as a zealous parish priest. An obituary, probably from the *Western Mail*, stated that Griffiths, along with Dean Vaughan, had taken part in all movements of public interest within the diocese, while Bishop Hughes of St Asaph wrote to Gladstone commending Griffiths for episcopal office, arguing that he had brought new life into many parishes in his archidiaconal capacity.[25] This may have been true, but Griffiths could equally stand upon the dignity of his office and ride rather roughshod over individual preferences. This emerges in his dealings with Canon Lewis, vicar of Ystradyfodwg in the Rhondda valley, relating to the building of Ton Pentre Church. Lewis had approached Griffiths about building a church on land owned by Crawshay Bailey, the archdeacon being a trustee of the estate, and having "dandled" the young Crawshay Bailey on his knee. The Bailey family had not only given the land but had also built the church, spending on it the same amount as Canon Lewis had spent on 13 other building projects. The good canon, following the other precedents, took the initiative and asked the Ecclesiastical Commissioners to inspect the new church on the assumption that they would act as the trustees of the property. Griffiths was furious, and insisting that he and another person friendly with the Bailey family should became trustees instead, wrote a succession of stinging letters to Lewis. This happened again on another occasion when the church needed repairing and the wardens applied to Griffiths as a trustee for assistance from the Bailey estate. The implications of this trusteeship were catastrophic for the church, as it could not be consecrated until it was placed in ecclesiastical hands, nor could it become a district or parish church for the same reason.[26]

Throughout his life Griffiths remained an evangelical churchman and he frequently expressed the view that too often the Church of his day was elevating the altar at the expense of the pulpit. Peter Williams records: "He had intense dislike of sacerdotalism in all shapes and forms. He knew and felt that ornate services and high ritual were not the means to bring back the Welsh people to the Church of their fathers." Rather, he was one, Williams wrote, of that noble band of evangelical men, such as Hughes Tregaron, Griffiths Machynlleth, Hughes Llandovery and others. Like them he was "fired by intense enthusiasm and love for evangelical truth – from which he never wavered – he consecrated his whole life to the service of his country and of his God." Speaking to the 1872 Leeds Church Congress Griffiths asserted that as the Welsh people were so Biblically based in their faith any "coquetting" with the doctrines of Rome would rouse an opposition which would crush the Church. Speaking in 1894, at a conference of Welsh evangelical clergy, he urged them to be "united, fearless and uncompromising" in the face of a growing secularisation on the one hand and ritualism on the other, as well as the threat of disestablishment. "Even if they should feel left out in the cold as regards popular or ecclesiastical favour, their work was known to God, and would bring its own reward."[27]

Preaching was his forte: "the simple, warm, energetic preaching of the pure Gospel of Jesus Christ – who will carry that Gospel to the homes of the people", was his own homely description of it to a CPAS meeting of 1884. His great ambition was to be known as an extempore preacher. In his first parish he started cottage meetings, taking along with him the bellringer to start the singing, a simple but gracious Christian man. Alas, though Griffiths determined to preach extempore on the first such evening to his cottage audience, he collapsed after five minutes, and only the encouragement of that bellringer enabled him to persevere. Griffiths came into prominence, says Peter Williams, when a new church in the Vale was to be opened and one of the Church's more celebrated Welsh preachers, "Jones y Faenor", was due to preach. A large congregation was drawn there by the preacher's reputation, but he was unable to attend, and Griffiths, arriving late, had a surplice placed on him and was told he had to preach instead. All resistance was useless, he was forced into the pulpit, and all eyes became fixed upon him. "He prayed, and God blessed his efforts."

It became sufficient to announce the archdeacon's name (or rather his description as Griffiths of Neath) as a guest preacher in order to draw a large congregation together. Dissenters and church people all fell under the spell of his eloquent and expository preaching. It is recalled that preaching at a outdoor temperance meeting at Gellionin near Pontardawe, Griffiths was able to draw in the thousands of scattered people into a packed group before the platform as soon as he started. It was not an uncommon experience. His favourite subject was justification. "He felt the sympathy of numbers, and as he warmed with his subject, his eye would kindle, his fine and expressive face would be lighted up, and he would pour forth a torrent of eloquence which held the listeners spell-bound." Though he could sometimes lose the thread of his argument and might wander from his text as a new thought occurred to him, a congregation would not grow tired of listening to him for three quarters of an hour and more.

This is Peter Williams's description, which is confirmed by J. Vyrnwy Morgan, who added that while he was no theologian or profound thinker, Griffiths never lost his grip on his congregation, even though sometimes he had periodic moments of spiritual ecstasy which he was never able to communicate to his hearers. Rhys Phillips in his *Vale of Neath* quotes a person who wondered which of his two languages, Welsh or English, Griffiths felt more at home in, for he was able to move from one to the other with such consummate skill and natural ease. John Morgan of Llanilid, however, suggested that Griffith did not always come up to his own standards but at his best could thrill congregations with his oratory and feeling.[28]

Preaching to the Volunteers in 1860 (a sermon which exemplified the theory of the just war and the need for a peacetime force of soldiers), Griffiths concluded with this Gospel peroration which must remain as a solitary example of his style:

> There is a Standard raised, and you are asked to rally around it; there is a Leader, who knows the enemy's strength, and He invites you; an armoury is open, and the weapons it contains are the free gift of your Eternal King; the Gospel trumpet loudly calls to the work of preparation. – "Is there not cause" for this wonderful provision, and this call to arms? There is a cause! and every true feeling within your breast, bids you not delay; commissioned by the Great Captain of salvation, I to-day summon you to the place of duty. To arms! Brethren; "Put on the whole armour of God;" do not be half equipped – do not forget a single weapon; strictly obey the direction of your Commander; and He will lead you to victory and to glory. – We press these considerations upon you, knowing that the Christian service, like that to which you belong, is a volunteer service. If you come, it must be of your own choice; we cannot compel, but we must exhort, and we must direct. We direct you to Jesus Christ, as the only powerful and appointed Leader – experienced in the contest that you are called upon to engage in; choose him to-day, choose him at once! Fighting under Immanuel, the Prince of Peace, no victory was ever lost. Here, however, there is no victory, no crown, without fighting; you

must not only carry weapons, but you must use them – "Resist the devil." To do so successfully, you must use *means* of resistance. What are these means? Prayer is a powerful weapon – *"Pray always."* The Scriptures are valuable means; - "the Sword of the Spirit, which is the Word of God;" - frequenting God's House; – the Church is the place where Christ meets his waiting followers; – here he meets them to strengthen, to console, and to instruct them – "Where two or three are gathered together in my name, there am I, in the midst of them."[29]

"A tolerable preacher," suggested H. A. Bruce of Griffiths, and Lady Llanover added that he was a man who had set aside preaching in Welsh because he knew he could never compare with the Welsh preachers of his day.[30] Yet these remarks sit strangely with what has already been stated, or with such assertions as Archdeacon Buckley's that Griffiths was a born extempore preacher who had the gift of swaying multitudes, or of an obituary writer in the Llandaff diocesan magazine who suggested that he was one of the most eloquent preachers and speakers of his day. John Morgan commented that such was Griffiths's reputation that he could be called upon to preach six times in a week. Dean Vaughan, who knew him well, wrote that he was accounted by those who could tell a good preacher in Welsh. Buckley, however, provides one clue for the disparity. He never did justice to himself, he commented, when preaching in the cathedral, perhaps because he felt he had to read his sermons or because he was overawed by the presence of Dean Vaughan, one of the most noteworthy English preachers of his day. It seems that his cathedral sermons were in English.[31]

****

An obituary writer wrote that Griffiths was a man ready to take up unpopular causes.[32] By the 1880s three of the most unpopular causes he could have advocated were the use of the Welsh language in the Church, his patronage of the eisteddfodau, and his interest in the university movement within Wales. This was at a time when the Welsh language was identified by many with Nonconformity, and was believed to be an inferior language which should be allowed to die out in the name of progress and opportunity. His cultivation of these causes made Griffiths a rather notorious figure in the eyes of the more progressive churchmen, especially of the growing Anglo-Catholic school, which had no love for Nonconformity and no desire to perpetuate the Welsh language. As such they claimed Griffiths was more of a Nonconformist than a Churchman.

This was untrue as the evidence given below declares. But what was true was that Griffiths would have described himself as a Christian rather than as a Churchman. Yet his parochial work and his concern for the Church were true and genuine. He rejoiced in the Church revival in Wales which he believed had been assisted by the work of the Church Pastoral-Aid Society, whose followers had helped turn the Church from a mere concern with outward duties into one providing a real ministry for people.[33]

Yet although it was a time of Church revival and growth it was also a time when some Nonconformists were endeavouring to disestablish the Church and transfer much of its monetary resources to other causes. Griffiths saw this movement as a warning to the Church in Wales to put its own house in order. While he accepted there were some dissenters who were motivated by political causes, who wished to attack the Welsh Church because it was weak and as a prelude to general disestablishment all round, he refused to accept that every Nonconformist wanted disestablishment or that others wanted it merely for impure motives. But if the Church was weak, he argued it had been made weak not by its enemies but by its professed supporters, that is, the tractarians or anglo-catholics. Furthermore, Griffiths saw within Nonconformity a strong attraction for the old Church and its worship: "[t]here is a looking back to the old home, and I feel perfectly that were it not for the suspicions which hang around that home we should have a great many more return to it."[34]

During 1893 the Liberal government introduced the Suspensory Bill as a prelude to the disestablishment of the Welsh Church. In a speech of protest Griffiths made his position perfectly clear. He was against disestablishment, but he was equally concerned at the way in which the Church was being called upon to fight it "tooth and nail" by Bishop Edwards and others, although he did not name them. "Harsh measures and hard words are poor substitutes for argument," he declared, and while they might rouse the passions of men, they would never influence minds. "Do not let us go into wild hysterics. Do not let the enemy suppose that our strongest weapons are opprobrious names. Calling our opponents 'robbers, men of sacrilegious passions, despoilers of Churches, &c.,' will have little effect on them." "Indiscriminate charges," he continued, "are as abundant in mischief as they are generally deficient in proof. Let there be no imputation of ungodly motives; let there be no resort to injurious epithets on either side." What body of men had practised greater self denial, had shown greater energy in advancing Christian truth, and in promoting Christian morals than the Nonconformists? Though he would not defend his Church "one inch" beyond what she deserved, Griffiths hoped that this contest would soon be a thing of the past, when the fight would be exchanged for a nobler conflict between superstition and evangelical truth, between mental slavery and scriptural freedom. "I am no prophet," he wrote, "but I feel sure that this is a near battle field, when the combined Churches will have much to do to hold their own." He continued:

> Let the old Episcopal Church be faithful to herself, and she has a glorious destiny before her. I know no organisation like hers for the work of her Master; and I feel sure that if fidelity to her marching orders is maintained; if she exhibits the spirit which is rightly hers, she will be a greater power in the future than she has ever been in the past. Her strength, her endurance, are not to be found in her establishment – in her connection with the State. If this bond is her only strength, her only prop, her only trust, then I pity her. She casts away a far nobler inheritance if she makes this earthly bond, her strength.

It was natural for the Church to fear any change in her position, and equally right to believe that her work would be greatly hindered if disestablishment took place, but (he continued) it was still necessary "to make clear the difference between that which is essential and that which is fortuitous; between that which has been ever hers, and that which, in the course of years, has fallen to her lot, giving her aid in carrying on her work." Let every honest plea be put forward in defending the possessions of the Church, argued Griffiths. But why should people who love religion act in a way which was imperilling "the Christian brotherhood, which the Great Head of the Church has laid down as an essential of his Church ...? Is it too late for thoughts of peace, for serious reflection? What are the grievances of Nonconformity? Let them be honestly discussed, especially the fear of sacerdotalism and the opposition to religious endowments and state connections. The Church is on trial, and she must remain a Protestant Episcopal Church." Reform was clearly needed, but the paramount need of the Welsh Church was to be a Church of deep doctrines and wide sympathy, "with a very large heart, and with very long arms, to embrace, not a few, but a nation", and thus to be a real National Church. When a people found such a Church they would not fail to cherish it, claimed Griffiths.[35]

Such words are the words of a man who loved his Church and desired its spiritual prosperity. Griffiths expressed his concern that its ministry was becoming professionalised, rather than being understood as a holy vocation, so that men of decent morality and financial means were being ordained, even though they lacked spiritual qualifications or an aptitude for the cure of souls. The Church should go out to find rather than wait for, "the material she wishes to get; and, when this is found, no pains or efforts should be deemed too great to convert this material to her use." He found fault too in the training offered to candidates. Too much was based on a course of secular theological study and too little attention paid to the heart, or to the more spiritual aspects and motivation of their calling. More emphasis was needed on pastoral theology and practical training, especially in the art of preaching. Many Welsh candidates needed not only intellectual training but also social elevation. While this could be gained at the ancient universities, the expense of residence, their lack of Welsh, and the fact that few Welsh ordinands educated there ever returned to Wales, made this a difficult option. Consequently St David's College, Lampeter, where discipline was stricter, education more helpful and temptations less insidious, needed to be both improved and also properly supported. At a later date Griffiths argued for an evangelical college in Wales (a sort of equivalent to the Anglo-Catholic St Michael's College, then at Aberdare), and others claimed that its foundation "would strengthen the hands of those who are fighting for the Reformation in Wales."[36]

If Griffiths was concerned for the preparation of men for the ministry, he was equally concerned for men at the end of their ministry who, because of the lack of an adequate pension scheme, had to remain in their parishes and see the good work they had done in previous years undone by their failure to sustain it through old age and infirmity. As an archdeacon he probably saw many such examples. He longed to provide a diocesan association which would assist such men in obtaining retirement pensions, as the Methodist Church had already done. It took many years, however, for this dream to come true.[37]

Another concern of Griffiths was that the Welsh-speaking clergy should be represented in Convocation, and in the memorable contest

for the office of proctor between Thomas Stacey, who represented
the interests of the Anglicised clergy, and John Griffith of Merthyr,
who represented the Welsh speakers, Griffiths seconded the latter's
nomination. Even though he travelled at railroad speed and had his
peculiarities, said Griffiths, Griffith knew the Welsh Church
thoroughly and could represent her interests with conviction and
experience. It would be a disgrace to send up a man who was
unacquainted with the Welsh-speaking press and who was even less
of a Welshman than their bishop who was competent in the
language. Griffith lost by 49:45, amidst great bitterness, as the Welsh
clergy generally looked after huge industrial parishes compared with
the English clergy's small rural parishes, and commonly felt that
their interests were almost entirely neglected by the Church at
large.[38] Equally, Griffith was concerned that the Church should
make use of lay assistance (what we might term today lay ministry),
especially as he attributed the strength of Nonconformity to this
cause. If the Church in Wales, Griffiths remarked, was ever to
recover her position, she had to use "this instrument to an extent far
beyond what she has hitherto done." Had the Church in Wales done
so, he suggested in 1893, and allowed the laity to be more involved
in its ministry and presumably in its counsels, then the crisis of
disestablishment might have been shorn of much of its severity.[39]

Griffiths had an equal concern for the Welsh-speaking part of the
Church in Wales. Depreciating those, even bishops, who denied the
existence of the Welsh Church, Griffith begged in 1872 for the
appointment of more Welsh-speaking bishops, and was one of the
earliest advocates of a separate province for Wales with its own
archbishop. Griffiths was also to argue for an extension of the
episcopate. Bishops needed to exercise an oversight as well as a
pastoral care of clergy, and if this was impossible, much injustice
and misrepresentation could occur. How much unhappiness had
many honest, earnest men received through such a lack of pastoral
care and understanding? he asked. Suffragan bishops were not the
answer; what was needed was an extension of the episcopate, but
without the necessity of cathedral structures and palatial edifices. At
least another three dioceses were required in Wales, being based
upon such places as Llanbadarn Fawr and Brecon. And equally, the
bishops needed diocesan councils for their own good as well as for
the good of their dioceses. These synods needed both clerical and lay
membership, and care was required that the laity were not all drawn
from the privileged classes. His views were reflective of many within

the wider Church, although he was in advance of most people in his own country.[40]

Griffiths was therefore a loyal son of his Church. So we now turn to his involvement in those unpopular causes which made many question his loyalty.

There were many who accused Griffiths of being over-friendly to the Nonconformists. This of course was at a time when militant Nonconformity was seeking to disestablish and disendow the Church, and some of the schemes proposed would have left the Church in Wales with only a small percentage of its income. While he deplored sectarianism and longed to see unity, Griffiths recognised there was no fundamental difference between the doctrines of the Church, as generally understood in his day, and that of dissent. Year by year he met the Nonconformist leaders on holiday at Llandrindod, such as Thomas Gee, Henry Richard, and Hiraethog, and with them discussed the events of the day. Furthermore Griffiths was quite happy to appear on Nonconformist platforms, to the annoyance of many church leaders. Bishop Ollivant, for example, expressed his concern that Griffiths had presided at a Wesleyan missionary meeting held in a Neath chapel. Nothing is to be gained, the bishop wrote, by popularity with dissenters, and perhaps Griffiths had forgotten that the Church had missionary societies of her own. Perhaps they were using him for their own purposes? Dissent, he continued, was "evil", and it was right not to shrink from saying so; indeed, how could Griffiths pray for unity and yet join others in schism. These associations were giving offence to many church people and might well injure his own ministry.

Griffiths thought otherwise, perhaps appreciating the spiritual content of dissent far more than his bishop did and having a broader sympathy of outlook. Nonconformists, he argued, had little hostility to the Church "or to her doctrines when honestly taught." With such a viewpoint it is not surprising that Griffiths later depreciated the tone of the Welsh Church press when it wrote about Nonconformity. He also expressed dismay at "the language of some of our young unfledged curates, who think that the chief work they have to do, when they get into a parish, is to pour down reproaches on the heads of Dissenting ministers and their flocks." Thankfully he believed that the Church's charity was often far wider than that exercised by her sons. As a result Griffiths became a great favourite with, and had an influence over, Nonconformists, a point made by Henry Richard to

Gladstone, while Bishop Joshua Hughes told the premier that Griffiths might be able to heal the divisions between Church and dissent if he was appointed a bishop.[41]

This so-called espousal of Nonconformity made Griffiths unpopular with many church people. Some of them were the Anglo-Catholics who saw Nonconformists as heretics, and others were church defenders who could not appreciate that some Nonconformists wished the Church to be disestablished for its own good, or that others had such close links with the Church, through background and family, that they stood aside from the controversy altogether. By and large Nonconformists in Wales were Welsh speaking, so that any enthusiasm by churchmen for the Welsh language and culture, or any manifestation of nationality, was regarded as either disloyalty to a Church which was appealing to its English connections as a defence against disestablishment, or as near insanity by those who saw the English language as the vehicle of progress and refinement. It must be admitted, as is noted later, that Griffiths gave expression to this latter view at times so that his own relationship to the Welsh language was ambivalent. Thus Griffiths's concern for the Welsh language and its institutions was capable of much misunderstanding and aroused considerable annoyance in various quarters.

Speaking on the subject of the linguistic condition of Wales at the 1889 Cardiff Church Congress, Griffiths revealed that he was well aware of the tension in his and in others' support of the Welsh language. Two languages were struggling for mastery, and each claimed for itself superior dignity and usefulness. The new language brought with it influence and power as well as prestige, and bid the old depart. This it refused to do, asserting its superiority, not in ordinary matters of every-day living, but in matters relating to a cultural and spiritual appreciation of life. The language of one people could never be effectively adopted by another until they could assimilate its inner life, and this would take generations to complete. The grand mission of the Gospel was to reach the heart, but "the heart has its language as well as its lips" and so the language of the heart must be used. Regretfully many clergy, no doubt with good intentions, discouraged the use of Welsh in their spiritual ministry and in their schools. Griffiths considered this to be a tragedy, for "Welshmen are not going to be won to the Church by organisations, nor by the press; but by words spoken warmly, idiomatically, spoken from a full heart, by a fluent tongue ..." People would be alienated from the Church if the language used for the intimate spiritual dealings with God was replaced by one alien to their spiritual heritage. But Griffiths accepted that there was an inadequate supply of clergy to undertake this Welsh-speaking work, while much more attention needed to be given to it in the theological colleges.[42]

In his capacity of examining chaplain to the bishop of Llandaff Griffiths endeavoured to inculcate these views to those ordinands who were being placed in Welsh or bilingual parishes. He was also required to examine candidates for institution to those parishes where a knowledge of Welsh was required. His bishop trusted him implicitly, and told him, after Griffiths had said he had some doubts about the quality of some candidates, that if he said a candidate was not qualified, then he would not be permitted to proceed further. Peter Williams wrote of a young friend of his, Oxford educated, who fancied himself as a Welsh preacher, being examined by Griffiths. There was a friendly greeting and a chat before Griffiths requested him to read a passage from the Welsh Bible, "but my friend had not gone on far before he heard the grave old man thundering forth, 'Stop, Stop! young man. None of your nice namby-pamby Oxford twang. That style will not suit the Welsh. They must have the real genuine article, without any 'llediaith' at all. Listen.'" He then gave him an example as to how the passage should be read. Then he talked to him, and such talks, Williams commented, "were indeed precious things, and never forgotten. He acted like a father in God to the young men who were just entering the ministry, and gave them, from his long and varied experience, advice that would always prove useful to them." In fact Griffiths is credited with coining the term "Wenglish", to describe "the horrible mixture sometimes found in speaking and preaching the Welsh language." The language needed to be cleansed from these defects.[43]

Responding to Dean Vaughan's comment that his and others' concern in these matters was just another instance of the cry "Wales for the Welsh", Griffiths denied the accusation, arguing that the sons and daughters of Wales were not so foolish as to confine themselves to the narrow limits of the Principality.[44] Nevertheless his associations and interests did tend to suggest that this theme of Wales for the Welsh was a motivating force in his life, as witness his desire for a Welsh province and archbishopric. He was one of the founding members of the Welsh Utilisation Society, which sought to establish the teaching of Welsh in the schools, and he was its president for many years. Principal Viriamu Jones of Cardiff,

Thomas Gee, Dan Isaac Davies, T. Marchant Williams and others
were associated with him in this venture, as a result of which,
suggests Kenneth Morgan, the language gained a greater ascendancy
and became more culturally secure.[45] Griffiths was also a member of
the Cardiff Cymrodorion which initiated and furthered many of these
concerns.[46]

Most Welsh speaking people knew Griffiths not so much as a
church dignitary but as a leading member of the eisteddfodau
movement. This is where he gained his reputation as a Welsh
speaker and personality, for his oration at the Denbigh eisteddfod of
1860, delivered without a moment's notice, was said to be one of the
most notable ever recorded. On its platform he consorted with all the
leading Welsh Nonconformists. Perhaps he felt the irony of the
situation. For the modern eisteddfod had been created by the Welsh
literary clergy in face of Nonconformist distaste, but now it was
almost the preserve of these people and the Church had all but
abandoned it. He saw the eisteddfod as the focus of a nation which
had no real institutions of its own, and as a means of bringing
together in peace and goodwill all the different factions in Wales,
whether divided by religious or social distinctions or by geography.
"Why should we not bring the aristocracy of the land to meet the
labouring classes?" he asked on one occasion. It was his influence
and that of Hugh Owen which established the union of the eisteddfod
in 1862, with meetings being held alternately in north and south. It
was Griffiths who chaired the national council which brought this
about together with other reforms. Although Griffiths had a high
vision of the eisteddfod, he had no wish to exclude from it those who
could not understand the language. In 1867 Griffiths eloquently
denied that the eisteddfod was bent on obstructing the spread of
English, and gave a list of its English-speaking activities. "Oppose
the spread of the English language," he argued rather ambiguously,
"nothing more preposterous ... I think that our time might be better
employed than in bolstering up a language that may be of
questionable advantage."

At that Carmarthen eisteddfod of 1867 (which he and Latimer
Jones, vicar of Carmarthen, promoted, and also had to take
responsibility for its heavy debts), Griffiths used the platform to urge
a greater understanding between the Welsh and English
congregations of his own Church, and an end to the class distinctions
within churches as exemplified by the appropriated pew. His rapport
with the audience was substantial. At the same eisteddfod when an

adjudicator's decision failed to win acceptance, it was Griffiths's intervention that brought a nasty scene to a close. And when Matthew Arnold failed to obtain a hearing at the Aberdare eisteddfod of 1885, due to the dampness of the day and his poor voice, Griffiths brandishing his "gamp-like umbrella", counted up to ten and then wished he had a dozen *Cardis* to thrash the crowd for their discourtesy to their guest. Twice he produced order, but Matthew Arnold eventually had to give up. Griffiths's interest in the eisteddfod continued to the end of his life. Watcyn Wyn recalled the "electrical effect" of his speech at the London eisteddfod in 1897, appreciated not only by the Welsh speakers but also by the non-Welsh onlookers.[47]

A further concern of Griffiths, in which he was again misunderstood, related to his support of the Welsh university movement. At that time its only college was at Aberystwyth, and the feeling of the Church towards it could be summed up in Bernard Shaw's phrase "the Nonconformist academy by the sea", especially as the Church saw it as a rival to its own institution at Lampeter. Griffiths was said to be the only Welsh clergyman to take a part in the movement, along with a Welsh exile in London, the Revd Robert Jones, rector of Rotherhithe. Nevertheless he was prepared to withdraw his support if the college did not have daily public prayers asking for God's blessing upon its work, and he insisted that if the professor who officiated on these occasions wished to use the liturgy of his own Church (one was an ordained cleric) then he should be free to do so. Thomas Gee had denounced the religious sentiments of two of the college's professors, and had attacked its principal, Thomas Charles Edwards, for using the *Book of Common Prayer* on these occasions, but Griffiths wrote to Gee, however, asking him to allow the same liberty to these men as he claimed for himself in attacking them, appealing to their common Protestantism as against the real enemy of Rome. He also wrote to Edwards and asked him to be a little more sensitive in the face of widespread objections (although commending his choice), and suggested that a selection of prayers be made assisted by a representative of each Protestant religious tradition. It was a pity to cause shipwreck over such an issue when the ship had just been launched, he continued, especially when the new movement might help renew confidence and the cementing of religious friendships as well as forwarding the work of national education. He later endorsed the new service book which was produced, but he received little support within the Church for these activities. He was later to support Cardiff University College as well, becoming a member of its council, and was also one of the originators of the Welsh intermediate school movement.[48]

****

It is hardly surprising that Griffiths, with this national reputation, and in a climate of opinion which felt the desirability of appointing Welsh-speaking men to bishoprics in Wales, should have been regarded by many and recommended by some as an episcopal candidate. What is surprising, however, is the vehemence expressed by some of the prime-minister's official or would-be advisors whenever his name was mentioned, even though Richard Grosvenor, Gladstone's political agent, having canvassed opinion in Wales about the Llandaff vacancy of 1882, stated that Archdeacon Griffiths seemed to be the favourite. He was more qualified than any other Welsh clergyman in Wales for the appointment, wrote Henry Richard, and a thorough Liberal, decidedly evangelical, but not narrow-minded as such clergy generally were. He was the head of every movement designed to promote good in the Principality, and although his appointment might be distasteful to some because of his liberality in politics and religion, it would be very advantageous to the Church. Watkin Williams, MP, had also recommended him on that occasion as did Osborne Morgan, MP, who wrote in much the same terms as did Thomas Gee in 1882 who thought his appointment would be well received by all parties. He was respected even by those who differed from him. On the same occasion Bishop Hughes of St Asaph suggested that, if appointed, Griffiths could do much to heal the breach between Church and Nonconformity. Furthermore, he wrote, Griffiths was already a man of influence in the vacant diocese, and although he had no university training he yet possessed what no university could confer, namely the qualifications for ministry. Henry Richard also made this point, arguing that if elected Griffiths would be a popular choice, as he was a good man and a great favourite with the Nonconformists.[49]

Most of these recommendations came from Nonconformists or those members of parliament who wished to see the Church disestablished, such as Watkin Williams and Osborne Morgan. Gladstone probably paid little attention to them as he disliked the disestablishment campaign and was a decided high churchman. Nevertheless, he was a fair man, but other comments made about

Griffiths were probably sufficient to damn his candidature.

Lady Llanover's comments might be easily dismissed, for Gladstone probably knew that she had fallen out with Griffiths. Although she suggested his name for the vacancy in St Asaph in 1870 as one of the great preachers of Wales (as opposed to Basil Jones whose appointment she feared), even then she positively disliked him. He was, she wrote, an ambitious, scatter-haired Welshman with restless activity and no system of steady perseverance; a Welshman who seldom preached in his own native language and whose real ambition was to be an English platform orator, and a man who had presented the Princess of Wales with a medal at Carnarvon Castle but had allegedly still not paid for it. Twelve years later during the Llandaff vacancy she repeated her arguments with undisguised malice, indicating that she believed his name was being seriously considered. Griffiths's Welsh was so little used that it was no better than if he was ignorant of the language. Indeed he would not use it for he knew he could not compare with the real Welsh preachers. He did nothing in Welsh in his parish apart from a monthly communion service. Though he could talk "patriotism boldly with patriots" he was unstable and had no intellect. His sister had been her dairy maid and her husband her bailiff, but he had been dismissed for dishonesty, and then took a public house of a most ordinary description. The archdeacon had recently, in his old age, married a young wife who had no time for Wales, and her love of fashion and fine display, seen in all its bad taste at their marriage at St George's, Hanover Square, had not been forgotten by those who knew his first wife and her antecedents.[50]

Other voices were more persuasive and could not be easily ignored. In 1870 Lord Cawdor described Griffiths as "a popular preacher", but to this recommendation Gladstone's main advisor on Welsh affairs, H. A. Bruce, later Lord Aberdare, added the caution, "if this is my friend of Neath, I must bid you beware, he has no real stuff in him". He was not to be compared with David Howell or Pryce of Bangor. Though Bruce had no doubt that Griffiths's appointment would be a popular one, he was simply a glib speaker at eisteddfods, a tolerable preacher, and a very indifferent clergyman.

On the occasion of the 1882 vacancy Bruce described Griffiths as yet another platform speaker who carried no moral weight with the clergy and laity, though a certain fluent facility of speech made him popular with the multitude. Although these may be the comments of Anglo-Welshmen who did not understand or who failed to appreciate the Welsh temperament, Dean Vaughan was equally decisive though much fairer. Writing to Dean Davidson as advisor to the Crown during the 1890 Bangor vacancy, he described Griffiths as a very popular Welshman and a good man. Although he was a little large in his ideas of the Welsh, as of himself, nevertheless he was a good hearted and pleasant man and was accounted a good preacher in Welsh. Though he was probably 70 years of age he was as strong as a root. But Vaughan knew all too well these were not the attributes of a bishop. The position was put a little more crudely although publicly by a writer in the *Western Mail*. If the qualifications were governed "by private influence, electioneering stumping, and toadying" then Griffiths might stand higher than any other candidate. But in all the higher qualifications for the episcopal office he was deficient. He was intolerant and hasty, and no manager of his own or parochial affairs. Part was malicious, but part was true.[51]

Griffiths was a man of genial humour, human touch and kindly sympathies, although an opportunist, suggested Vyrnwy Morgan. Watcyn Wyn (Watkin Hezekiah Williams), a Nonconformist minister and literary figure, remembered his great kindness to him at the eisteddfodau, helping south Walians to understand the idiosyncrasies of the north Walians, giving him a box of white ties (the colour of the Gospel, he said) when he was ordained, and travelling from Neath to Aberaeron in a coach drawn by two horses each summer for his holidays. The *Record* in its obituary noted him as a man who always upheld the rights of his own Church; though others described him as a Nonconformist in all but name. However, Peter Williams regarded Griffiths as the best known of all the Church's dignitaries in Wales, and quoted an obituary writer who stated that he had popularised the Church amongst the masses. Griffiths's fellow archdeacon, William Bruce, called him a man of notable presence who had won the respect of a whole people. He continued that although Griffiths was involved in every organisation for the good of the nation, and was acclaimed by the whole of Wales as a national leader, he practised what he believed, namely that sectarian differences were better healed by patience than by controversy. Griffiths died at his residence in Neath, Aelybryn, on 1st September 1897, a few months after he had resigned his benefice, and his body was buried near his old childhood home, at Hen Fynyw, near Aberaeron. We can only conclude that in spite of all his faults and inadequacies, he served his parish and his nation to the best of his ability, and was an "able minister of the New Testament."[52]

ENDNOTES

1 *Young Wales*, III (1897) 235, cf. *Report of the Llandaff Diocesan Conference*, 1897, pp. 12-13.

2 Peter Williams, "John Griffiths", in J. V. Morgan (ed.), *Welsh Religious Leaders in the Victorian Era* (London, 1905), pp. 86-7; E. T. Lewis, *North of the Hills* (Haverfordwest, 1972), p. 255; *Geninen*, 16 (1898 - St David's Day issue), 36-9, 233-5; 19 (1901) 29; 20 (1902 - St David's Day issue), 1; WM, 24 February 1873, p. 3. His clerical brothers were Arthur, rector of Llanelli, Breconshire, and Alban, who died aged 33 as vicar of Llanallgo, Anglesey: Francis Jones, *Historic Cardiganshire Homes and their Families* (Brawdy, 2000), p. 91. For Cardigan Grammar School see Joseph Morgan, *Rev. David Jones, Panteg* (Pontypool, 1925), pp. 4-6.

3 *Church and People* (CPAS), III (1891) 91-2; Roger L. Brown, *The Welsh Evangelicals* (Cardiff, 1986), p. 120.

4 Williams, "John Griffiths", pp. 96-7.

5 NLW, Aberystwyth, Church in Wales Records, LL/LB/5, Llandaff Diocesan Letter Book, fol. 48b; and Glyn Simon Deposit 1968, Box 1, Diocesan Memorandum book. Morgan in his *Geninen* article states he built a new parsonage: 1898 - St David's Day issue, p. 39.

6 The papers of the Ecclesiastical Commission and Queen Anne's Bounty relating to the parish of Neath are in the custody of the Representative Body of the Church in Wales. An article of mine based on these papers appeared in the *Neath Antiquarian Society's Transactions*, 1995-6, pp. 30-41. See also CMG, 27 April 1861, p. 7.

7 Jane Ross, *A Light upon the Road* (Aberystwyth, 1989), pp. 56-7; CMG, 27 April 1861, p. 7.

8 Bruce to Gladstone, 13 January 1870, British Library, Gladstone Manuscripts, Addit. MS. 44086, fol. 84, and Lady Llanover to Gladstone, 14 January 1883, Addit. MS. 44479, fol. 121; WM, 16 June 1874, p. 7.

9 Williams, "John Griffiths", p. 94; Ecclesiastical Commission papers for October 1866; CMG, 29 March 1856, p. 5 and 27 April 1861, p. 7. Part of the difficulty may have resulted from an attempt to impose a church rate to cover the cost of the additional services. Rhys Phillips in his *History of the Vale of Neath* (Swansea, 1925), p. 106, states that the parish determined to establish a licensed room for Welsh services in 1850 at "Melincrythan".

10 Ecclesiastical Commission papers; *Church and People*, III (1891) 91-2; CPAS Reports, 1878, p. 23 and 1884, pp. 19-20; CMG, 29 March 1856, p. 5. For the curates see a cutting from the WM in John Griffith's cuttings book, South Glamorgan Library, Cardiff, MS. 5,157, and J. R. Buckley, typescript at the same depository, *Recollections and Reminiscences*, p. 31.

11 CMG, 29 March 1856, p. 5; Phillips, *History of the Vale of Neath*, pp. 600-1; George Eaton, *From Castle to Civic Centre* (Neath, 1975), p. 72.

12 Howell Williams, *The Romance of the Forward Movement in the Presbyterian Church of Wales* (Denbigh, 1946), pp. 121-2; T. Mardy Rees, *Seth Joshua and Frank Joshua* (Wrexham, 1926), pp. 15-16, 104.

13 Pamphlet: *The Arbitration of the Archdeacon of Llandaff* (Neath, 1885).

14 Williams, "John Griffiths", pp. 99-100; W. R. Lambert, *Drink and Sobriety in Victorian Wales* (Cardiff, 1983), pp. 89, 92, 136; *Neath Total Abstinence Society: Report of a Meeting in Memory of the late Evan Evans* (Neath, 1859); Buckley, *Recollections*, p. 34. Eben Fardd, the Welsh bard, commented in his diary for 1859 that Griffiths had visited him. He found him agreeable company even though he spoke strongly to him in favour of total abstinence: quoted in *Wales (OME)*, III (1896) 487-8. See also Griffiths's evidence to the Royal Commission on the Operation of the Sunday Closing (Wales) Act 1881: *Report*, 1890, pp. 174-7. Noting the improved condition of the streets of Neath as a result of that legislation, he felt it had loopholes in it which made it socially unfair. One of his leading parishioners, H. B. Coke, expressed some reservations about his temperance activities: CMG, 27 April 1861, p. 7.

15 George Eaton, "Neath Mechanics' Institute", *Neath Antiquarian Society Transactions*, 1978, p. 92, and Gareth Williams, "Battling for Books", in ibid., 1980-1, pp. 157-8.

16 CMG, 10 January 1857, p. 5; 17 January 1857, p. 4; 10 July 1858, p. 8; Connop Thirlwall, *A Letter to J. Bowstead, Esq., concerning Education in South Wales* (London, 1861), pp. 63-5; CPAS Report, 1878, p. 21.

17 *Record*, 3 September 1897, p. 882; Lambeth Palace Library, Benson Papers 146, fols. 6, 8-9.

18 *Record*, 19 February 1897, p. 181. A contributor to the *Church Times*, 19 February 1897, p. 192, stated that the Alderman Davies Schools had not been handed over to the School Board as the offer had been withdrawn by the Archdeacon, though all parties accepted that the Schools could be used by the Church on Sundays and weeknights.

19 *Report of the Bath Church Congress*, 1873, pp. 261f. Griffiths tried to promote a private grammar school at Neath, for which he was taken to task by the editor of the local *Neath Times*: T. G. Davies, *Neath's Wicked World* (Swansea, 2000), pp. 32-6.

20 NLW, Church in Wales Records, Ll/Ch/2746.

21 *Record*, 24 September 1897, p. 959.

22 NLW, Church in Wales Records, Ll/MISC/191-7.

23 A cutting from the scrapbook already described as MS. 5.157.

24 *Church Times*, 12 February 1897, p. 167; *Record*, 19 February 1897, p. 181.

25 *Report of the Llandaff Diocesan Conference*, 1897, pp. 12-13; cutting in MS. 5,157; Bishop Hughes to Gladstone, 22 December 1882, Addit. MS. 44478 fol. 164. CMG, 14 July 1854, p. 3, states that Griffith took his BD from Lampeter in that year.

26 Muriel Evans, *The Story of the Parish of St David's, Ton Pentre* (Pentre, 1960), pp. 12, 16-18, 21, 25; T. J. Prichard, *Representative Bodies*

(Llandybie, 1988), p. 152.

27 Williams, "John Griffiths", pp. 100, 90; (J.) V. Morgan, *The Church in Wales in the Light of History* (London, 1918), p. 157; *Report of the Leeds Church Congress*, 1872, p. 457; *Church and People*, VI (1894) 121-2.

28 Williams, "John Griffiths", pp. 97-8; CPAS Report, 1884, pp. 21-2; Morgan, *The Church in Wales*, pp. 157-8; Phillips, *History of the Vale of Neath*, p. 116; John Morgan in *Y Llan*, 11 November 1898, p. 3; *Geninen*, 19 (1901) 29. Griffiths became equally well known as a preacher at the Clerical Meetings of the 1840s and 50s: Brown, *Welsh Evangelicals*, p. 64.

29 John Griffiths, *Britain's Cause: A Sermon at the Parish Church of Neath to the Glamorgan Rifle Volunteers* (Neath, 1860), p. 19.

30 Bruce to Gladstone, 13 January 1870, Addit. MS. 44086, fol. 84; Lady Llanover to Gladstone, 14 January 1883, Addit. MS. 44479, fol. 121.

31 Buckley, *Reminiscences*, p. 31; *Llandaff Diocesan Magazine*, March 1899, p. 5; *Geninen* (1898 - St David's Day issue), 234; Dean Vaughan to Davidson, 13 March 1890, Lambeth Palace Library, Davidson Papers 522, fol. 95.

32 *Record*, 24 September 1897, p. 959.

33 *Church and People*, VI (1894) 122f. and III (1891) 33-4; Brown, *Welsh Evangelicals*, pp. 120-1; CPAS Report, 1884, pp. 19-20. Griffiths expressed his concern that the more Anglo-Catholic Assistant Curates Society was taking over from the CPAS in the provision of curates' grants: CPAS Report, 1878, p. 21.

34 CPAS Report, 1878, p. 22; cf. 1884, p. 21.

35 John Griffith, *An Address to Protest against the Suspensory Bill* (Neath, 1893), *in passim*, cf. CPAS Report, 1884, pp. 20-1. Griffiths felt that disestablishment could turn to the benefit of the Church, by making her think less of trifles and more of realities. During the tithe disturbances he was much criticised for allowing a rebate to his Neath and Llantwit tithe payers, but he argued that he had no wish to lose the goodwill of his parishioners and that clergy were there to exercise spiritual good not for their own benefit but for the good of their parishioners. He also argued that the landlord was ultimately responsible for the payments, a position established by legislation in 1891: *Report of the Llandaff Diocesan Conference*, 1886, pp. 105, 121-6.

36 *Report of the Swansea Church Congress*, 1879, pp. 268-71; *Record*, 18 May 1894, p. 492.

37 *Report of the Llandaff Diocesan Conference*, 1886, pp. 98-101.

38 Convocation was the so-called parliament of the Church, although it had little effective powers. Those elected to it by the clergy were termed proctors. CMG, 22 June 1861, p. 8. See also WM, 4 March 1874, p. 5, in which Griffiths supported Powell Jones of Llantrisant as he was not only qualified to represent the Welsh Church and to point out its real condition, but also because he had upheld evangelical doctrine in a celebrated controversy with Rowland Williams. Powell Jones lost the election.

39 *Report of the Bath Church Congress*, 1873, p. 68; Griffiths, *Suspensory Bill*, pp. 3-4.

40 Griffiths, *Suspensory Bill*, p. 9; *Report of the Leeds Church Congress*, 1872, p. 456; and *Report of the Bath Church Congress*, 1873, pp. 257-62; Williams, "John Griffiths", p. 92.

41 Williams, "John Griffiths", pp. 91-3; Ollivant to Griffiths, 19 November 1857, in NLW, Church in Wales Records, John Morgan Deposit, Box 10 (he expressed reluctance to interfere); Henry Richard to Gladstone, 1 February 1882, Addit. MS. 44479, fol. 36, and Bishop Hughes of St Asaph to Gladstone, 22 December 1882, Addit. MS. 44478, fol. 164; *Report of the Leeds Church Congress*, 1872, pp. 456-7; *Church and People*, III (1891) 34.

42 *Report of the Cardiff Church Congress*, 1889, pp. 553-7; cf. *Report of the Leeds Church Congress*, 1872, p. 456. G. H. Jenkins, in his introduction to *The Welsh Language and its Social Domains, 1801-1911* (Cardiff, 2000), p. 8, suggests that Griffiths was one of many Welsh speakers who was traumatised by the 1847 educational report (which had castigated the Welsh language) "and lived in further dread of further mockery and humiliation at the hands of the English." Griffiths was appointed a member of the committee for the revision of the Welsh New Testament: *Bye-Gones*, May 1881, pp. 262-3, and Griffiths to Professor T. R. Powel, 24 July 1890, NLW, MS. 8541b.

43 *Report of the Swansea Church Congress*, 1879, p. 578; Williams, "John Griffiths", pp. 95-6; H. T. Edwards, *Gwyl Gwalia* (Llandysil, 1980), p. 361.

44 Fred and V. A. Holley, "An Australian Visitor, Sir Samuel Griffith, in South Wales, 1887", *Merthyr Historian,* 5 (1992) 99, 101-2. Dean Vaughan was said to have been rather discomfited by Griffiths's reply.

45 Williams, "John Griffiths", p. 94: K. O. Morgan, *Rebirth of a Nation: Wales 1880-1980* (Oxford, 1981), p. 95. See also *Report of the Cardiff Church Congress*, 1889, pp. 555-6 and *Bye-Gones*, January 1888, p. 6.

46 David Williams, *Thomas Francis Roberts* (Cardiff, 1961), pp. 26-7.

47 Williams, "John Griffiths", pp. 90-1, 93; Dillwyn Miles, *The Royal National Eisteddfod of Wales* (Swansea, 1878), pp. 57-8; D. L. Baker Jones, "The Carmarthen Eisteddfod of 1867", *Carmarthenshire Historian*, 9 (1972) 44-70; John Morgan in *Y Llan*, 11 November 1898, p. 3; *Geninen*, 16 (1898 - St David's Day issue), 235, and 19 (1901), 29; K. V. Jones, *Life of John Viriamu Jones* (London, 1915), p. 137; Edwards, *Gwyl Gwalia*, p. 86; H. T. Edwards, "The Welsh Language in the Eisteddfod", in Jenkins, *The Welsh Language and its Social Domains*, p. 311; and see *Report of the National Eisteddfod of Wales, Chester 1866* (pp. 16-17) for Griffiths's letter regarding the need for reform, though adding that the intellectual, social and moral condition of the people could not be improved by excluding from it the experiences, learning and sympathy of "our English neighbours". There are a number of Griffiths's letters regarding eisteddfodau matters, and in particular arguing for suitable

liberality to visiting choirs and speakers, in NLW, MS. 3291E.

48 T. T. Lucius Morgan, *Rupert of Glamorgan* (Dolgellau, c. 1920), p. 51;
John Morgan in *Yr Haul*, 11 November 1898, p. 3; T. I. Ellis (ed.),
Thomas Charles Edwards Letters (NLW Journal Supplement 1952-3), pp.
46-7, 50-1; E. L. Ellis, *The University College of Wales, Aberystwyth,
1872-1972* (Cardiff, 1972), pp. 38-40 gives a background to this long and
involved debate. It has been suggested that Griffiths used his influence
with Lord Aberdare to obtain a grant from Gladstone for Aberystwyth:
Williams, "John Griffiths", p. 93. He also wanted schools for the middle
classes to feed the university colleges, and made the suggestion that the
colleges at Lampeter and Aberystwyth should be united: *Report of the
Welsh Education Conference at Aberystwyth*, January 1870, p. 30.
Griffith also gave important evidence before the Royal Commission on
the Working of the Elementary Education Acts in 1887.

49 Letters to Gladstone from Grosvenor, 31 December 1882, Addit. MS.
44315, fol. 102; Henry Richard, 8 March 1870, Addit. MS. 44425, fol.
226; Watkin Williams, 14 March 1870, Addit. MS. 44425, fol. 256;
Osborne Morgan, 19 January 1870, Addit. MS. 44424, fol. 121; Thomas
Gee, 22 December 1882, Addit. MS. 44428, fol. 160; Bishop Hughes of
St Asaph, 22 and 26 December 1882, Addit. MS. 44428, fols. 164, 224;
Henry Richard, 1 February 1883, Addit. MS. 44479, fol. 36. Some
confusion was caused, however, as another episcopal candidate, John
Griffiths of Llandeilo, had the same name: see, for example, Archbishop
Tait to Gladstone, 10 February 1870, Lambeth Palace Library, Tait Papers
167, fols. 26-7.

50 The letters of Lady Llanover to Gladstone, 17 November 1869, Addit.
MS. 44423, fol. 165; 19 February 1870, Addit. MS. 44425, fol. 25; 16
December 1882, Addit. MS. 44478, fol. 141; 14 January 1883, Addit.
MS. 44479, fol. 121. It was also claimed that John Griffith of Merthyr
was doing his best to prevent Griffiths's candidature: WM, 22 December
1882, p. 3. In a letter to John Griffith of Merthyr from the clerical
columnist of the WM, David Williams, of 20 February 1873, Williams
claimed that a column he had written about Griffiths had been suppressed
by the editor because it was too severe, although all to whom he had
shown it had said his portrait was very true: South Glamorgan Library,
MS. 3,508. The portrait of Archdeacon Griffith in the "Portraits of Welsh
Preachers" in the WM of 24 February 1873, p. 3, appears to have been a
revised version of this "column". It started by quoting a vehement attack
on Griffiths as a temporiser, a Dissenter masquerading as a Churchman, a
hypocrite, idler and intriguer, whose one desire was to become a Welsh
bishop. Although the writer defended him against these allegations, the
difference in tone from the other articles in the series is quite
extraordinary. Griffiths's first wife was Mary, daughter of Caleb Lewis a
book seller of Cardigan, and his second Jennet Matilda, daughter of Rees
Morgan of Neath.

51 Letters to Gladstone by Lord Cawdor, 17 January 1870, Addit. MS.

44424, fol. 62; of Lord Aberdare, 13 January 1870, Addit. MS. 44086, fol. 84, and 19 December 1882, Addit. MS. 44087, fol. 135; Vaughan to Davidson, 13 March 1890, Davidson Papers (Lambeth) 522, fol. 95: WM, 16 June 1874, p. 7.

52 Morgan, *The Church in Wales*, p. 156; *Record*, 10 September 1897, p. 906 (for Bruce), and 24 September 1897, p. 959; Williams, "John Griffiths", pp. 88, 101-3; Watcyn Wyn in *Geninen*, 19 (1901) 29.

6
GEORGE HUNTINGTON, RECTOR OF TENBY

"The tattered figure of the Rector as he tottered through the town, exchanging greetings with his parishioners, lent a pleasantly theatrical touch to the scene which the handsome old comedian was well aware of. He felt that he was playing the leading role in this pantomime and playing it well."[1] Thus wrote Augustus John, the artist, of his early days in Tenby and in particular about its rector, George Huntington.

Born in Hull during 1825 into a middle-class family, Huntington was later able to tell Bishop Wilberforce an impertinent story about his father's statue there which set the bishop laughing. Huntington's grandfather, whom he remembered, was a Norfolk parson who served three parishes, keeping a horse saddled and bridled in order to travel from one church to another, and arranging the times of service as best he could. A first cousin was John Bacchus Dykes, the church musician.[2] At the age of 21 Huntington entered St Bees College in Cumberland, which specialised in preparing non-graduate men for the ordained ministry. Possibly his family could not afford a university education for him or he changed vocational direction mid-stream, but his sense of inferiority may be glimpsed by what he wrote about St Bees in his most noteworthy book, *Random Recollections*. In his day there were between a 100 to 120 men at the college, he wrote, some of whom had been trained for other professions, but there was also a considerable number of Scripture readers and former dissenting preachers, as well as younger men like himself. The entrance requirement was "to be able to read and construe the Greek Testament readily and grammatically at sight; to read and parse a piece of Latin; and you were supposed to try your hand at a Latin theme. Butler, Pearson, Hooker, and Paley were text-books, and you had to pass an examination in *Grotius de Veritate Religionis Christianae* in the original Latin; and if you were ambitious to stand well, you were expected to cite the Articles and Creeds in Latin, as well as in English."[3] It was clearly equivalent to a university education, and Huntington was to speak highly of its principal,

Richard Parkinson, who gave him much assistance during his earlier years in Holy Orders. Huntington must have been gratified to have received an honorary MA degree from the Archbishop of Canterbury in 1855, one of the so-called Lambeth degrees, which entitled him to wear the hood of the archbishop's university, in his case that of Cambridge. It is not known why or how he obtained the degree, but it is known that they were not given for trivial reasons nor could they be purchased.[4]

Huntington was ordained in 1848 to a curacy at St Stephen's Salford (where he was later to serve as rector), and between 1850-5 served another curacy at Wigan Parish Church. From circumstances described by G. W. E. Russell, who records reminiscences of Huntington, this was a parish with a Tractarian tradition, having daily services.[5] In 1855 he became a clerk in orders or chaplain of Manchester Cathedral, or as he preferred to put it, The Old Church. He served in this capacity for 12 years, and for the last three years he cared in addition for the parish of St Stephen's, Salford. His entry to this clerkship might have been assisted by his former principal, Parkinson, who was also a canon of the cathedral, or possibly by William Huntington, rector of St John's, Manchester, who may have been a relation. Nevertheless his appointment was made by selection, as Dean Bowers reminded him in the chapter house when he was officially told of his election: "Now there are nine of us, and we cannot be expected to think all alike. Now remember you're two ears and one tongue." It is clear that Huntington was extremely happy in Manchester and wrote of it, and the men under whom he served, with much affection in later years. One of these men was Canon Wray, a kindly old-fashioned clergyman who merely held out two fingers for curates to shake, only giving his full hand to his fellow canons. He claimed to have baptised more children and married more couples than any other clergyman in the Church of England. When Canon Wray took exception to Huntington's extempore preaching the dean suggested he simply took notes up to the pulpit in order to gratify the old man. The advice worked and Huntington received a special commendation on his performance together with an encomium on written sermons. Whereupon the dean accused him of being a poor deceiver, "for you forgot to turn over the leaves".[6]

Clearly these were happy days, but in 1867 Huntington was unexpectedly offered the rectory of Tenby by the Crown's appointment secretary. Huntington may have attracted the attention of the Crown as he had served for a time as domestic chaplain to the

Earl of Crawford and Balcarres, although it is more probable that Parkinson had recommended him for a parochial appointment. It is hard to understand why Huntington accepted the dull and fashionable watering place of Tenby, for his previous ministry had been confined exclusively to working-class parishes in industrial areas. It may be that he hoped that an appointment to a Crown living might be the prelude to better things. If that was so, it was a vain hope.

Huntington, who was already a voluminous writer by the time of his appointment to Tenby, was later to become well known in his day for his polemical books and pamphlets. If Tenby gave him the leisure and space in which to write, his books indicate that his heart remained in those dark northern mill towns with their vibrant life. As one of his curates, D. Ambrose Jones, remarked in an obituary which appeared in the *Haul* of 1905, Huntington remained an Englishman to the last.

His book *Amusements and the need of supplying Healthy Recreations for the People* was published in a second edition during 1868. This was an extended lecture, with an appendix of quotations, dedicated to the loyal and intelligent working men. But its underlying thesis was the need to return to the days of "merry England" when Church and Society worked together for the well-being of people. Such was his dream, idealised and clearly tractarian in shape. Bodily exercise was to be encouraged by using the Church festivals as occasions for rural sports or beating the bounds. The clergymen, after celebrating the morning eucharist – hopefully choral in tone – should be foremost in these activities, thus affording the strongest security against drunkenness and disorder. Cricket (but not on Sunday, walking only was to be permitted), gardening, allotments, and splendid and cheap excursions were also recommended. Working-men's clubs could be organised by the parish clergy. These clubs, Huntington suggested, should contain reading rooms with well-selected novels and games such as chess, draughts and backgammon (but certainly not cards). Indoor gymnastics, dancing (if properly regulated), cheap concerts and penny readings, magic lantern lectures, guest speakers, and scientific lectures could also be arranged. The room should be well lit and have a good fire, while refreshments such as coffee, tea, bread and butter could be provided. Men should be allowed to smoke, and although wives and children were not to be admitted, at least the wives would know their husbands were not liable to come home intoxicated. Furthermore, there could be occasional tea parties for wives and children. It was clearly right for clergymen to mix with their people, Huntington advised, but woe to the priest known to be a card-player, a dancer or frequenter of theatres, for he would be the last person to whom a penitent would "open his grief" or a sick man send for on his death bed.

Another but more major work appeared around the same time as this pamphlet on amusements and recreations. This was *The Church's Work in the Large Towns*, which was first published in 1863 and attracted some favourable reviews from the tractarian press. It was compiled from articles which had been published in *The Church Review*.[7] Huntington's main thesis in this book was to point out the spiritual destitution of the large cities, thus furthering the impact caused by the statistics of church attendance produced by Mann's religious census of 1851.

Huntington's remedies included the re-distribution of the Church's wealth and clerical manpower, in order that all livings should be made up to the value of £300 per annum. New dioceses should be created, and the cathedrals made into centres of diocesan life as well as places for devotion and study. There was a need for "colleges" of priests and laity to serve in what might be described as mission parishes. These mission clergy needed to be both preachers and confessors, combining the sacerdotal and prophetic ministries. Huntington stressed the need for laity to be far more effectively used in the work of the Church, and argued the case for a permanent diaconate in the inner city areas of London. Churches for the working class should never be shabby, for the poor must not be excluded from God-given beauty, which would inculcate a sense of reverence in the Church's worship. Huntington thus wrote: "I believe that the right thinking among them are utterly adverse to the burlesque indulged in by those who think themselves especially called to minister to the working classes. However unfamiliar some may be with the Church's worship, they will soon learn to appreciate what is beautiful and true." A real effort was required to win back dissenters to the "true" Church, though there should be no compromise of truth. The provision of free seats was essential to achieve this for not only was the Gospel meant to be "without money and without price", the lack of free seating had contributed to the spread of Nonconformity. Furthermore, social conditions in the large towns needed to be remedied. This could be achieved by the closing of public houses on Sundays and a better control of lodging houses and "vicious literature". By such means, rather than by the so-called revivals which too often exhibited heresies and blasphemies, the masses would be won back to the Church of their forefathers. There was little new in this book. Other men, far more experienced than Huntington, had written on similar lines, but at least he gave coherence to these arguments and was sufficiently outspoken to attract attention.[8]

Huntington, though an outsider, had thought much about the position of the Church in Wales, on which subject he spoke at the Church Congress held at Leeds in 1872. This was his only contribution to these annual events, which suggests that he kept a low profile during his Tenby years. These congresses, independent in character and designed to provide a forum for all kinds of churchmanship, debated matters of concern within the Church and soon acquired a quasi-official status. Though he accepted that he spoke as an Englishman in Wales, regretting that he did not speak the Welsh language, Huntington was sufficiently bold to suggest that its problems were five fold, namely isolation, a scattered population, poverty, the existence of two languages, and immigration into the industrial areas. His answer to poverty was, once again, a redistribution of resources and an increased liberality from the property owners. Isolation however would only be removed in time with the ever-increasing links between England and Wales and by the spread of the English tongue, which was now the only language used in the day schools. Rural deaneries should have a full-time missioner attached to them who, in rural areas (one assumes) could be sent forth with a horse, a priest's bag containing a surplice, communion vessels, a Welsh Bible and Prayer Book, and a few hymn-books, in order to preach in the open air, or to hold services in farmhouses. Church services needed to reflect the character of the Welsh people. An excitable and imaginative people required music and preaching to match their mood. Missions, such as the Aitken mission at Swansea, were wanted in the new towns. All this, Huntington concluded, should cause hope for the Welsh Church, and would allow her to take part in that great wave of religious and social improvement which was already occurring in England.[9]

Possibly the one work for which Huntington was well known during his lifetime was his *John Brown the Cordwainer: shewing what part he took in the spread of Church Principles among the Working Classes*. Although described as "edited" by George Huntington, and published during the 1870s, it appears to have been modelled on Spurgeon's *John Ploughman's Talks*, being a dialogue in a reasonably simple style which commended particular principles. In

Huntington's book these principles were eminently Tractarian and ritualistic, and the frontispiece carried an illustration of a large Tractarian church, with an eastward altar richly covered by a frontal, a surpliced choir, and a congregation sitting in chairs rather than pews. But another illustration – shades of Pugin's *Contrasts* – illustrated the low church coventicle, with its boxed pews for the rich and benches for the poor, empty galleries, the royal arms, and a clergyman dressed in a silk gown pontificating from the central three-decker pulpit, with the altar dimly hinted at in the corner surrounded by a reredos containing the decalogue. John Brown, the working man, relates the building of a new church which, with its free seats, bright choral services, the ritual and colour of the ceremonial, and daily services, extended a warm welcome to working class people. Church schools, an almshouse and a church institute all consolidated this work. A sub-plot describes the attempt of the liberal-Nonconformists to disestablish the Church and to denounce its ritual. But the attempt is doomed to failure as the working men are not to be deceived, recognising that this attack has come because the Church has revived itself. Once again we see the Tractarian ideal of a contented society dominated by the benevolence of a Church whose ethos is medieval in doctrine and tone, but it is significant that the setting is the mill area of Lancashire, even though the book was probably written at Tenby. *John Brown the Cordwainer* is the literary equivalent of Huntington's essay on the Church's work in the large towns.

Only one of Huntington's works appears to describe his Tenby days, and it has the tone of a "swansong". This was *The Autobiography of an Almsbag or Sketches of Church Life and Social Life in a Watering Place*, published in 1885 under the pseudonym of "by the author of John Brown, Cordwainer". Many of the stories found in this book are also contained in his *Random Recollections*; Checkington-on-Sea is clearly Tenby, and the bishop of St Vortigern's is obviously Thirlwall.

The work for which Huntington is now best remembered, *Random Recollections of Some Noted Bishops, Divines and Worthies of the "Old Church" of Manchester,* a new edition of which appeared in 1896, is an exercise in sheer nostalgia. Seven of the 15 chapters deal directly with Manchester, and only three with his contemporaries in St David's diocese, namely Bishop Thirlwall, the saintly Birkett of St Florence and the learned if eccentric Smith of Gumfreston.[10]

His essay on Thirlwall, for example, leads us happily into an account of his ministry at Tenby. Noting his bishop's inaccessibility to his clergy and his inability to speak to them or even encourage them, Huntington related his own experience:

> I went to be instituted to my living of Tenby, to which I had been nominated by the Crown, and it is considered one of the most important benefices in the diocese. Three other clergymen were ushered into his presence to take the oaths. The secretary instructed each of us to take the New Testament into our hand, and to pass it from one to the other, and to repeat the usual formula. The Bishop was stooping down looking at the folios on the lower shelves of the bookcase, and when the business was over, he took us all in with one sweeping bow, and then disappeared.

Nevertheless he records Thirlwall's kindnesses to his daughters and son. His son was at school in Oxford with two of the bishop's great-nephews, and journeyed there with them, staying overnight with the bishop at Abergwili Palace. On one occasion a children's party was in progress, and the bishop told his son to find the prettiest girl he could find, and take her in to dinner, and later whispered into his ear, "I commend your choice". It is these little details that make his book so valuable.[11]

Huntington must have felt that the coldness of the bishop was a suitable prelude to his ministry at Tenby, for within a few months of his arrival in 1867 he was to be embroiled in storm after storm. This was due to his desire to put into effect his high church practices. In fact, Huntington has been termed the pioneer of the Oxford movement in the western part of the diocese of St David's. As Nigel Yates notes, his predecessor, Archdeacon George Clarke, had introduced a twice monthly early (9.00 am) celebration of the Holy Communion on Sundays, and though an early morning celebration was almost a badge of advanced churchmanship at that time, D. Ambrose Jones suggested that Clarke was more a churchman of the black gown and white cravat variety than a ritualist. Huntington immediately brought the service forward an hour and made it weekly. Other practices soon followed. The surplice was used in the pulpit rather than the preaching gown, the exhortations in the communion service were omitted; *Hymns Ancient and Modern* introduced; the communion elements were brought in after the service had begun and the eastward position taken; choral services established along with processions of "persons in surplices", while

Huntington endeavoured to introduce (without success at first) the offertory and a lectern.

All these were marks of high churchmanship, but it is probable that Huntington simply continued his Salford practices almost without thinking, but when challenged, dug in his heels. It is hardly surprising that he was challenged. The Victorians disliked innovations in their pattern of worship and they disliked having offertories in churches even more, believing that the church rate or pew rents should suffice for the maintenance of the building and its worship. Perhaps they clearly saw that the offertory was an attack upon their cherished private pews, which sat 688 people in comfort compared to the 340 not-so comfortable free seats. But the other innovations were seen as an attack upon the Protestant Church, at a time when tractarianism and papal aggression were still matters of anxiety. Many believed that Tractarianism would open the door to a Roman Catholic take-over of the Established Church, and this in turn would have major political repercussions. Mr Huntington's changes were thus affecting their security as Christians and citizens.

Within a few months of Huntington's induction the good citizens of Tenby had called a public meeting to "consider what steps should be taken to put a stop to ritualistic practices" in their parish church. As a result 248 aggravated parishioners signed a memorial complaining about the practices noted above to Bishop Thirlwall. The bishop, one of the few independent liberal thinkers on the bench at that time, refused to take sides, supporting Huntington in all the points of conflict, save for that of the eastward position, though even here he felt unable to interfere. He made the suggestion, rather surprisingly, that much of the opposition sprang from Huntington's membership of the English Church Union, which organisation the bishop personally distrusted as it tended to lead the Church in a Rome-ward direction. Though Nigel Yates quotes the *Church Times's* blatant comment that Thirlwall supported the rector "most cordially", and read "the fussy Protestants a lesson which they will not soon forget", he also notes his private letter to Miss Elizabeth Hill-Johnes of Dolaucothi which would have given the editor of that paper some cause for reflection. In this letter Thirlwall wrote: "[t]he Ritual plague has broken out at Tenby, imported by a new rector, in a mild form indeed, but yet accompanied by fever, restlessness, ill blood and other bad symptoms." The two parties had appealed to him but the bishop felt that his intervention involving "endless letters to both" and revealing the confidences of one side to the other, had "put both sides in a worse humour with me than they were before with one another." The dispute also annoyed Thirlwall in another way, for this "disastrous interruption" had forced him to change many of his planned activities that month.[12]

In that same letter Thirlwall wrote that he wasn't sure if he had heard the last of the matter. He was correct, for a lengthy correspondence continued in the local press while matters were stirred up from time to time by his opponents. Nevertheless Huntington was not the man to take too much note of the opposition, for he was financially independent of his parishioners, and he must have felt reasonably sure that if his bishop did not actually support him he would not effectively oppose him. Within the next four years more innovations took place. The church was decorated at Easter; a choral eucharist established; a jewelled cross, candlesticks and floral decorations introduced; the already surpliced choir taken from the gallery into the chancel; processional hymns allowed; a costly altar frontal purchased; a temporary rood-screen erected in the chancel and regular weekday communions begun. In the 1872 parish magazine Huntington claimed that there was no church in Wales, and few in England, where there were more numerous and beautiful services, or where a larger and more devout congregation could be found. During Holy Week and Easter Tuesday there had been 44 services held in the church, 18 of them Communion services, and 5 of these "solemn choral Celebrations". The Harvest festival of that year, the choral services, the richly decorated church, the dignity and beauty of the ritual, and the processions with the clergy in their new and richly decorated white stoles, gave added emphasis to his earlier claim.[13]

Huntington's assertion that he had a large and devout congregation was probably true. Tenby was sufficiently large to have a reasonable number of people who liked ritual and ceremony while others were probably loyal to their parish church although perhaps not all that approving of his innovations. On the other hand one wonders how many of his congregation were visitors. But not all his parishioners were sympathetic or prepared to remain passive and quiet about these new practices. One, who described himself as *An Old Churchman*, wrote a strong attack on Huntington in the *Tenby Observer*, taking up comments made by the *Church Times* in its account of the Whitsunday services of 1872. It was later published as a separate pamphlet whose title was suggestive: *Letters on Medievalism in the Parish Church of Tenby*. It may be that the writer was a visitor to Tenby, when visitors stayed for months rather than weeks, but the fact that this was published separately surely indicates that there was widespread support for his views within the town. Indeed the writer notes that Huntington had to refute some of his opponent's arguments (rather badly he thought), through the medium of his parish magazine, in the hope of reducing their impact.

Old Churchman used a familiar tactic, in suggesting that while these ritualistic innovations might not seem too alarming at the present time, they yet constituted a clear if muted attack on the reformed Church. He warned the fathers and mothers of families, in particular, that to ignore as unimportant "the beginnings and symptoms of this defection from the Reformed Catholic Faith is as unwise and reckless as to disregard the premonitory symptoms of a prevailing epidemic or the prognostics of a coming storm." The eastward position was condemned as an act of flagrant disobedience against the canons of the Church (by one whose theology, he suggested, gave a high place to church order). Huntington was accused of teaching the intermediate state in his sermons, while the writer felt obliged to leave the church before the communion was administered, feeling "excluded from the Holy Communion by the medievalisms of these pseudo-Catholic revivalists." Such men as Huntington would introduce their ceremonies step by step, he argued, for "they never lose a step, or miss an opportunity, great or small." A choir was introduced for congregational singing, but it was soon being used for the introduction of Romish costumes or ceremonials, such as processions. The teaching of the Catechism in the afternoon children's service received *Old Churchman's* strongest condemnation, for it contained "a mass of absurdities" and allowed the introduction of a "quasi-religious parody". The catechism had been followed by the Litany of the Holy Family, which he believed owed its origin to some Romish office, and would have the result of leading the little ones into superstition. The evening sermon was equally condemned for suggesting that "men were not to go straight to Christ for themselves, but to the clergy, to be by them brought to Christ." *Old Churchman* thus argued:

> In laying before you the fallacies, the sophistries, the inaccuracies, the confusion of thought and language, the lack of any clear or definite view of what they were talking about ... my object has been this – to point out how utterly unfit these men are to teach you, when they wander one hair's breadth

from the language which our Church has put into their mouths: how unsafe it is for their parishioners to take their teaching upon trust – a duty which they continually urge upon their parishioners as the first thing needful to those who would be brought to Christ ... They may be ... estimable men, but they are not, in my opinion, men to whom you can safely trust implicitly as independent expounders of Christian truth. [14]

A new bishop of St David's, Basil Jones, was embroiled in yet another dispute relating to Huntington's practices at Tenby. True to his beliefs, Huntington had organised various missions to the people of his parish, but their high church character aroused considerable opposition, and a medical man, William Cust Gwynne, wrote a very strong letter of protest to the bishop. This letter, with George Huntington's letter of explanation to the bishop, and the bishop's reply to Gwynne, were later printed by R. Mason, the Tenby printer, in a pamphlet of 1878, *Three Letters on the Subject of the late Tenby Mission*. Might it have been Gwynne, one wonders, who had also written under the pseudonym of *Old Churchman*?

The first mission had been conducted by the celebrated Father Ignatius of Llanthony, whom Gwynne described as a man "of notoriously Roman Catholic proclivities, calling himself 'a Monk of the Church of England,' and habited in frock and cowl, and sandals ..." The second mission had been conducted by a Revd H. C. Wilkinson, who used the priest-confessor's title of "Father", and by a Revd J. Douglas, who belonged to some semi-monastic order which the good doctor felt "savoured" of Roman tendencies. Although the initial services and addresses were good, and most of those who attended "were loud in their praise of the fervour and eloquence of the preachers, in their testimony to the deep impression made on the hearers, and the good likely to result from the Mission", Gwynne was horrified that half way through the mission the tone of the teaching changed. As a result of this change "the congregation was astounded at hearing Confession to a priest, which had not been so much as alluded to before ... advocated with an earnestness and enthusiasm worthy of a better cause, and perhaps seldom exercised in a worse one."

Furthermore, a tract entitled *Sin Absolved*, containing similar teaching, had been widely distributed. Deeply concerned about the sacerdotalism which appeared to be rife amongst the clergy of the Church, as well as the lack of any legal method of restraining it,

Gwynne's particular resentment was reserved for the practice of auricular confession. This he described as the "last and most repulsive development" of sacerdotalism, and which could cause spiritual havoc to the young, the feeble-minded, and "the trusting and credulous natures of the younger portion of the weaker sex." As for himself, he regretted that he hardly entered his own parish church. The teaching of the Real Presence from the pulpit, and the impression given by the clergy that they regarded themselves as sacrificial priests, made it essential for his own peace of mind to accept "the inconvenience" of attending a neighbouring parish church in common with many others who felt excluded from their own church. It was his hope that the bishop would "devise some means of counteracting an agency so inimical to the well-being and purity of the Church, and of at least preventing any future Mission here being prostituted to the purposes of propagating doctrines" which were never intended to be taught in the Reformed Church of England.

Huntington who had received a copy of this letter from his bishop, wrote an extremely defensive reply. This could have been because he had had to substitute other missioners for the ones whose names had been given to the bishop, and who were presumably licensed by him for this work. But it may also have been because Gwynne had touched on some very raw nerves. Of course, Huntington wrote, he could not hope to please everybody by his ritual and teaching. If only a few had left many others had joined, and he made the claim that "our vastly increased congregations and communicants testify certainly that our labours are not unrewarded." He was grateful to the doctor for his testimony as to the number who attended these mission services, and for the moderate tone of his letter, which was rather different from his letters in the local press when he wrote as a member of the Church Association. It was a pity he had listened to hearsay evidence, for he had not been present at these meetings. Yes, confession had been taught, but it was only recommended in those special cases for which the prayer book itself made provision. If a confessional had been used, in reality it was only a place where the mission clergy could go and be consulted for spiritual counselling or advice, or even for people to sign the temperance pledge. As for Gwynne's arguments against the confessional Huntington felt they were the usual stock charges, but most of the so-called "penitents" were men unlikely to be wrought upon by mere sentiment, such as military officers of high rank, employers of labour, or seafaring men who were also grandfathers. He denied that a doctrine of the real presence had even been taught which was inconsistent with the recognised teachings of the Church of England, and the clergy of the parish had never put themselves forward as sacrificing priests. Rather he believed that the mission had assisted himself and his brethren "to renewed earnestness, not in the direction of any phase of doctrine or ceremonial, but in that of a desire to win souls to the Redeemer." Huntington thus concluded: "[p]ersonally I feel that no ministrations have ever effected me more deeply since the first fervour of my Ordination."

The bishop may have accepted such assurances, but he considered Huntington to have been a little devious, to say the least. Writing to Gwynne he expressed his regret that the missioners had been changed (one of them as a member of the Society of the Holy Cross would have been most objectionable to him), and that the mission had been advertised as having taken place under his sanction. Although the tract on confession given out was not against the teaching of the Church in a doctrinal sense (for the teaching of the Church allowed people to come to a clergymen for his "ghostly counsel and advice"), yet in a practical sense the bishop was concerned to note that it suggested that absolution depended on the judgment of the priest rather than upon the reality of repentance. The bishop also expressed his regret that "a Tract of what I cannot but call a very pernicious character [was] circulated in Tenby, at a time when the minds of some of the parishioners must necessarily have been in a condition of unusual religious excitement." Though the mission appears to have been blessed, yet it was unfortunate that this tract had been circulated, and that the rector "had transferred the care of his parish to strangers".

It is perhaps not surprising that at some stage rival services, conducted by laymen, were held in the Assembly Rooms, and, equally unsurprisingly, that they were denounced by Huntington. At some stage a branch of the Free Church of England was formed by these laymen. This Church, which had a number of branches throughout England and Wales, claimed to offer a pure liturgy and a Protestant theology. But matters settled down, though Huntington was mortified when he discovered that some of his congregation were attending or even contributing to the new Roman Catholic church in the town. That was the Italian mission, he argued, whereas St Mary's Church represented the true Church of this Christian nation. But it was hardly surprising that some of his parishioners should have frequented that other church when their taste for ritual had been developed by Huntington, and when many of his teachings had been backed up by reference to authorities in better standing with the so-called Italian mission than with the Church of England.[15]

On one occasion, if his *Autobiography of an Almsbag* is autobiographical, Huntington had the last word against some of his opponents. He wrote about it in this way:

> The queerest things, indeed, used to be said about the goings on of the clergy; but, as usual, these false reports went to the bottom when the inventors and spreaders were tired of keeping them afloat, for the vicar had a knack of drawing people out and asking for their authority, and so the truth came uppermost at last. On one occasion he had heard so many strange stories told about himself and his curates by two well-meaning ladies in a railway carriage on their way to Clackington, that, concealing his identity, he drew out their confidences and they told him all their mind. He heard that, though married himself, as before hinted, by a Papal Dispensation, he demanded vows of celibacy, not only from his curates, but from every young lady he prepared for confirmation. Now the vicar being, as may be gathered from the notices already given of him, a plausible kind of man, and much given to humour, not to say sarcasm, made himself as agreeable as it was in his nature to these good ladies, who, not knowing who he was, in the fullness of their hearts expressed their wish that he had been the parson of Clackington instead of the dreadful man they expected to find there. "I am the man," quoth he. "Oh, we sincerely beg your pardon," was the reply. "We were only telling you what we heard." "My dear friends," replied the vicar, ... "promise me one thing that you'll go to church and judge for yourselves." The ladies went, never missed a service during their month's stay, and what was more, presented five pounds for the local charities as a thank offering before they went away.

The book goes on to notice the sewing society, mission meetings, Sunday school, children's services, penny readings, and all the other activities of a successful Victorian parish. This note of "success" is confirmed in D. Ambrose Jones's account of his vicar. He did not know of any other town in Wales where Nonconformity had so little strength, where there was such a continuous flow of young people to the Church, or where people took such an interest in church services.[16]

Apart from these parochial issues and problems which Huntington had to face, there were more personal ones. The rectory house had been repaired during 1852-3, and the then incumbent had taken out mortgages for this work from Queen Anne's Bounty in various sums totalling £535. The house had been previously let for many years by a previous rector, Dr Humphreys, as rector, who in 1832 certified that he lived in lodgings as he did not need the use of the house. The total income of the benefice then was £375. By 1877 a survey found that the certain income was £318, derived mainly from the glebe which was let at £72 and from the tithe rental charge of £239, but from this sum deductions of £79 had to be made. But in addition the Easter offerings produced £76 and the surplice fees £28, thus giving a total income of £394. But there were other charges which could not be claimed as deductions, such as the payment of the curates' stipends (for that was the rector's responsibility though he might be assisted by diocesan and other grants and by his parishioners), the maintenance of the rectory, and the cost of chancel repairs.[17]

Writing in October 1873 to Queen Anne's Bounty, a Church charity which had given the mortgages for the rectory and to which he, as the successor in title, had to make the annual repayments, Huntington respectfully begged to lay before them the circumstances of his case. The loans previously given had been expended on work

which it would have been better for the living had a sixpence never been laid out. *The Rectory of Tenby is in plain English uninhabitable.* Owing to its low and damp situation, aggravated by the raising of the road, and the sewerage of the Town, which discharges itself into the brook running through the Rectory garden, it is never without smells, and its lower stories so moist that I have had to remove my books to the upper story and to discontinue living on the ground floor as far as possible. My predecessor, Archdeacon Clarke, makes no secret of the fact that one of the reasons, if not the principal reason, for resigning the living was the unhealthy nature of the house. He had two attacks of gastric fever in it, and I have hardly had a day's health, one of my children has died of rheumatic fever and one has had a very severe attack of scarlet fever (the only case then in town), and one of my servants has left in ill-health, apparently when she came she was a strong and healthy woman. Three of my children are showing unmistakable signs of delicacy for which the medical attendant can assign no sufficient reason but the character of the House. Add to this, that the Rectory is built of rubble, that it is always needing repairs, that during the recent gales it was partly unroofed, that it has three times been inundated during the heavy rains.

A further letter indicated that the sea breezes brought the unmistakable smell of the local gas works to the house, while the local sanitary inspector had advised them that the only way to obtain a healthy home was to built one on a new site. It was impossible to patch up the house to make it a decent residence, and thus Huntington requested the governors of the Bounty either to free him from the amount of debt still remaining on the house, or to assist him in building a new house elsewhere. A doctor's note was enclosed indicating that in his opinion the ulcerated throats and a case of scarletina in the rectory family were all due to the unhealthy nature of the house. The governors unhappily replied they were unable to forgo the debt, as it was made out of their capital, and pointed out that to sell a parsonage house needed the consent of the diocesan bishop, the patron and the archbishop.

This was not the only problem. A large family, an expensive house, a substantial mortgage, and a reducing income due to the fall in the value of the tithe, meant that Huntington was not able to meet his mortgage payments when required. There was still £385 due on the house with an annual charge of £24. By November 1873 he owed a sum of £47 10s.6d. One Herbert Huntington, writing from Narberth, sent a draft for £14, and another £5 was paid by Huntington, but there was still £28 10s.6d. owing, and the Governors felt constrained to sequestrate the living for these arrears. This meant that a trustee would be appointed to manage the income, pay the debts and outgoings, and hopefully have sufficient in hand to enable the rector and his family to somehow stay alive. Thankfully it did not come to that, for the balance was paid by the same Herbert Huntington.[18]

It seemed to be accepted on all sides that a new rectory house was required. After a long delay due to legal complications the governors of the Bounty and the Ecclesiastical Commission, which was also involved, agreed that a site could be given for this purpose by the trustees of the Tenby Church Charity. By the end of 1874 the old rectory had been sold to Messrs Roden and Adams, of Stoke on Trent, for the sum of £1,500, and 15 acres of glebe land was sold for the sum of £4,500 (possibly to Roden's brother-in-law, Mr R. Fothergill,

MP, who to complicate matters was later declared bankrupt). This latter sum was invested to augment the living, producing an annual income of £50, as it could not legally be used for the provision of a new house, thus upsetting Huntington's calculations. The negotiations for the sale of the house were said to be most protracted and troublesome, while the costs of the sale were disputed by all the parties concerned and appear to have been finally paid by Huntington. They came to nearly £25, besides which there was another charge of over £7 for dilapidations. As the patronage was vested in the Crown the prime minister's consent had also to be obtained, and the cost of obtaining this from Mr Disraeli was six shillings and eight pence. The remaining mortgages were paid off from the sale of the old rectory, and meanwhile, it appears, Huntington and his family had to obtain rented accommodation until their new house could be built.

A London architect, William Newton Dunn, designed the house, which had to fit in with the specifications required by the commissioners. Three large reception rooms together with the usual kitchen offices were on the ground floor, four bedrooms were on the first floor with a bathroom and two dressing rooms, and four bedrooms and a boxroom on the second floor. The cost was estimated at £1,950, the land having been given free of charge. But the total cost, including extra work and the architect's charges brought the total to £2,498. Some of the additional work was due to the exposed situation of the house being built above the sea front, thus requiring the installation of a lightning conductor and shutters for the windows. The sum also included additional gas fittings. The remaining monies from the sale of the old house and the sale by the Bounty governors of some securities belonging to the parish held by them, helped pay most of the costs of the new house. The remainder was obtained from private subscriptions; Queen Victoria gave £500 as patron of the living, while a two-day bazaar which had a Christmas tree as one of its principal attractions realised £150. A further £500 was allowed by the Ecclesiastical Commissioners from the sale of the glebe land. Huntington may well have hoped that the governors of the Bounty or the commissioners would have assisted him with a grant, but the first body could not give to benefices whose income was over £200 per annum, and the second tended to reserve its grants for the populous manufacturing parishes. Tenby lost on both counts. Nevertheless, Huntington did apply for assistance to the commissioners, asking that if he could raise a benefaction of £100 to £150 from his parishioners, would they be able to meet it with an equivalent grant? He could not afford to borrow any more money with the claims made on him by the parish and the debt still due to the Bounty governors, while the parish was daily increasing in population and he needed to keep a large staff of curates. The reply was polite if blunt; his chance of success was remote.

Unfortunately the new house was built on a very exposed site, as Huntington made clear in a letter to the Bounty governors in October 1886. A new porch was needed as well as alterations to the back of the house, for "beautiful as the situation is, it is so exposed especially to the north and south-west winds that at times it is hardly habitable and both family and servants take colds thereby ... I suppose one feels these things more as one gets older, especially of late years when within the memory of that historic individual, the oldest inhabitant, there never has been such a constant succession of storms." He had paid hundreds of pounds from his own pocket in an attempt to keep the draughts out, but he would have to double-glaze those windows which, as the sailors say, "is in the wind's eye". Thankfully some more money appears to have been found from sums held on behalf of the parish by the Bounty treasurer.[19]

A surprising glimpse into the workings of his parish is found in an evangelical paper, the *Record*. In 1894 its editor sent a questionnaire to all incumbents in Wales which asked them what effect disestablishment and disendowment would have on their parishes. Huntington replied that Tenby would not be affected to the same extent as other parishes, being a watering place, although disestablishment would certainly hinder the work of the Church there as the incumbent would lose his income from the tithes. Voluntary offerings given by the congregation supported two to three licensed curates, two mission churches, and the large voluntary day and Sunday schools, besides maintaining the fabric and services of the parish church. This meant that the resources of his people were "taxed to the utmost". If disestablishment came it might mean they would need to give up the mission chapels and lose some members of the parish staff, while the incumbent would forgo his position of comparative independence as he would need to be paid by the congregation. This he felt would be an enormous loss, for such financial independence "seems to me to be necessary, or if not absolutely necessary, most conductive to his usefulness." The local parishes might have to be grouped together and served from Tenby. Nevertheless he believed that the prospects of the Church in Wales were highly favourable if she was left to pursue her work, for she was prospering daily, and were it not for political agitators there would be the best understanding between clergy and laity.[20]

His remark was significant. Had Huntington been under the control of his congregation at Tenby then there would have been no Tractarian advance in the town, or in the locality, for Huntington's curates, when instituted to their own parishes, followed his example, notably at St Martin's Church, Haverfordwest. By the end of his time in the parish (he died in April 1905), Huntington's churchmanship had been accepted by the parish, possibly because of his personality, and by the assistance of the many friends he brought in to further his cause, such as his cousin Dr Dykes, Bishop Ellicott of Gloucester and Dean Farrar.[21] Although not all of these people were tractarians and some of them were more summer visitors than personal friends, all gave an air of respectability to his innovations as they were probably encouraged to take part in and to preach at his services. A personal picture of Huntington during the latter stage of his life is given by D. Ambrose Jones. Plagued by arthritis, dressed like a Jesuit, he spent more time in the church vestry than in his own study, and continually delivered Latin tags which he expected people to reply to in the same language. Although he had no business sense and accounts drove him crazy, many wondered why preferment to higher office had never come his way.[22] In addition it appears he was a good preacher in an age which valued that ability. A Gloucestershire squire, Dearman Birchall, visited Tenby in 1882, and wrote in his diary:

> May 7. We are perfectly charmed with the large old parish church, its services and clergyman Mr Huntingdon [*sic*], who is almost inspired it seemed to us. In the morning he preached on the text "In my Father's house are many mansions"; in the evening, "This is life eternal to know the only true God and Jesus Christ whom thou hast sent." He spoke of Darwin as one of the greatest thinkers who had in his last utterances confessed his true faith. His eloquence amazed and delighted us.[23]

A pioneer of the Tractarian movement in Wales, exiled in Tenby from his beloved Manchester, beset by family illnesses and the anxieties of bringing new life into a parish where the old tradition dominated; a comedian playing the pantomime well, and no ordinary man, such was George Huntington. One only wonders what he would have made of Aelred Carlyle who came with his revived Benedictine order to Caldey Island the year after his death?[24] Would he have greeted him as a fellow innovator, or seen him as part of the same divine pantomime?

ENDNOTES

1 Augustus John, *Chiaoscuro* (London, 1954), p. 10.
2 George Huntington, *Random Recollections* (London, 1896), pp. 58, 61-2, 119, 224 [in this book he mentions a relation, Frederick Huntington, a medical man who was especially good to the poor of Hull, which may be a reference to his father: p. 227]; *Report of the Leeds Church Congress*, 1872, p. 428.
3 Huntington, *Random Recollections*, pp. 268f.
4 "An Old Churchman", *Letters on Medievalism* (Tenby, 1872), p. 3, complained that he wore his Oxford hood in a medieval style much disliked by the writer. Huntington pointed out that that those who held such degrees were entitled to wear the hoods of either university.
5 G. W. E. Russell, *The Household of Faith* (London, 1902), p. 337.
6 Huntington, *Random Recollections*, pp. 257, 161, 285, 288.
7 *Ecclesiastic* 25 (1863) 507-12 contained a press report of this book. A second edition was published in 1871.
8 He attributed the rise of dissent in Wales to the failure of the Church to provide Welsh language services: p. 144. This was possibly an afterword for the second edition.
9 *Report of the Leeds Church Congress*, 1872, pp. 457-60. Surprisingly, he refers to Aitken's mission at Swansea, which he commended, although Swansea was an evangelical parish. Aitken, however, was more an old-fashioned high churchman who was able to work with all schools of churchmanship.
10 Huntington preached the funeral sermon for Birkett in 1877 which was published under the title *The Sleep and the Awakening of the Holy Dead*. It is a remarkable tribute to a quiet life lived in the style of George Herbert.
11 Huntington, *Random Recollections*, pp. 87-8, 96-9.
12 Nigel Yates, "The Parochial Impact of the Oxford Movement in South-West Wales" in Tudor Barnes and Nigel Yates, *Carmarthenshire Studies* (Carmarthen, 1974), pp. 234-8, quoting the local and church press as well as the parish magazine; A. P. Stanley (ed.), *Letters to a Friend* (London, 1882), pp. 157, 159; Nigel Yates, *Anglican Ritualism in Victorian Britain 1830-1910* (Oxford, 1999), pp. 115-6. See also *Church Times* of 5 March 1897, p. 252, for Huntington's remarks on fasting communion. Two of Huntington's curates became vicars of St Martin's, Haverfordwest, making that church the temple of Tractarianism in Pembrokeshire when Tenby stagnated under Huntington's successors: see David Smith, *They Did it Their Way* (Haverfordwest, 1992) pp. 16-17.

13 Yates, *The Oxford Movement*, pp. 236-7.

14 Anon., *Letters on Medievalism in the Parish Church of Tenby* (1872), pp. 15-16.

15 Yates, *The Oxford Movement*, pp 237-8; Yates, *Anglican Ritualism*, p. 116. However vestments were not introduced until 1898.

16 *Autobiography of an Almsbag, by the author of John Brown, Cordwainer* (London, 1885), pp. 95-6 [note his probable description of Mr Gwynne, p. 94, as the sole surviving member of the Church Association, voting himself into the chair, passing resolutions, and drawing up addresses and letters to the press]. D. Ambrose Jones's obituary of Huntington is in the *Haul*, 1905, pp. 484-6. In it he suggests that Huntington wished to keep to the middle ground of high churchmanship but found great difficulty in holding back his curates.

17 A previous legal case of 1853 regarding the chancel repairs attracted much interest, see *Ecclesiastical Gazette*, XVI (1853-4) 5. As the rector of a parish received the great tithes he was obliged to repair the chancel of the parish church.

18 In 1905 Huntington's widow received a grant from the Pembrokeshire Sons of the Clergy, indicating that her circumstances were not particularly good: Church in Wales records, National Library of Wales, SD/MISC/677.

19 This section is drawn from the papers of Queen Anne's Bounty and the Ecclesiastical Commission.

20 *Record*, 22 March 1894, p. 269.

21 Huntington, *Random Recollections*, pp. 121, 240-1.

22 Ambrose Jones in the *Haul*, 1905, pp. 485-6.

23 David Verey (ed.), *The Diary of a Victorian Squire* (Gloucester, 1983), p. 137. Huntington published a number of volumes of sermon aids, based on the communion lectionary readings. The first was published in 1856, and the last in 1872. The series was entitled *Sermon Aids*.

24 Though Caldey was an extra-parochial territory, Huntington took pastoral care of the island and held a monthly communion service there during the summer: Huntington to Bishop John Owen, 25 November (1899?), NLW, Bishop John Owen Papers, Box 7, file 1.

PHILIP CONSTABLE ELLIS
taken about 1870
(courtesy of Llanfairfechan Historical Society)

7
THE STORMY PETREL OF THE SEE OF BANGOR
Philip Constable Ellis: Rector of Llanfairfechan

During the mid-nineteenth century there were two Welsh clergymen, at least, who were prepared to speak their mind about the state of the Church in Wales as they saw it, whatever might be the consequences of their actions. One was John Griffith, rector of Merthyr Tydfil; the other, a slightly younger contemporary of his, Philip Constable Ellis. Both faced the scorn and anger of their bishops. Both found themselves frequently denounced by many of their fellow clergy, though equally applauded by others, and both, in spite of their considerable ability, died without preferment – not even to a honorary canonry – although both served for a time as rural-deans.[1] Nevertheless Ellis was known to have declined the deanery of Bangor in 1884, a fact recorded in an open letter to Ellis from John Griffith, though by that time they were not on the best of terms. Ellis had heard a rumour that Griffith, who supported the disestablishment of the Church as the only means of sorting out the ritualists he disliked, was to appear on a pro-disestablishment platform in a Llanfairfechan chapel. He thus challenged Griffith to appear in a public hall before an impartial audience and defend his position. If he failed to do so, then he and the public would see it as "an indication of your reluctance to expose the failure of your work at Merthyr to the light of day." Griffith replied that there was no truth in the rumour whatsoever, and was surprised that Ellis – a man who had been offered a deanery – had given any countenance to it. Furthermore, Griffith took such exception to "the sting in the tail" of Ellis's letter that he sent it back without comment in a registered envelope and used his own channels with the press to register his strongest protest at such discourtesy.[2] Griffith could certainly hold his own with Ellis though few others could.

Born in 1822 of a family domiciled near Pwllheli, Ellis's father was described as a fearless and eminent lawyer. After attending Beaumaris Grammar School, Ellis entered Jesus College, Oxford, in

1840, and from which he graduated in 1843. He was powerfully influenced by the tractarian movement during those years in Oxford, though its seed had already been planted in his mind by his former headmaster, Dr Hugh Jones, who later became rector of Beaumaris. Ellis was to become the leading contender of this movement throughout north Wales. Ordained in 1846 he became curate of Holyhead to Charles Williams, then a fellow and later principal of his old college. His stipend as the "second curate" was £80 per annum (Williams expecting his curates to have private means of their own), and Ellis was required to take two or three services a Sunday as part of his parochial duties. He later recalled with much affection the homeliness of Williams's mannerisms, and how he could reach down from the three-decker pulpit and tug Ellis's surplice in order to attract his attention during the service. As Bishop Bethell of Bangor belonged to the old High Church school he possessed a ready sympathy with the doctrine, if not with the later ritualistic manifestations, of the movement. This made the diocese a congenial place for tractarians such as Ellis.

An incident from these early days is remembered which indicates that right from the start of his ministry Ellis upheld his Tractarian principles though making it clear he was no "Romanist". At a public meeting the then member of parliament for Caernarvon, Bulkeley Hughes, endeavoured to prove that the Book of Common Prayer was "full of papalism." Ellis took out his own prayer book from his pocket, held it up, and declared that if anyone could show him anything in that book which was "papalist" he would give up his post immediately.

While at Holyhead a cholera epidemic broke out, and Ellis's bravery and ministry to its victims was remembered for many years. As the undertakers refused to put the victims into their coffins Ellis performed that service for them. Surprisingly he remained unscathed.[3]

It may have been as a reward for this bravery that Sir Richard Bulkeley presented this quite young man to the united benefice of Llanfaes and Penmon. Its income was £180 per annum, the joint population about 500 people. Part of Ellis's concern for the wider Church was that each church should have double duty on Sundays, that is, a morning and an afternoon or evening service. At that time such duty was widely neglected. In fact, as we note later, Ellis became involved during these years in a considerable controversy regarding this subject. In order to accomplish this desire in his own parish he obtained a curate and paid his stipend from his own pocket. Ellis's courage and willingness to sacrifice for his convictions impressed many of his fellow clergy, and made him, in some respects, a dangerous man for any bishop who wished for little more than a quiet and untroubled diocese.[4] This was certainly not to be the case, for during those years there was a formidable debate about Nonconformity and its claims, in which Ellis was deeply involved.

James W. Vincent, rector of Llanfairfechan since 1834, was appointed dean of Bangor in 1862, and Bishop Campbell, in whose gift the parish lay, offered it to Constable Ellis. He had certainly revitalised the parish of Penmon and had restored the old priory, and there was much to be done of a similar nature at Llanfairfechan. The Nonconformists were strong and the Church comparatively weak at a place which was rapidly becoming a watering place for English tourists, who included many senior English ecclesiastics, such as Bishop Tait of London, who was later to become archbishop of Canterbury. For the honour of the Welsh Church a man was needed who would revitalise the parish and make it a showpiece of ecclesiastical life and good churchmanship. In addition a number of English people had moved into the area who needed a strong English-speaking ministry which would complement the new English church which one of the wealthier of their number, John Platt, an Oldham manufacturer, was planning to build. Ellis was to remain in this parish until his death in 1900, although growing infirmity meant that he preached his last sermon in 1889. Nevertheless, he seems to have remained active within the parish, if only as a driving force, for many years thereafter.[5]

It is hardly surprising that Ellis, a pronounced Tractarian, should have introduced his theological views into his new parish straight away. Almost immediately the uneasy truce which had existed between the Methodist cause and the Church disappeared. It seems that the services had been held at separate times to enable people to attend the services of both traditions if they so wished, for there were many people who liked the Anglican liturgy but preferred Methodist preaching. But this would not do for Ellis. There were to be no feet in both camps. And consequently the times of the church services were so altered as to coincide with those of the Methodists. The break was complete.

An English church, Christ Church, had been planned by Dean Vincent in the early 1860s. Writing to the Ecclesiastical Commissioners on 16 November 1861 Vincent noted that as his parish was on the sea coast and had a railway station it was being much frequented by English visitors as well as attracting English settlers. He wanted to build an English church for these people and in so doing obliterate "a very great injury" which had occurred in many similar parishes to his own where the language of the inhabitants was Welsh. This injury was the inability of the Church to give the requisite number of services in both languages at convenient times. This was impossible when there was only one church. The result was that "a most injurious effect" had occurred "with regard to the influence of the Church's teaching on the Welsh population."

Vincent made it clear that he wished to accommodate the English people while at the same time doing justice to the claims of the native Welsh. The new church would not be a district church, or a separate parish church, for the English and Welsh people were intermingled throughout the parish, and the bishop had stipulated that a permanent endowment would be required for a curate's stipend. He wondered therefore if the commissioners might meet with an equal grant a sum of £1,000 promised him from a private source for this object. His last paragraph revealed a hidden agenda. One important advantage of such an English church and ministry from a national point of view, he added, would be the advantage of familiarising the native population "with the public worship of the Church in the English tongue." As was usual with these requests, a commission was appointed of three clergymen to examine the income and position of the parish. It reported that the population was 1,200 but that the church could only accommodate 200, though all the seats were free save eight. There was a glebe house or rectory and the income of the parish in 1860 was £422, made up of the tithe rental charge of £399, land let for £3 10s. and houses for £9 10s., and fees of £8. Outgoings in rates and other charges amounted to £65, but there was also a mortgage to Queen Anne's Bounty for rebuilding the rectory in 1854 which amounted to £42 per annum (Ellis later expanded the place to cater for his growing family). Upon consideration the commissioners refused their assistance. There were far needier parishes than Llanfairfechan.

The new church and the land were given by John Platt. In his letters to the commissioners he made it clear that his concern and generosity were for an English language church where divine service would be held twice each Sunday. Although Ellis repeated Vincent's request for assistance from the commissioners in July 1864, noting that a Welsh parish with a bilingual policy could not be compared with an English parish of the same population where only one language was spoken, he was equally unsuccessful. In a further letter of 23 April 1866 Ellis pointed out the impossibility of complying with the trust deed of Christ Church while at the same time holding services in the old parish church. A curate was necessary, and although he did not say so, he broadly hinted that a good curate needed a decent place of residence, which Mr Platt was willing to provide, and possibly covenant to keep in repair (otherwise the dilapidation costs would have to be met by the incumbent, a point noted in an earlier letter). Alas, the commissioners could not see how they could assist. Eventually an endowment for a curate who would serve this church was given by a number of subscribers, of whom the principal subscriber was Richard Luck, another English settler and industrialist. The money was eventually invested with Queen Anne's Bounty on behalf of the living with the specific condition that its interest was to provide for these two English services in the Christ Church chapelry. An additional curate was supported by the offertory collections.

Mr Platt continued with his generosity. In 1868 he purchased at Ellis's request 15 acres of the glebe for the highly inflated price of £1,063. Ellis referred to this in 1876 when he noted in a letter to the commissioners of 10 April that Platt had bought this land "at an exorbitant price" in order to increase the value of the living. In that year about two and a half acres of this land were purchased back from the estate of the then late Mr Platt for £275 (utilising part of the proceeds of the earlier sale) in order to ensure that the rectory and Christ Church had a "green belt" around them in a village which was rapidly expanding and growing outwards. This 1868 sale of the glebeland meant that the value of the living remained at a reasonable level at a time when the value of the tithe rent charge had seriously eroded causing much distress to many clergy and their families. Although the gross income of the living as a result of Platt's generosity and the curacy monies invested with Queen Anne's Bounty increased to £419 (the tithe income now being set at a much lower £309), deductions for rates and other outgoings, plus the £120 stipend paid to the curate under the terms of the endowment, meant that the net income was just over £200 per annum. Without a private income Ellis could hardly have managed in that parish on just over one and a half times a curate's stipend. The Platt family, though generous, had thus caused some economic hardship to the incumbent of their parish by the requirements, though no-one could have anticipated at the time the endowment was given that there would be such a devastating decline in agriculture and thus in the value of the tithe rent charge.[6]

It is clear that Ellis was uncompromising in his teaching about the value of the sacraments, the dignity of the Church, the efficacy of its priesthood, and the importance of tradition. The outward sign of a new church, built in the new approved style and with a fine east end, which the priest occupied in majesty as the representative of Christ, further enforced these strong Tractarian views. The final completion of Christ Church with its new and ornate chancel and sanctuary in 1892 was rightly regarded as the culmination of all these years of Tractarian teaching and worship. A new and vigorous congregation had been formed, aided no doubt by the many distinguished clergymen who preached there, a number of whom were constant visitors to the place, such as Dean Farrar and Archbishop Benson.

The congregation in the old church was not forgotten. They perhaps were more resilient to the new ritual, and probably felt inferior to the new and wealthy English church. Indeed, they may well have considered that Ellis favoured the English people rather than the Welsh. If they did they were a little unfair as Ellis's public statements made clear. When speaking to the Swansea Church Congress of 1879 he argued that the Welsh language was far more alive than most of his hearers believed, for even in Swansea where the impression had been given that the language was dead, 28 out of its 50 chapels were Welsh-speaking causes. Though he would certainly not mourn the death of the Welsh language, he believed that while it still survived and the soul of a Welshman was Welsh then the Church needed to be fair to both languages. Certainly it would be easier to have but one language and this would be a great relief to many clergymen as they would not have to duplicate services, but while the language remained the Church had to recognise it.[7] Nevertheless there were English language services in the afternoon at the old church (and later, with the permission of its members, a second English service during the holiday season), although this never replaced the Welsh evening service. Speaking in Convocation, of which he was a proctor elected by his fellow clergy in Bangor, Ellis argued that in Wales it was the evening service which most people attended, and though he had in a parish of 2,047 people 870 who considered themselves to be church people, of whom 340 were communicants, he felt his parish would be seen as spiritually dead if it lost these evening services. Instead people would attend

Nonconformity or the Salvation Army.[8]

What of his impact in the parish? Speaking at the Leeds Church Congress of 1872 Ellis maintained that he believed in lay co-operation, and had about four to six men, some of whom were orators, helping him and his curate in the parish. Their earnestness and power of speech made him feel quite small, especially those able to speak to the Welsh mind. These helpers were used constantly at communicants' meetings where their talks were based on the Church's teaching as found in the epistle and gospel for the following Sunday. Some of these men had been dissenters when he first came to the parish, but had, it seemed, been captivated by his teaching about the centrality of the Lord's Sacrament. Others led the Sunday Schools, including a working man of great ability who would walk back from his employment in the quarry nine miles away in order to attend. A recent literary meeting in connection with the Sunday school had produced 33 expositions by children on the chief characters of Scripture, and two elaborate essays on the three orders of ministry.[9]

His daughter in her later years remembered the introduction of daily services, the communicants' meeting for the Welsh population, and the preparatory meeting for youngsters called "The Young Soldiers of the Cross". One of the main rules of these guilds was that members should never enter a Nonconformist chapel. The Welsh Sunday School, she pointed out, was an all-age one, not simply confined to children, and they regarded the catechising as almost equal in importance to the service. Later a temperance meeting was started. The Harvest Thanksgiving was held on a weekday, so that the Sunday lessons might not be lost, and people might show their thankfulness by giving up work for that day.[10] By the 1880s Ellis's brand of churchmanship was entrenched in the parish and generally accepted by his parishioners, possibly because it had given new life to the Church and provided a focus for social entertainment as well.

****

Constable Ellis was a reformer both in his parish and within his Church. A tractarian or even an evangelical could hardly be less. He was fortunate in some respects that he was able to take with him his deanery chapter, or at least such a significant part of it that he was able to speak in the name of the deanery of Arllechwedd. Not only did it lend a certain prestige to his remarks, it also meant that the newspapers would not fail to notice the chapter's comments.

His first major controversy involved the need for double duty in the churches of Anglesey. This took place during his days at Penmon. It has already been noted how he won a great deal of support by employing an assistant curate out of his own pocket in order to ensure that his churches had two services each Sunday, and we have noted too his remarks in Convocation about the need for an evening service. His concern was twofold: not only was the dignity of the Church's worship being lost, but people were attending Nonconformist chapels instead.

During 1850 and 1851 an anonymous writer wrote letters to the *Carnarvon Herald* using the pseudonym, "The Voice of Mona". In these letters a strong protest was made about the state of many of the island's churches, especially in the neglect of the second service or double duty. The rector of Llanbeulan, Chancellor Trevor, replied in a letter defending the local clergy, whereupon the writer castigated the state of his parish. Trevor, noting that Ellis was busy forming a society to secure the reform of the Church, accused Ellis of being the author. He replied regretting he was not, but added insult to injury by indicating that he wished he was the author, for the writer had revealed the wickedness of a system which could lead to the extinction of the Church in Anglesey. In fact it appears the writer was W. O. Stanley, MP, of Penrhos, a cousin of Dean Stanley of Westminster.

Trevor had informed Bishop Bethell about these matters, and in defence of himself Ellis sent to the bishop copies of his correspondence with the chancellor, revealing all too clearly his sympathy with the anonymous writer. The bishop replied in a letter of prelatorial art. While he gave Ellis credit for "desiring to fulfill his own ministry faithfully", he advised him to stop interfering in other people's affairs "and to be more respectable to those who had given many more years and service to the Church." Ellis refused to let this be the last word, and courageously replied that his youthfulness had nothing to do with the matter. Rather he was saddened to think that Mr Trevor might be encouraged by the course the correspondence had taken to persist "in what is regarded by the people generally as a neglect of duty. The effect of it must be to damp and discourage those who are striving to supply the spiritual craving of their flocks."

The controversy entered a new phase when Trevor wrote to the Methodist minister in Amlwch expressing his concern about "Arfer y Wlad", the courting system known as bundling. Claiming it was prevalent in Anglesey, and that it led to much immorality and promiscuity, Trevor admitted not only that the Church had neither power, influence nor discipline to deal with the matter, but hinted that the Church was so tied to the state that she had no moral influence whatsoever. Ellis, inflamed, wrote in reply to the *North Wales Guardian:*

> How anxiously have I looked for some indication of our insulted Church from some senior clergyman more fitted and more able than myself ... Mr Trevor little thinks that his letter is cast in the teeth of his brethren as an authority in confirmation of the opinion of Dissenters that the Church is without discipline. If I could recognise with Mr Trevor in Methodism a divine system, and in the Church a paltry engine of State, I would become a Methodist at once. I never would be party to adding a feeble sect to the too many already in existence ... I would beg to suggest that Mr Trevor would do more towards putting a stop to *Arfer y Wlad* if he would give his parishioners an opportunity of worshipping God twice a Sunday in the churches of his Incumbency, and by exercising the discipline which the Church empowers him to exercise over his flock.

When Trevor met a number of dissenting ministers soon after and repeated his claim that his Church had neither power nor authority to deal with the position, but offered to co-operate with them in order to restrain the evil, Constable Ellis and others engaged in an explosive newspaper correspondence. Let the Church cease to be an engine of the State, roared Ellis, but rather let her be seen as

> the Church of Christ, instituted to furnish the souls of men with the bread of life, the pure doctrine of the Gospel ... I doubt not, if we could all be more faithful, that in ten years from now we should have larger flocks to instruct, but if the present system is to continue, I for one care not how soon our pride is humbled in the dust by the destruction of the Church as an Establishment. One's heart dies within one when the mind is allowed to range over the parishes of Anglesey, and to reflect on the forlorn condition of many a locality.

Indeed, the zeal of any reformer would be chilled by the miserable system which prevailed in that county. Furthermore, Ellis wrote, it was impossible to co-operate with Nonconformists, for they were outside the apostolic succession. The Church had sufficient resources and discipline of her own to deal with these moral problems, he continued, as witness the second rubric of the Holy Communion service. There was no need to go outside their own structures in order to co-operate with a religious association whose lack of moral principles had to some extent caused the problem in the first place. The Church's position and its truth should not be compromised in order to gain a fleeting popularity. The bishop protested with a stern rebuke to Ellis, though admitting he had not read the letters, but Ellis, knowing the support he was receiving from others continued with the attack:

> Mr Trevor hesitates not to award to Dissenters a position vastly superior to our own, himself meanwhile cleaving to the system which he degrades. I consider it more honest that the Ministers of the Church should set themselves in earnest to develop the Church's resources, and to make her more efficient for accomplishing the great ends she was designed to bring about, and yet our Bishop seems to regard all Mr Trevor does to be right, and pronounces my acts wrong. Mr Trevor could empty our Churches for us and yet do no wrong, while the exposure of the evils which are ruining the Church with a view to their remedy, is a mark of ignorant and mischievous zeal.

By now Ellis had many supporters, and while Dean Cotton of Bangor started his own enquiry to discover how many churches in Anglesey could have double duty but did not, others drew up a petition to the bishop asking for an enquiry into the condition of parishes and the opportunities available for worship and instruction. It was presented by W. O. Stanley, to show that laymen were equally concerned, and hopefully to save the supporting clergy from further episcopal anger. The petition was moderate in tone and read as follows:

> To the Right Rev. The Lord Bishop of Bangor,
>   The Petition of the undersigned Clergy and Members of the Established Church in the Diocese of Bangor sheweth –
>   That your petitioners are much concerned to witness the continued estrangement of the mass of the people from the

Church of England.

Your Petitioners are persuaded that such estrangement is, in a great degree, the result of insufficient number of Services provided for the spiritual wants of the people, in many of our Churches on the Lord's Day, rather than from any decided objection to the tenets of the Church of England.

Your Petitioners have, several of them, promoted the building of new churches, in many populous localities, and the restoration and enlargement of other existing churches, with a view to afford every facility for the people to attend the services of the Church on the Lord's Day; and they all feel most anxious for the efficiency of the Church throughout the Diocese.

Yet it is with deep felt regret that your Lordship's Petitioners are compelled, by a sense of duty, to avow their belief that, in numerous instances, only one service and sermon is provided in those churches where, on ground of population and revenue, two services can by Law be enforced.

Your Petitioners could point out many instances of such neglect; but refrain from any mention of individuals; respectfully submitting this representation to your Lordship, in the confident hope that an enquiry will be instituted into the truth of these statements, and, if found accurate, that your Lordship will take steps, as by Law empowered, to remedy the evils here represented, in order truly to remove so just a cause to many earnest minded men, and to promote the growth of religious truth through the instrumentality of the Church as established in the country and Diocese of Bangor.

The 80-year-old bishop's reaction was anticipated: Bethell was a man of strong views who expected to rule a Welsh diocese with his English tongue and manners. The petition, he asserted, was a reflection on his own work (at least he was correct in that) and an assault on his prerogatives. Cotton was told not to meddle in the diocese, and Ellis, regarded as the ringleader of the "plot", was accused of exciting a "mischievous agitation" and promoting insubordination and disobedience. In particular he was charged with giving publicity to the petition against the bishop's wishes. His offence, declared Bethell, was aggravated by the "ungrateful returns you have made to me for the forbearance and kindness which I shewed you in pity for your youth and inexperience on a former occasion." By this he meant the controversy with Trevor. Though

Ellis wrote to say he had not published the petition (W. O. Stanley had done so), he unwisely added that he had concurred in its publication. Bethell accordingly demanded a public recantation and apology, and if this was not forthcoming he threatened that the matter would be referred to the senior Church court, the Court of the Arches, in London.

Ellis replied by saying he was sorry the bishop "should have considered himself justified in applying to me terms so harsh and unlike what I should have expected from a Father in Christ." It might have been thought that he "stood convicted of the grossest immorality, or of denying the fundamental articles of the Christian Faith" in the face of this demand for a public recantation. He continued, adding yet more fuel to the fire:

> What misbehaviour have I been guilty of? What am I to recant? Is it a greater offence to invite your Lordship's attention to churches infrequently served, and to ask for the Bishop's interference, in accordance with the Law, than to acquiesce in such a state of things? I know that two or three Rural Deans lament over the neglect existing in some cases in their several deaneries, and yet scarcely know how to remedy the evil. I wonder at your Lordship's thinking it possible that I should consent to anything you might think proper to dictate. I know not what my offence is, at least your Lordship does not define it in this case. Does your Lordship hold that to address a petition to your Lordship, inviting enquiry into certain specified neglects, constitutes an offence against the Ecclesiastical Law? Then let the case be tried in the Court of Arches. I had rather give up my living and retire into private life than subscribe to such a doctrine. Unable as I am, to bear the cost of a suit in the Court of Arches, the trial would have this advantage: it would lead to such an investigation of the state of the Church in your Lordship's Diocese as must result in the carrying out of the improvements which it is now sought quietly to effect.

Bethell replied in a letter expressing his outrage that any incumbent of his diocese should so address him. He was aware that Stanley had publicised the address by having it inserted into the newspapers, but whether that was his or Ellis's doing made no difference. Ellis had had "the presumption to manufacture this insolent attack on your Diocesan and to issue circulars to several of the clergy, inviting their concurrence with you in your mischievous proceedings." If he did not make the concessions he required, that is (it seems) a private apology, the bishop threatened to

> fix a day and hour at which you are to attend in the Chapter Room at Bangor, before the Chancellor of the Diocese and a few other clergymen of some standing in the Diocese; and you shall then read and subscribe the *recantation and apology* which shall be drawn up for you, and promise that you will not in future be guilty of such insubordination and disobedience to me and my successors, and the same publicity must be given to your subscription as has been given to your so-called Petition. The recantation will be confined to your *present offence*, without any reference to your former headstrong insolence and breach of faith.

In response to this incredible (even to nineteenth-century eyes) display of episcopal arrogance and temper Ellis pointed out that the sole aim of the petition was "to represent to your Lordship that, in certain cases, a single service only is celebrated each Lord's Day, where your Lordship might require two; and to invite your Lordship to institute an enquiry, with a view to ascertain which those cases are." If the bishop continued on this course then the previous controversies would have to be re-opened, and as he still possessed all the correspondence, he would be able to show that the bishop had admitted that the chancellor might have been wrong on that former occasion! If the bishop insisted on a court case that court would have to investigate a number of points. The first would to identify who wrote the petition. The second whether there was "anything in its language disrespectful and insolent? And again, whether any person circulating a Petition, not in itself disrespectful, and asking for the exercise of the authority, with which the law has armed Bishops for the redress of evils, admitted on all hands, be an act of insubordination, rendering the person accused amenable to the Ecclesiastical Laws."

As soon as Bethell's threats became known Ellis received the support of a considerable number of the senior clergy of the diocese. They included, amongst others, Charles Williams, his former vicar and now principal of Jesus College, Vincent of Llanfairfechan, later dean, Dean Cotton and Archdeacon Wynne Jones. Although he was aware of this support the bishop persisted in taking the matter before the Court of Arches, but difficulties soon presented themselves and he decided to drop the case. He thus wrote a rather amazing letter to Ellis:

> Owing to the delays and technical difficulties that met me in Doctors' Commons, I was unable, during my abode in London last year, to bring to a conclusion the suit which I had commenced against you. As some months must have passed before it could be recommended, and the same difficulties would still have occurred, and under the hope that, if you would not confess, you would, at all events, perceive that your behaviour had been unjustifiable, I determined to drop the suit altogether, unless I should receive some further provocation. What has passed between us since has, I hope, convinced you that I bear no ill will, and am desirous to communicate with you on such terms as a bishop is always anxious to do with his clergy.
>
> Whilst I do not, in the slightest degree, alter the opinion which I expressed of your behaviour, which I willingly ascribe to infirmities of judgment and temper, I freely and fully forgive you, as I hope to be forgiven my own follies and faults by the Great Searcher of Hearts, and shall always, except in the case I have mentioned, carry on my intercourse with you as if nothing of the kind has ever occurred. But I have entered into the explanation that you may not suppose that my change of conduct indicates any change of opinion. I do not wish you, or rather, I must ask you not to make any reply to this letter. And I pray God that your time and talents may be henceforth devoted to the glory of God and the edification of your flock.

Much later Ellis met an assize judge who told him that many years before Bethell had asked his opinion about a young clergyman whom he wanted to bring before the Court of Arches. He had advised him that there was no case whatsoever. "I am the man," replied Ellis. Nevertheless, Sir Stephen Glynne's comment on Ellis's involvement in this controversy was apt: "[t]hough he was often right in his facts & the conduct complained of was not defensible, ... his way of dealing with it was not wise & not likely to promote improvement."[11]

****

Ellis's concern about the need for double duty was linked with a real concern about Nonconformity. The 1851 religious census of Horace Mann had revealed all too clearly to the Church its own failure to retain within its fold the people of Wales. Ellis clearly believed that the Church's failure to live a full sacramental life and to teach the catholic doctrines about the Church was to blame for this. To him dissenters were pseudo-Christians, aliens from the true Church, and without valid sacraments as their ministers were self-ordained and thus outside the true apostolic succession. Without that succession there could be no valid Church, no ministry, no sacraments and, though he never put it as crudely as this, no hope of eternal life. This, of course, was orthodox Tractarian teaching. We have already noted his practical application of this doctrine in his own parish, by his exclusion of the dissenting folk from the Church's worship, his insistence on an evening service so that people would have no excuse to go elsewhere, and his attempt to prevent members of church guilds from attending Nonconformist places of worship.

A long newspaper correspondence took place during 1857 as a result of what Ellis had said to a meeting of Sunday school teachers at Beaumaris. He had argued the need for teaching Church principles in the schools, especially about baptism, the nature of the Church's ministry, and its connection with the state as the Church of the nation, as well as the need to see church buildings as consecrated places of worship. Ellis also stated that Nonconformists were schismatics who needed to return to the true Church. An independent minister, William Williams (under the pseudonym of "Cromwell"), replied to a press report of this meeting, and started an acrimonious correspondence in the *Carnarvon and Denbigh Herald.*

The correspondence was translated and published in a Welsh pamphlet in 1859, and twenty years later the original letters were republished as *Letters to a Dissenting Minister, in which the Church is Defended, and the position of Dissenters proved by Scripture and History to be Untenable.* The pamphlet (which only contain Ellis's letters) comprises 63 closely printed pages. Both men, however, were arguing from different premises, although Williams must have found his defence hard going against a ruthless opponent who probed every chink in his armour, as Lloyd Hughes notes. The Church of England was the Church of the nation, maintained Ellis, and preserved her apostolic ministry as constituted by divine authority throughout the turmoil of the Reformation. This meant that "nothing can affect her right to be what she is, 'The Church of the Living God, the ground and pillar of the Truth.'" The dissenting minister, he proclaimed, shared with the popish priest in Ireland the distinction of being "infallible oracles in the estimation of misguided thousands". If Williams attacked the bishops by asking when did the apostles live in palaces, wear mitres, sit in parliament, ride in carriages, and be men of wealth, Ellis could sarcastically reply, when were they ever in a dissenting meeting house, wearing hats and black coats, or members of the "Congregational Union", or "possessed the ease and dignity and wealth of dissenting doctors of divinity", driving around in two-wheeled gigs or four-wheeled phaetons? The principles of dissent, he concluded, were the principles of disunion, which had been opposed by the prayer of Christ. Was not dissent, therefore, the Anti-Christ as compared to the Church which was "one united visible body from the beginning, 'continuing in the Apostle's doctrine and fellowship, and in the breaking of bread and in the prayers', and so one with Christ, 'the Head of the Body, the Church'."[12]

Dissenters should not be won to the Church by concessions, claimed Ellis, nor by arguing there was no excuse for their separation now that the Church was reformed. Rather they would only be won for the Church on doctrinal grounds, namely on the truth of its catholicity. Unfortunately Ellis never seemed to be particularly successful in stemming the tide of dissent within his parish, for between 1863 and 1900 eight new chapels were built in his parish by four denominations, although it is also true that its population increased substantially.[13]

It should come as no surprise, therefore, that all Ellis's recorded contributions to the debates in Convocation (the Church's parliament) concerned the various burial bills which came before Parliament on a regular basis. These bills endeavoured to redress a major Nonconformist grievance, namely that Nonconformists were not permitted to bury their dead in churchyards with their own form of service conducted by their own minister. Instead they were required to have the Church of England service read by a clergyman. A bill was finally passed in 1880, prompted by Osborne Morgan, a liberal MP who was the son of a former vicar of Conwy. Ellis's main fear about this agitation was that the dissenting bodies, headed by the Liberation Society (which existed to disestablish the Church), were using the graveyard issue as a means of obtaining admission to the church buildings. He was even more disturbed when an amendment to this bill proposed in the House of Lords suggested that the Church should not be entitled to the sole and undivided enjoyment of any property which had been acquired during the previous 50 years. This meant, he argued, that it was useless to add to the Church's property as it might eventually be used for the benefit of dissenters rather than for church people. The church property in his parish had been increased by £15,000 during the previous 18 years. Was all this to be handed to the dissenters? Unless this proposed amendment by the marquess of Salisbury was defeated, churchmen would be reluctant to build or restore churches or support such organisations as the Church Defence Society or the Church Building Society. This amendment if carried would paralyse the Church, and he could not understand the bishops voting for it as they did. Perhaps Ellis was mistaken in his interpretation, but the amendment was lost in the House of Commons.[14]

****

Constable Ellis's most famous controversy was his protest, linked to that of the rural deanery of Arllechwedd (of which he was rural-dean), about the appointments by the Bishop Ollivant of Llandaff of Bishop Perry to a canonry at Llandaff Cathedral, and of Dr Vaughan to the deanery of the same cathedral. Before we note this, it is important to realise that this was one of many protests made by this chapter about the state of the Church in Wales, and in particular about the way in which patronage was administered. In a sense, this chapter almost took over the role of the Association of Welsh Clergy in the West Riding of Yorkshire, whose reports during the 1850s were strongly critical of the Church in Wales and its abuses. The chapter proposed a fund to assist aged and infirm clergy. It petitioned against the Pluralities Act Amendment Act, considering that "the obnoxious clause limiting the bishops' power of enforcing services in the vernacular to one service in the Welsh language every Sunday" ought to be removed as they knew of no case where the English inhabitants were neglected, but many cases where the Welsh people were. They asked the bishop to investigate the need for double duty in churches and make better provision for the religious needs of people. They drew up a petition to the House of Lords in 1874 for the repeal of the Cowper-Temple clause about religious education in schools, and asked that church schools should benefit from rate-aid in those areas where school boards existed. Protests were made about the dissenters' demand to use the churchyards for their own burial services, and they asked their bishop to inform the archbishop of

Canterbury that their chapter wished to have a fuller representation of parochial clergy in Convocation.

A member of the chapter, Archdeacon Evans, was requested to inform both the archbishop and the bishop of Lincoln that they believed that the substitution of the bishops by laymen as judges in the Church courts would be "a violation of the essential and inherent rights of the episcopal office." The chapter later petitioned Convocation about the same measure. They even held a conference for clergy and laity about Church reform in 1886. This requested, for example, lay representation in the patronage of parishes; a diocesan voice in the appointment of bishops; the equalisation of the income of benefices; better provision for retired clergy; an increase in the representation of Convocation, and that the landlords and not the tenant should pay the tithe rent charge. The conference also considered that parochial church councils could cause much mischief, especially by substituting congregationalism for the system of the Church. On another occasion Bishop Campbell complained that the chapter had ensured that some irregularity by the vicar of Llanbeblig had become a matter of newspaper controversy. He accused the members of the chapter of making themselves into an ecclesiastical court by naming this particular person. Though the bishop later retracted some of his strictures, and gave them credit for acting from "pure and high motives", Constable Ellis was not prepared to accept they had no right to address the bishop on any subject relating to the well-being of the Church, and wondered if the bishop was aware of what was happening in his diocese![15]

It will have been noted that many of these concerns were ones which Constable Ellis had himself expressed on previous occasions. Although there were a number of strong characters in the deanery, such as Archdeacon Evans and David Walter Thomas of St Anne's Church, Llandegai, it seems reasonably clear that Ellis was the forceful leader of the chapter in its efforts to reform the Church, even if this had to be done in a negative sense by pointing out the abuses which needed reform. As Ellis wrote to the bishop of Llandaff in 1886, the members of the chapter believed they had a right to address any bishop on any matter affecting the well being of the Church, and he added that they frequently drew up petitions to Parliament or others, "without considering it necessary to ask the bishop's sanction for doing so."

On the 18 March 1879 Constable Ellis addressed a remonstrance in the name of the chapter to Bishop Ollivant of Llandaff, in relation to the appointment of two men as dignitaries in his cathedral church, one as canon and the other as dean. Both, he claimed, were unconnected with the Principality, being "strangers to the national feeling, and unable to minister in a tongue understood of the people." This remonstrance was signed by many of the clergy of the deaneries of Arfon and Arllechwedd, who claimed that because the Welsh dioceses were so specially united by their particular circumstances that if "the Church suffers in one diocese, she suffers in all." The slow growth of the diocese of Llandaff was attributed to the inability of the cathedral dignitaries "to appeal to the sentiments and affections of the people", and the alienation of its people was "in no slight degree" due to this fact. Neither were there any Welsh services in the cathedral, although there was a Welsh-speaking chapel in Llandaff. Deep concern was expressed that the Church was not more involved in the literary and cultural activities of the nation. It was in this area that the cathedrals were failing, the remonstrance suggested, for as the mother churches of their dioceses they ought to be giving a lead to the parishes in these matters. Instead people were seeing the cathedrals as the preserve of the rich, whereas their endowments had come originally from the Welsh people. To allow such endowments to be utilised for those who could not exert any influence over the Welsh people was to divert them from their real purpose. The bishop had obtained the patronage of ten parishes in the diocese of Bangor on the plea that he had insufficient patronage on his own to reward his meritorious clergy, but these appointments were inconsistent with his claim. While the members of the chapter expressed their high regard for the bishop, his learning, high Christian character and venerable years, they yet felt it their duty to point out that his action was injuring the life of the Church of the Principality.

Ollivant replied, clearly hurt, that his first feeling on reading their letter was to suggest that if he felt they could have helped him in the administration of his diocese he would have asked them, but this would have been impolite. Denying that his diocese was a Welsh-speaking diocese in the sense the chapter had indicated, and pointing out that Monmouthshire in particular was English speaking, he refused to accept that his patronage had resulted in an increase in the strength of Nonconformity. It was unfair to make it a *sine qua non* for the Llandaff clergy to be able to speak Welsh, for he saw the offices of dean and canons as posts whose occupants could assist the clergy to obtain a higher standard of spirituality and learning, as well as offering them an example which they could emulate in their own parishes. Besides, this was the first occasion in three vacancies in which he had appointed a man from outside the diocese as dean, while all but two canons had been appointed from within the diocese. The bishop named these two men as Perowne, a man who had trained many of the Welsh clergy at Lampeter, and Bishop Perry, a distinguished former colonial bishop who was able to assist him in the work of the diocese. Furthermore, Ollivant pointed out that only 20 of the clergy of the two deaneries had signed. Presumably the other 40 felt it was not a matter which should concern them.

Constable Ellis could not forbear a further reply. The cathedral clergy, he argued, if they were to function as Ollivant suggested, would need to be Welsh speaking. The bishop was obviously deceived as to the state of the Welsh language in his diocese, and if he claimed his diocesan clergy supported his appointments it was because they would be unlikely to reveal the truth to him. The bishop had stated he had been bishop for 30 years in the diocese. If, during that time, Ellis hinted, he had been doing his job properly as a father in God he would have known that he had clergy fit enough for the jobs he had given to outsiders.

Ollivant's reply was swift, and according to one commentator (when the chapter protested once again about an appointment to Cowbridge in that diocese), it was "so scathing and so contemptuous as effectively to quench their disposition for future interference with his undoubted prerogative." His only desire had been to appoint to the vacant office (of dean) in order to promote the interests of his diocese, and he would not have made such an appointment if he felt it would injure the Church elsewhere.

The letters were published in a pamphlet by Ellis and a considerable newspaper controversy was aroused. There was truth on both sides. Ollivant was concerned that men of wide experience and culture should be appointed to his cathedral as a means of influencing the clergy and enriching the Church. Vaughan, a former head of Harrow who had turned down the bishopric of Rochester, was a distinguished preacher and a well-known trainer of men for ordination. Few of the Welsh clergy had such a background of learning and culture. On the other hand a man of such ecclesiastical importance, if he could speak Welsh, would obviously have a powerful ministry within the diocese, and might bring back to the Church many people who had strayed from it due to its lack of Welsh preaching. The appointment also suggested to some that the native clergy were not good enough for the higher offices of the Church, and that the plums of episcopal patronage were not for them. The issue raised a huge hornet's nest of discontent about the inferior position of the Welsh-speaking clergy, in much the same way as the campaign for Welsh-speaking bishops had raised the same arguments and fears. The rector of Crumlin, for example, James Hughes, argued that many of the clergy in the diocese of Llandaff welcomed Ellis's intervention, as few in the diocese were prepared to expose themselves to the "obloquy and misrepresentation" that would take place if they made clear their sentiments. Ollivant, writing a memorandum to himself about the whole business expressed his deep hurt and bewilderment. He believed he was fully supported by his own clergy, but the Llandaff clergy no longer wished him to speak in Welsh, not because his Welsh was so "worthless and unintelligible that it may as well be given up", but because the language was no longer used. Surely his Welsh was still adequate: had not Evan Lewis said, when he came down from the pulpit at Aberdare, "You have not forgotten your Welsh", and had not Joshua Hughes, then bishop of St Asaph, told him "you are a great success"?[16]

✳✳✳✳✳✳✳✳✳✳✳

One may argue that Ellis's heart was in the right place. He asked for justice in the Church, even though he may not have been the beneficiary of it. Though he preferred English, he yet championed the Welsh causes, although one suspects that his main aim was to use the Welsh language in order to eliminate Nonconformity! But his besetting sin was that he could not refrain from the harsh comment, the insinuating remark, or from demanding the last word. Had this not been the case Ellis might have been listened to with more attention, for much of what he said needed to be said, but his action in taking the argument too far so hurt and angered people that little was done to put his suggestions into effect. Neither did his churchmanship help, especially with its abrasiveness to Nonconformity. It alienated many, because once again he seemed to be unable to present his convictions in an attractive light, being only able to see the negative side of what he stood for as against his opponents. His was the way of denouncing others, rather than of affirming his beliefs. He could have done so much more had it been otherwise for he was a man of vision, courage and integrity.

David Griffith, then curate of Llansadwrn, summed up much

when he wrote in his diary his impression of Ellis who had preached at that parish's harvest thanksgiving service in 1885. It was disappointing, he wrote, and the people were spiritually famished, "High Church husks fed not hungry souls, they need the Evangelical grain."[17] Sir Stephen Glynne, writing to his brother-in-law, the premier Gladstone, on the occasion of the 1870 episcopal vacancy at St Asaph, commented upon the claims of Ellis for the post. Though he was "a good and active Parish Priest" and "decidedly far above the average of Welsh Parsons, clever, well read, a graduate of Oxford, and of rather pronounced Church views", he had "an irritable temper and a most provoking way of speaking." He continued: "[i]f it were not for this fault of temper and want of judgment he would be a considerable man, but I fear he would never do as a Bishop for his manner of doing things even with the best intentions would cause much angry feeling." [18]

Twenty years later, Dean Vaughan, over whose appointment Ellis had protested, wrote to Randall Davidson, then dean of Windsor and the archbishop's confidant, regarding his fear that the wrong sort of men would be appointed to the Welsh bishoprics. He feared the appointment of one "of the flaming Churchmen who live in antagonism to the vast multitude who are unhappily estranged from us, and triumph in every proselyte made to the nominal ranks of the Church. Such men as Mr Constable Ellis and (I believe) the Dean of Bangor [H. T. Edwards], are the *real* enemies of the Church in Wales."[19] In some respects it was a mistaken judgment, but Vaughan was not entirely unfair for it could be argued that Ellis's statements about Nonconformity went far to cause its distrust of the Church and its desire to see the Church disestablished.

ENDNOTES

1   Ellis is alleged to have been offered three deaneries in Wales in DWB, but *By Gones* for 10 May 1900, pp. 379-80, specifies the deanery of Bangor only. Elizabeth Constable Ellis (edited Lloyd Hughes and Gweneth Lilly), *Fresh as Yesterday* (Caernarfon, 1988), p. 16, notes he was offered this deanery on two separate occasions.

2   A cutting in a scrapbook of cuttings relating to John Griffith, probably from the *Western Mail* of early December 1884: South Glamorgan Library, Cardiff, MS. 5,157.

3   E. H. (Edward Hughes), "Y Diwedder Barchedig Philip Constable Ellis" in *Yr Haul*, 1901, pp. 521-4; 1902, pp. 167-8 (he notes that even before

his ordination Ellis had been in correspondence with Bishop Bethell regarding the pitiful condition of Llanengan Church); M. Lucy Williams, "The Portionary Church of Caergybi and Jesus College", *Anglesey Antiquarian Society Transactions*, 1947, p. 52.

4 E. A. Williams, *The Day Before Yesterday* (Beaumaris, 1988), pp. 176-7. According to the *Clergy List* of 1849 Ellis's predecessor kept a curate, but he was also headmaster of Beaumaris Grammar School!

5 Ellis, *Fresh as Yesterday*, pp. 11, 100, 106. Tait's visit is noted in his life by R. T. Davidson and W. Benham (London, 1891), I 496.

6 Ellis, *Fresh as Yesterday*, pp. 11, 85-8. The papers of Queen Anne's Bounty and the Ecclesiastical Commission for the parish of Llanfairfechan are in the custody of the Representative Body of the Church in Wales. The parliamentary return of 1832, lodged in the Ecclesiastical Commission papers, states that the net income was £303, with payments of £4 to the schoolmaster for teaching poor boys and £13 to a schoolmistress for teaching ten poor girls.

7 *Report of the Swansea Church Congress*, 1879, pp. 277-8; Ellis, *Fresh as Yesterday*, pp. 13-14. Ellis's children were not taught Welsh.

8 *Chronicles of Convocation*, 1884, p. 270. Ellis added he had six Sunday services.

9 *Report of the Leeds Church Congress*, 1872, pp. 467-8.

10 Ellis, *Fresh as Yesterday*, pp. 92-3, 98-9.

11 E. Maldwyn Evans, "A Voice Crying", *Province* 14 (1963) 56-60; Edward Hughes in *Yr Haul*, 1902, pp. 167-70, 263-6; 1903, pp. 89-93; Williams, *The Day Before Yesterday*, pp. 176-7; Glynne to Gladstone, 19 January 1870, Glynne-Gladstone Correspondence at Flintshire Record Office, Hawarden, file 689. Bishop Campbell, Bethell's successor, accepted the concern about double duty and endeavoured to achieve it throughout his diocese.

12 Constable Ellis, *Letters to a Dissenting Minister* (Rhyl, 1879), pp. 33, 39-40, 63 in particular; Edward Hughes in *Yr Haul*, 1903, pp. 124-7; CDH, 6 June 1857, p. 6, and 18 July 1857, supplement, p. 2. In these letters Ellis carefully defended the idea that a State Church could also be a spiritual body. He concluded one of his letters with the assertion that unless his opponent could prove that the Church had failed and the sects could be seen as Christian, "to say nothing of their ministry", it was pointless to waste time over "all the farrago of revilings, which the malice of Dissent can invent against the Church of the living God, the ground and pillar of the truth.": p. 20.

13 *Report of the Swansea Church Congress*, 1879, pp. 277-8; Ellis, *Fresh as Yesterday*, pp. 14-15.

14 *Chronicles of Convocation*, 1877, p. 348; 1878, p. 116; 1880, pp. 242-3.

15 Gwynfryn Richards, "The Rural Deanery of Arllechwedd: An Old Chapter Minute Book", *National Library of Wales Journal* 18 (1973) 149-80, *in passim*.

16 *The Welsh Church and the Welsh Cathedrals: A Correspondence between*

the Lord Bishop of Llandaff and the Clergy of the Deaneries of Arfon and Arllechwedd in the Diocese of Bangor. 1879. *in passim.* See also *Western Mail,* 6 September 1883, p. 4. The newspaper correspondence is contained in the Llandaff Cathedral files at the Glamorgan Record Office, Cardiff, DD/L/DC/P7; and Ollivant's own note of 1879 regarding these allegations is at the National Library of Wales, Aberystwyth, Church in Wales Records, John Morgan Collection, Box 10. The chapter also petitioned against the patronage exercised by St John's College, Cambridge and Jesus College, Oxford, in their diocese, as well as the patronage transferred to the bishop of Llandaff of ten livings in the diocese of Bangor in order to increase his diocesan patronage. His exercise of this patronage gave much disappointment to the 70 curates in their diocese, it claimed, and it suggested that the bishop ought to return this patronage back to the bishop of Bangor as his patronage had sufficiently increased due to the creation of many new parishes in his diocese.

17 R. O. Roberts, "David Griffith", *Province* 12 (1961) 105. Evans in *A Voice Crying* (p. 59) suggests that Ellis lost his position as rural dean as he defended the principal of St Mary's College, Caernarfon, against Campbell's charges of high-church teachings.

18 Glynne to Gladstone, 19 January 1870, Glynne-Gladstone Correspondence, file 689.

19 Vaughan to Davidson, 13 March 1890, Lambeth Palace Library, Davidson MS. 522, fol. 95.

8
IN CONTROVERSIES UNLIMITED
THOMAS WALTERS, DD, of LLANSAMLET

Honestly, who in Wales has done more to benefit the Welsh
Church during the last 30 years than Dr Walters has? Yet who
has been more neglected by the Bishop of St David's than the
doctor has? I know the doctor is an awkward customer, and the
sort of man no Bishop of an Established Church would like to
have near him. The doctor is not what Welsh Bishops like so
much to have near them; that is, a "Shôn-bob-ochr" ["Johnny-
both-sides"]. But, for all that, he is a sterling fellow. Look what
he has made of the most miserable parish, perhaps, that ever
existed in the world before he went into it – the parish of
Llansamlet. Even the Bishop himself when he first visited it said,
"he never saw such a place". Yet the doctor is not preferred. Oh,
yes, the Bishop offered him, I forgot, some place in North Wales,
I think it was Darowen, with the hope, I imagine, he would take
it; and be for ever forgotten, at any rate in the Diocese of St
David's. But the doctor did not take it, and he would not have
been forgotten if he had, even in the Diocese of St David's. This
is one of the mistakes Bishops make. Men like Dr Walters
cannot be put under a cloud and forgotten. They are made of the
stuff that Bishops cannot extinguish.[1]

Thus wrote John Griffith of Merthyr of his friend and adversary,
Thomas Walters. Both men were firebrands, hot tempered and quick
to use the press to their advantage. Another writer, this time
anonymous, gives us a further picture of Walters:

Waiting, however, is not Dr Walters's weakness. If he waited
more, he would, I think – like the tortoise over the hare – get on
faster in the Church than he does or has done. He sees a point to
which his hopes and natural expectations lead him, and off he
starts to get there. If a wall intervene, down it must come at once

or be scaled. If neither is possible, then a more roundabout way must be tried, but get to the goal he must. Brambles may intercept – and in the case of your determined and adventurous spirits these things generally do intercept, being carefully strewn about by unfriendly hands; but they are waived aside, and the restless battler passes on. The timid man would put on his gloves for the purpose. Not so with the Rector of Ystradgynlais. He is callous of little stings, and the thorn of the controversial bramble has no terror for him ... [He] writes as he thinks and speaks – ruggedly and earnestly. The diamond is in the rough. It might be polished into brilliancy with very little trouble, did not the irresistible impetuosity of the Cymry step in to prevent such mathematical peddling with a strong nature imbued with Welsh instincts that have never known complete control ...[2]

We must forgive the writer for this turgid prose, but the points he makes, namely that Walters was a rebel in word and speech, refusing to accept defeat, and often saying things on impulse which he knew would upset people, are ones we will note again and again.

A big man in every way (he was six feet four inches tall and turned the scale at 18 stone),[3] Walters's beginnings were obscure, and his background was the *gwerin* society of the Welsh countryside. Born at Trallwng, Breconshire, in 1823, the son of a shoemaker, we know nothing about his early education, but in a letter of complaint about Bishop Ollivant's closure of the Abergavenny Divinity School in 1866, Walters was recorded as one of its more distinguished students. This school, for literates, was mainly patronised by Welsh-speaking men who lacked the means, and sometimes the scholarship, to enter one of the universities or even Lampeter, whose course was more extensive and required an additional third year. Made deacon by the bishop of St David's on *letters dimissory* from the bishop of Llandaff in 1846, Walters served his title or first curacy in the large and growing industrial parish of Bedwellty in Gwent. This was a parish whose incumbents at this time were well-known evangelical men, such as Leigh Morgan, later of St Mary's Cardiff, and his cousin, Edmund Leigh. Two other curacies followed; Ystradgynlais, which he later served as incumbent, 1848-51, and Kilvey, Swansea, 1851-3. At the same time as this last curacy, and for two years afterwards, Walters served as the Welsh secretary of the Church Pastoral-Aid Society, an evangelical society which gave grants for curates and lay-workers in like-minded parishes. While living at Swansea, in 1855,

Walters's impetuousness led to a major dispute with his bishop, the redoubtable Thirlwall of St David's. As the dispute also involved Bishop Ollivant of Llandaff, Walters's position as the Welsh secretary of CPAS was badly compromised. Possibly he was lucky to be presented by the patron, Richard D. Gough of Ynysedoyn House, to the rectory of Ystradgynlais, where he had served his curacy and was obviously known.

In one sense it was a surprising appointment. Walters had alienated many of his parishioners by the reforms he had instituted during his curacy (when he seems to have been in sole charge), while his Welsh, not so good in those days, was inferior to that of their previous well-loved and elderly curate. As a result many members had left for Nonconformity, while there had been a rebellion against the church rates. His appointment as rector resurrected this hostility, which did not die down for many years. Walters remained as rector of Ystradgynlais until 1874 when Bishop Thirlwall, in one of the closing acts of his long episcopate, presented him to the parish of Llansamlet in the Swansea area. Although it is said that the bishop when he made the presentation remarked it would be "a sphere of duty somewhat less laborious than that which you have long filled", it might well have been seen by others as a punishment station, for the parish was in considerable difficulties. Nevertheless Walters accepted the offer, remaining in Llansamlet until he retired in 1892. Having bought the lordship of the manor of Trallwng (the local lad-made-good syndrome), he built a house there for his retirement but died soon afterwards.[4]

Walters's doctorate was a legitimate one. It was not from an American university (where many Welsh Nonconformist ministers had obtained their doctorates) nor was it from Lambeth, where to keep up scholarly pretensions *vis-à-vis* the Nonconformist doctors, the archbishop of Canterbury had awarded numerous Welsh clergymen the Lambeth BD and DD degrees. Rather Walters took advantage of a now defunct Cambridge privilege of being "a ten year man". By this Walters was enabled to enrol as a mature student at St John's College, in 1853, for the degree of BD. The number so chosen was very small and all were carefully selected, but by studying externally over a period of ten years Walters was awarded the BD in 1863; he then incorporated at Trinity College, Dublin, and in 1871 took his doctorate in divinity from that college, probably by examination rather than by thesis. This doctor was clearly a man to be reckoned with.[5]

The rectory of Ystradgynlais, linked with the perpetual curacy of Capel Coelbren, had a population of 3,758, an acreage of 10,000 or so, and an income of £350 per annum, according to the 1859 *Clergy List*. By 1874 the mainly Welsh-speaking population was estimated as between 5,000 and 6,000 people. According to a later return of 1887, most of its income came from the tithe-rent-charge; in that year it amounted to £336 although its commuted value was £372. Although its full value was obtained in 1867, outgoings diminished this sum to £266.[6] But if the net value was reasonably high (at least for a Welsh living), the parish of Ystradgynlais was both extensive and also demanding. It consisted of two districts of scattered villages containing colliers and quarrymen, at Cwmtwrch and Abercrave. The church accommodation consisted of the parish church and a licensed schoolroom at Abercrave which had been built in 1860. Cwmtwrch itself, three miles from the parish church, was spread over two other parishes, Llanguicke and Llangadwg. But as the nearest parish church of the two was seven miles away, it was obvious that their incumbents preferred to leave the care of this area to Walters.

As Walters pointed out, people could remember Cwmtwrch as a hamlet of two or three small thatched cottages and the whole parish as having a population of about 100 tenant farmers and a few mountain shepherds. By the mid-1860s it had a population of 1,250 miners, and a large number of dissenting chapels. Although Walters had tried to start an English service in the afternoon in the parish church (the Welsh services taking place in the morning and evening), it had to be discontinued as funds were not available to employ another curate. There were no resident landed proprietors in the parish, which, apart from these mining districts, consisted mainly of small tenant farmers who, as Walters observed, were neither in position nor intelligence superior to common labourers. Most were Nonconformists. A letter of 1867 indicates how the parish was worked. Walters had a curate in Abercrave and a Scripture teacher at Cwmtwrch. Each Sunday Walters officiated at three services preaching at each one, and on the third Sunday he did "a missionary tour" of the parish, performing six services (three of them communion services), and riding between 17 and 18 miles.

Much of this information is gathered from the letters Walters wrote to the Ecclesiastical Commissioners requesting grant-aid for a second curate, utilising as the benefaction (for the parochial share) a projected CPAS grant of £50 per annum. He had already received one temporary grant for this purpose in 1865 as the parish was a mining community. This was one of the first grants made by the commissioners for this purpose, and a CPAS grant had been found acceptable for the parochial share on that occasion. Although Walters indicated that the second curate would be able to establish two Sunday services and one weekday service at Abercrave, utilising the school-church which held 300 people, and thus maintain a Church presence in a place with five large dissenting chapels, the commissioners declined to assist. However they were prepared to increase the existing grant by another £10 to £60, provided the parish also paid an equivalent increase. However, Walters characteristically refused to take the commissioners "no" for an answer, and appealed against their decision, specifying again the circumstances of his parish, and making it clear that an additional grant would not relieve him of any part of his own duty. Thankfully his appeal was accepted and the grant allowed. But curates were not easy to obtain, however necessary they were for a parish like his, as witness Walters's concern that the commissioners would allow him to employ a man without an episcopal licence on a temporary basis in order to keep the work functioning. "It is my experience that church people in the outlying districts of parishes are very sensitive," he wrote, "unless they are at all times provided for they will think themselves neglected and perhaps in that feeling will leave the church altogether, and the work of so many years ... may be lost in a few weeks ..." Such a calamity was to be feared.[7] Walters was equally robust when the commissioners were late sending the quarterly cheque for the curate's stipend. It had put the poor man to considerable inconvenience if not hardship, he wrote, for with a wife and family to support out of this income he could ill afford to wait for it.

Walters had made it clear that on his income, without a parsonage house, and with a wife and a large family of boys to maintain and educate, he could not make any contribution to the payment of curates (though legally it was his responsibility). The parsonage house belonged to the patron of the living, who leased it to the incumbents, and it was not until 1880, after Walters had left the parish, that the commissioners offered a grant for its purchase, using the land on which it stood as a benefaction. Queen Anne's Bounty also allowed a mortgage for its repair.[8]

The work for which Walters was best remembered in Ystradgynlais was not this hard work of building up a parish and forming a church community, but rather that of rebuilding the parish church on a new site. Unfortunate it may be that outward things, rather than inward and spiritual, are best remembered, but in this case the proposed rebuilding generated so much heat and controversy it is not surprising this was so. Walters sent his plans to the Ecclesiastical Commissioners on 10 April 1856, unaware that they were unable by their terms of reference to assist in the building or re-building of churches. The parish, he wrote, was an agricultural parish thinly inhabited amongst the mountains of south Wales. In more recent years it had become a manufacturing area of no small importance, and the village, which once consisted of about half a dozen thatched cottages, was now a small town. Although the parish church was centrally situated, it had only 220 sittings, all of which belonged to the occupiers of the different farms to which they had been originally appropriated. Consequently, there were no free sittings. The church building was old and inconvenient, small and gloomy, and "a most unsightly building". A new building, to accommodate the new population and reflecting the enhanced importance of the parish, was urgently required. Land had been given for an extension to the graveyard by Beriah Botfield, Esq., but not consecrated, and Walters wished to build the new church on this land, provided he was sure the parishioners could not bring a case of misappropriation against himself and his wardens for this change of use. Indeed, he feared that his parishioners might be very troublesome in this matter, for Walters noted that there was such a strong feeling against church rates in the parish that there was no prospect of being able to borrow money on their security.[9]

By 1861, after years of dispute, a new church had been built and consecrated on this new site, 42 yards from the old church. It sat 640 people, and all its seats were free. The old church was abandoned and later demolished, its rights being transferred to the new one. The plans of the new church were possibly drawn up by Benjamin Ferrey, but the work is so idiosyncratic that it appears (as was asserted by Lord Glanusk in his edition of Theophilus Jones's *A History of the County of Brecknock*), that Walters acted as his own architect and possibly as clerk of works as well. The cost was £2,500.[10]

The controversy about its building was substantial and at times bitter. At first a number of inhabitants refused to accept that there was any need for a new church. The old was good enough. Mr Marryat, brother of Captain Marryat the novelist, was one of their number. They took strength from an earlier decision of the parish vestry of April 1857. This was to request a faculty in order to make certain alterations to the existing church, possibly in an attempt to prevent the building of a new church. But even this faculty application had been opposed by Mr Marryat, aided by Thomas Levi, a Nonconformist minister. Walters, however, received episcopal support for his original programme, and Thirlwall wrote a public letter to him at this time stating "[t]his is a case in which a new church is most urgently required in the place of the present small, gloomy, and most unsightly building, and I may add that I am at a loss to conceive how any friend to the Church can ever enter that building with any other feelings than those which I have experienced on every occasion that has brought me to it, viz., mortification, shame, and disgust!"

The next problem was raising the money. Although Walters's initial hesitation about promoting a church rate has been noted, it appears he was overruled by a vestry meeting of December 1859, which had been summoned after a specific request by some of the principal farmers and ratepayers in the parish. Though Walters had previously visited them and asked them to subscribe towards the cost of a new church, they felt that as the building was for the whole parish, the whole parish should be made to contribute towards its cost. The fortunate discovery that the Public Works Loan Commissioners were prepared to advance money on the security of the rates, at an interest rate of four per cent and repayable over a 20 year period was an added factor in the vestry's decision. The vestry eventually ordered a rate, after an inconclusive hand count had been followed by an informal ballot, and authorised the wardens and overseers to apply for a £1,000 loan.

At this point the opposition to the scheme became both vocal and active. Mr Levi maintained that the vestry had not authorised any rate, and insisted that Walters "having tormented the parish for a long time for permission to build the church", had been allowed to do so on the express condition that it would be built by a voluntary rate. Furthermore, he added, Walters had received generous contributions from Nonconformists. These generous contributions, Walters replied, amounted to £2 10s. Walters in turn complained that the agents of the Ynyscedwyn Iron Works, of which Marryat was the principal partner, had canvassed the parish against the granting of this rate, arguing that if Walters succeeded in gaining this £1,000 loan, he would shortly require a further £3,500 and would bring ruin to the parish. The agents had also "packed" the meeting with their senior employees whom, Walters claimed, "necessarily exercised a considerable degree of influence", Levi's other complaint that Walters had unduly influenced the meeting and prevented free and open speech was not supported by the facts, Walters pointing out that he had only declined to allow Levi a third speech because he had already made two, and that he was not aware that the tenants of two local estates had been told to vote for the proposal. Many of these tenants had not even been present at the vestry meeting. However, it was alleged that the local agent of the Tredegar estate and "a clerical gentleman" had gone round the estate tenants in order to persuade them to vote for the rate. Furthermore, Walters answered Levi's assertion that ale had been distributed amongst the "victorious party" by stating: "[h]ere again he seems not to be aware that it is always customary at public vestries of the whole parish always to allow one pound for the use of the room; and that it is the liberal spirits and good wishes of the worthy landlord, Mr Richard Lewis, to give the value of it in ale to all those who choose to partake of it." It was not an easy victory. Howel Gwyn, a local landlord, with the assistance of Marryat, took the matter further. It is alleged by T. G. Davies that the matter was taken to the consistory court of the diocese, and later went twice through the Court of Queen's Bench, though the evidence for this has not been found.[11]

Though Gwyn had opposed Walters over the church rebuilding, friendship was not lost. Walters appears to have frequently presided over the Gwyn rent-audit dinner, and did so two years after he had left the parish. Gwyn had failed to secure his parliamentary seat, and had been replaced by a liberal. His bitterness about his defeat was shared by Walters, who criticised those people, even "professing Christians", who had promised their vote to Gwyn, but had been persuaded "by interested and paid political agitators" that the newly introduced ballot box was sufficiently safe to enable them to break their word. It was, added Walters, a grief "to witness such utter want of moral rectitude and straightforwardness on the part of such a large number of the electors of his own dearly-loved native country." Before he left Ystradgynlais Walters had been elected a member of the School Board, and been nominated as a local magistrate. He summed up his achievement in the parish in 1869: when he had arrived there was one Sunday service in the parish church. By that date seven Sunday services were held and four weekday lectures. Five National and infant schools had been opened where before there had been none. Much of this improvement Walters attributed to the assistance given him by CPAS.[12]

The parish of Llansamlet, to which Walters was appointed in

1874, was in a deplorable state. Once again, Church life had to be established and the parish church rebuilt. And all this had to be done at a time of economic depression. Walters's predecessor, E. Lloyd Davies, had already started to prepare plans for restoring the existing building, but his death prevented their execution. Nevertheless he had formed a committee and issued a prospectus. In a letter to the bishop's registrar Davies revealed some of the problems associated with the old building. The singers had been evacuated from their gallery as the roof above them was unsafe. But their presence in the body of the church, together with the increase in the congregations, had meant that many had felt unable to attend divine worship as the stifling atmosphere gave them severe headaches. Davies also pointed out that this increase was largely made up of former Nonconformists, so that the local chapels bitterly opposed his plans.

Writing in July 1874 to the Ecclesiastical Commissioners, Walters forwarded the decision of a vestry meeting to demolish the existing church and to build a new one on a site alongside it. The question of rebuilding the church had been considered for many years, he wrote, and plans had been prepared by an architect, but the condition of the building was such that the matter could not "with dignity or safety" be delayed any longer. A new church was needed, one not only commensurate with the requirements of a rapidly increasing population, but also more in character with the importance of the parish, as well as "the honour due to a house consecrated to the service of Him, who is the giver of every good and perfect gift."

The new site, adjacent to the old churchyard, was given by the earl of Jersey (with the consent of his mortgagors, the Revd Lord John Thynne and Samuel C. Whitbread), together with additional land for an extension to the churchyard which was then "literally inconveniently full". The gift was valued at £1,000, while the directors of the Foxhole Colliery generously gave an undertaking not to work under this new site. After some hassle, Walters persuaded the parish vestry to pay for the enclosure of the new churchyard with money raised from the rates, on condition that paupers could be buried therein. Llansamlet, however, possessed one advantage denied to many parishes, for it was able to benefit from a local claim against the Ecclesiastical Commissioners. This was because the chancel had been historically maintained by the bishops of St David's, who held the impropriate tithes of the parish as well as 70 acres of glebe land. As the episcopal estate was now in the keeping of the commissioners, Walters, believing that they were responsible in law as well as by custom for the maintenance of the chancel, requested their assistance.

It was not that simple, however. While the commissioners accepted Walters's contention, they pointed out that the rectory had been let out at lease on a rental of £200 per annum to David Davies, Esq., of Henllan, Llandysil. The lease would not expire until 1888. While the lessee had covenanted to repair the chancel, he certainly could not be made responsible for its rebuilding. It seemed for a time that this difficulty would be a major obstacle to Walters's plans. Thankfully the commissioners arranged a compromise. The lessee was released from his chancel repair liability for a payment of £43 (estimated as the cost of repair to the old chancel), though he was still expected to make some contribution to the cost of the new chancel. All this took time, mainly because the trustees appointed by the lessee were not particularly obliging and delayed matters. It appears they had a hidden agenda, namely, that they hoped to purchase the reversion of the lease from the commissioners for themselves. Possibly in an attempt to make progress, Walters published the report on the state of the chancel and the church building produced by the commissioners' architect, Ewan Christian. Its opening words read as follows:

> Having to survey and report on the Chancel of your Parish Church, on behalf of the Ecclesiastical Commissioners for England, I have at the same time examined into the state of the remainder of the Church, and can have no hesitation in saying that it is unfit for its purpose, and from structural defects capable of little improvement. It is gloomy, damp, unwholesome, and insufficient in accommodation, and there are serious difficulties in the way of its enlargement, owing to the large number of graves, &c., and any scheme for that purpose would probably be more expensive than entire building on a new site.
>
> It would, I think, be better to pull down the whole of the Church, with the exception of the Tower, using the old materials as far as they are available in such boundary walls as will be necessary to enclose the new site, and to rebuild with new materials entirely. This would allow the old Church being used during the construction of a new one, and no loss would be sustained thereby.

The plans accompanying his report illustrate a chancel filled with box-pews, two of them actually abutting onto the east wall, and permitting only a narrow and very confined space for a communion table between them.

The bishop of St David's, Basil Jones, was persuaded to write a letter endorsing the parochial claim against the commissioners, in which he stated that this church was "everything but what a church ought to be". But the commissioners were not unduly impressed, and indicated that their total contribution would be only £150. On 10 February 1876 Walters replied to their offer in terms of disappointment and regret. The whole building would cost £6,515, he wrote, and the chancel, included in that total, £1,116. He had hoped that the commissioners, as holders of the reversion of the lease, would have contributed the full amount. Had they done so he would have felt able to appeal to the general public for the remaining £5,000. It was not an easy time to raise money. There was a recession in trade, so that the principal men on the building committee had "failed", and even the chairman had been bankrupted. There was neither a resident landed proprietor nor one of the owners of the works living in the parish. Instead his population of 7,000 to 8,000 people consisted mainly of small tenant farmers, working men, and a few agents. Under these circumstances he felt that the project would have to be abandoned. Instead they would have to concentrate their attention on the existing church, unless, of course, the commissioners could increase their offer. They did, to a sum of £400.

Taking the principle that if once successful then one should try again, Walters, in his letter of appreciation, made it clear that this sum was not enough. As his bishop had said, he could not imagine a more crying case of need than Llansamlet. Nevertheless, if the commissioners would not allow him more, could they permit him to modify the plans of the chancel? The reply was simple. No more money was available but modifications were permissible. Walters and his architect looked again at the plans. Alas, the architect felt unable to modify them. New plans would have to be drawn. Worse, the architect felt that he had been unfairly if not unjustly treated, for he had agreed to accept a five per cent commission on the earlier plans, and had already incurred expenses and labour which he could ill-afford to sacrifice. New plans would cause more expense and a great delay to the appeal then being launched for money. Two months later the modified plans were available. Although the original plan had been adhered to as far as possible, because of the paucity of the commissioners' contribution, only the chancel and a portion of the nave westwards would be built, and the tower would not be built beyond its foundations. This would save an estimated £1,300. Nevertheless Brian Jones, in his history of Llansamlet Church, notes that the architect, H. F. Clarke of Briton Ferry, had Walters to contend with apart from the commissioners. Walters demanded a number of detailed amendments to the plans, and later insisted on using contractors whom the architect considered incompetent.

An appeal for the money required was launched in December 1877. A broadside, entitled "Statement and Appeal", gave some of the information already recorded as to the state of the building and the need for a new church. It also included the names of the committee members and the initial subscribers. These included the earl of Jersey who gave an additional £500, Edward Bagot (chairman of the Building Committee who later became insolvent) who gave £105 and the Moore family £100. The list concluded with David Rees's humble but probably no less acceptable one guinea. The brochure added that the new church would have sittings for 800 people, and would cost £5,000, of which the promoters expected to raise about one half in the parish and neighbourhood. It added however in an expectant if not challenging mood: "the remainder must be sought for from amongst the widespread and generous sympathisers of Christian truth and gospel teaching, who are never asked in vain to help forward their Master's work for the benefit of mankind and for the Glory of God."

The appeal was rendered even more urgent by the rapid deterioration of the building. A letter from the bishop of St David's to Dr Walters was printed for circulation. It read:

> It is difficult to conceive a case of more urgent need than is presented by the Parish of Llansamlet to any one who has ever seen its most miserable Church. It is insufficient in size, inconvenient in its arrangements, and mean and ugly to the last degree. To crown all I am informed that it is unsafe, and this is perhaps, the single redeeming feature of the situation. But in consequence of the absence from the Parish of Residents of substance and influence, it is to be feared that even the fear of a falling roof, with which it appears that they are threatened, may not have the effect, which might be hoped for in another parish, of compelling the Parishioners to re-build their Church. There is, as I understand, every desire to do what is needed, but the means are sadly wanting.

One wonders if the bishop was hinting that Walters was exaggerating the position in order to obtain a new church. However, Walters's letter to the commissioners of 22 December 1876, asking them to upgrade their offer, was even more dramatic. It was impossible to sit in the chancel during wet weather, he alleged, as the rain poured down in torrents. The builder who had come to patch it up had indicated that it could not last another winter, and he would not be surprised if it all gave way. Services had to be conducted from the nave. If the roof fell and injured people he would have to hold the commissioners liable. While he was prepared to do what he could for the building of the new church, he expected the commissioners to be responsible for the chancel and not just for a part of its cost. It must have been a difficult Christmas for Walters, for two days after the festival he wrote once more to the commissioners. His building committee had collapsed because of the failures or "liquidations" of its principal members, and the full responsibility had fallen onto his shoulders. Consequently he felt unable to start work at all until he had an assurance that the commissioners would fund the whole of the chancel cost. Dr Walters, it seems, was holding the commissioners to ransom.

The commissioners did not oblige. A letter from the bishop to the commissioners of 6 July 1877 requested them, in view of the circumstances (reiterated once more), to give the highest possible contribution within their power. And a further letter from Walters, of the same week, itemised the poverty of the congregation and parish (he had 30 English communicants and 60-70 Welsh in a parish of working men and dissenters), and emphasised both the necessity of a new church, and also his own isolation - he had no one now to fall back on. As the commissioners had been in possession of the rectorial tithes since April 1876 he begged for further consideration. A further £100 was offered. This he accepted. In all the commissioners contributed £500 towards the cost of the chancel.

The foundation stone of the new church was laid with great and becoming ceremony by the Countess of Jersey in early May 1878. By this time it had been decided to go ahead with the full length of the 80-foot nave, together with the chancel and vestry. The cost of the whole was said to be £6,500, but the contract for the first portion built, of nave and chancel, was £2,380. It seems that the rest of the work would be done in stages as finances became available. A newspaper report stated it would cost a few hundred pounds to put a temporary wall on the south side, although the writer hoped that sufficient donations might be forthcoming to cover the full cost of this aisle (£1,410) before the building was consecrated, thus saving this needless cost. In fact the south aisle was built as part of the contract, although the money to do so was obviously borrowed from one source or another, while a sum of about £500 was raised by two bazaars, one held in the parish and another at Neath, where much help was given by the parishioners of that parish. The earl of Jersey, in his speech at one of these bazaars, mentioned the great depression "at present hanging over the neighbourhood" which had made it so difficult for Dr Walters to collect funds for the new church, but he hoped that with zeal, courage and perseverance "the difficulties which now seem oppressive will be overcome".

In January 1880 the commissioners' architect, Evan Christian, came once again and certified the work as complete. The bishop of St David's signed, and his butler witnessed the deed transferring the rights of the old church to the new one. The materials from the old and now demolished church were used to build an infants' school, an annex to the National School, for which the irrepressible Walters requested the commissioners' assistance during the following year, writing "we are only able to keep our struggling school afloat by dint of great exertion".

A deficit of about £2,000 still remained on the church, and although Walters was unsuccessful in persuading the commissioners to grant a further £500, a series of quarterly services were instituted as a means of clearing this substantial debt. In January 1881, for example, there were two special Welsh services and one bilingual service in the parish church, together with an English service in the National Schoolroom. An appeal was also made for subscriptions, and those offering half a crown or more were requested to put their offering in an envelope so that their names might be recorded. On this occasion the quarterly services produced collections amounting to £119. Preachers came to these services from far and wide, including Liverpool. The tower and spire together with an organ were still to be built, and it was estimated that this work would cost £1,800. For some years thereafter the needs of the local school replaced the desirability of finishing the work on the parish church, for by 1880 the school was so crowded that the medical and sanitary authority considered it to be a health hazard, and £350 had to be raised to improve matters and build new toilets and an additional classroom. As a result of this delay an organ was not placed in the church until 1895, the tower was not built until 1914 when the old one was demolished, and the proposed spire was abandoned. Finances were so tight that the Neath

Saw Mills was not paid the £250 due for the pews for ten years, when the owner reduced the cost by £10 in order to ease the parish's financial burden.[13]

Meanwhile the work of church extension in the parish continued for an ever increasing population. One cannot but admire the faith of Walters, when it is said that the offertory, introduced in 1874, only produced £2 on average per week, while his own income from the parish was about £300 per annum. Much of this sum had to be used to pay for parochial expenses as well as for his own needs.[14] St Paul's Mission Church was opened at Glais in 1881, and a large disused barn at Cefnygarth was converted into a church at a cost of £500 and dedicated to St David. Its owner, Mrs Wood of Stouthall in Gower, readily consented to lease the site and the barn to the parish for a term of 99 years at a nominal rent. The church sat 200 people, one in three of the then mining population of that district. Father Benson of the Cowley Fathers contributed £20 to the cost, having family connections with Gower, but perhaps this was kept secret from Walters who had no love of ritualists! Walters noted this mission church when he spoke to the CPAS annual meeting in 1882, stating he was glad of the support of a good number of laymen at this church. At times he had a staff of six curates, some of whom were supported by grants from the commissioners. His last activity in the parish was a mission to its Welsh-speaking inhabitants, held in 1892, during which a number of services were held in factories and mines. By the time of his retirement Walters had changed a neglected and dispirited parish into one with a strong and active church life.[15]

****

Thomas Walters was a thorough Church of England man. He saw his Church "as the great machinery established in this country by Providence for the evangelization of the masses." Like an old lantern it had preserved the light of revealed religion in the midst of the darkness of superstition and ignorance, and from it the Nonconformist churches had been lighting their "candles".[16] But he was also a native Welshman, and although not a nationalist in the later meaning of the word, Walters clearly felt that the needs of the Welsh people and clergy were not being adequately addressed by the Church of his own day. He became known for his controversial and outspoken statements and assertions on these matters which few others of his generation had the courage to mention.

His first major controversy ended in such disaster that one is surprised he ever took up the cudgels again. It concerned the patronage of the bishop of Llandaff, Alfred Ollivant. The Welsh paper, *Y Cymro*, contained a letter signed by "Candidus" in its issue of 27 September 1854. It was headed "Abuse of Church Patronage by the Bishop of Llandaff, and his appointments". The letter commenced:

> The preferment of inexperienced and incompetent men to valuable and important spheres of labour is one sure way to cripple the energies of the Church, depress the spirits of the hard-working and most deserving Clergy, and effectually disgust and alienate the national feelings, as well as render the Establishment a by-word and a proverb for those for whose welfare it is especially designed. But the Bishop of Llandaff, in several of the appointments made by him during the short term of his Episcopacy, seems to have lost sight of this, and has hitherto manifested considerable incompetence to judge for himself in this respect. He allows himself, when a vacancy occurs, apparently to be led by the relatives, connections, and friends of the respective candidates.

A number of examples were given. One man deceived the bishop and obtained a rural parish, but was later bankrupted. Another, the Revd W. Williams, then vicar of Pyle and Kenfig, was nominated by Ollivant for the living of Bedwas, one of the best livings in the diocese, although he had never distinguished himself, preached to bare walls in his own parish, and had only been a few years in orders. His father-in-law, who was churchwarden at Llandaff Cathedral, was alleged to have unduly influenced the bishop in favour of his appointment. But how much better, continued the writer, if an older man had been preferred, one who had borne the heat and burden of the day, and for whom Bedwas could have been an agreeable retreat in his old age. The bishop was accused of preferring to livings men who were gentlemen rather than primarily ministers of the Gospel. The result of this policy should have been obvious to him, for in the vale of Glamorgan where there were many gentlemen clergy the Church had become "pitiable". Such appointments were a deadly blow against the "self denying and meritorious efforts of the laborious Evangelical Clergy who are the substantial supporters and pillars of the Welsh Church."

A vindictive reply supporting the bishop was written by one who signed himself "Vindex", in which he accused the still anonymous "Candidus" of being consumed with envy and bitterness and wishing to gain revenge upon the bishop. Another writer agreed with "Candidus" and suggested that the new rector of Bedwas should exchange places with some of the older men of the diocese, who knew all too well the bitterness of non-recognition by their superiors. Regretfully the bishop, who was expected to be a tender father to his clergy, was treating his Welsh clergy – some of the most useful ministers in Wales – as "drawers of water and hewers of wood". It was no good crying peace when there was none, for too many of the bishops were acting as aliens to the Welsh clergy and allowing them to suffer privation and neglect. Ollivant, refusing to publicly enter the controversy, produced a privately printed letter in which he denied these allegations, and reviewed the whole of his patronage since his appointment as bishop four years earlier. No relations had influenced him, he asserted, although in some cases he had accepted the recommendations of local gentlemen who had had opportunity to judge the fitness of the candidates they were proposing. The bankrupted clergyman may have been unwise, but he was not dishonest. Williams had been offered Bedwas after a much more senior and Welsh cleric had declined it, but only after more careful enquiries had been made. Could a man who had served two curacies and been vicar of a parish for six years be described as a "raw recruit"? Ollivant asked, suggesting that his readers should judge for themselves if these appointments could be construed as a deadly blow to the evangelical clergy of this diocese.

Ollivant's reaction was cool, quiet and considered. He made clear that the controversy had caused him much pain but argued his case well and honestly. But another bishop reacted in quite a different way. This was Bishop Thirlwall, and Walters presumably held the bishop's licence to officiate as CPAS secretary in his diocese. By January Thirlwall had discovered that Walters was the alleged author. Walters denied this, but accepted that he had written an English letter commenting on the appointments made by the bishop of Llandaff which he had entrusted to the editor of the *Cymro* for his comments and inspection. The letter which had appeared in the paper was not representative of what he had written, although he was prepared to justify its content from comments made and letters sent to him by clergy in the diocese of Llandaff (presumably in his capacity as CPAS secretary). But Walters emphatically denied that he was guilty of "willful falsehood" or "fraudulent misrepresentation", and although he accepted his action was "an act of indiscretion" he asked Thirlwall to overlook "any impropriety into which I may have fallen". Thirlwall replied stating his action was "most reprehensible" and demanded that he should apologise to his episcopal colleague at Llandaff.

Walters did apologise, explaining the circumstances, and thankful for the bishop's "temperate and truly Christian-like reply" in his unpublished letter which had named Walters as the author. Requesting the bishop to accept that these "charges were not malicious or groundless fabrications of my own" but based on personal communications, Walters emphasised that his motives were not activated by personal hostility or disrespect to the bishop. Rather he had acted "in a mistaken notion that I was really doing good service" and promoting "the best interests of the Church by directing attention to the disposal of its patronage." It was a distressing subject, added Walters, and he much regretted the publication of the letter and his indiscretion which had led to it. Consequently he asked the bishop to overlook his impropriety. The apology was accepted, Ollivant stating that he retained no unkind feeling against Walters, and he hoped that his mistake would be "a lesson to yourself and others to abstain in future from pronouncing rash judgements upon matters with which they are imperfectly acquainted." Thirlwall, on hearing this, kindly intimated to Walters that he did "not think it necessary to visit you with any mark of my displeasure, and shall permit you to undertake any engagement which may be offered to you in my Diocese."

Alas, true to character, Walters wanted the last word, as well as to be cleared of the charges of wilful falsehood and fraudulent misrepresentation laid against him by his bishop, even though he accepted that the matter would remain "a salutary caution" to him, and hoped that his future conduct would merit the bishop's favour and approval. His letter was a mistake. A stinging rebuke came back from the bishop. While he was prepared to absolve him from such charges, yet "I am bound to observe that the plea by which you have sheltered yourself from this charge, namely, that you only reported what had been communicated to you by others, indicates such an excess of rashness and greedy credulity, and such an absence of openness and straight forwardness as it is hardly possible to attribute to any but personal and very unworthy motives." But Walters still needed to justify himself, and did so in a further letter to his bishop. He was thankful that the bishop had acquitted him of the initial allegations, and of his "error of judgement", but he was saddened that the bishop could put no better construction on his motives. Accepting that he had lost the bishop's confidence, Walters felt he had no other option but to seek an appointment in another diocese, painful though that course would be. If this was the case, he asked, would the bishop sign his letters testimonial? The reply was simple: "I shall be ready to countersign your Testimonials". As noted earlier, the offer of the parish of Ystradgynlais by a private patron saved Walters from some considerable embarrassment.

Whatever the true circumstances may have been of this nasty episode, there was certainly considerable feeling amongst the evangelical and Welsh clergy in Llandaff regarding the patronage of their bishop. There was a strong belief that Ollivant favoured the English and university men rather than the native Welsh clergy serving in the large valley parishes whose circumstances had made a university education impossible. It was a feeling which Ollivant failed to dispel by the recitation of his list of appointments. It left too much unsaid because he himself was unaware of the resentment the hard-working *gwerin* clergy felt against the soft-living gentry clergy in their comfortable rural livings. And Thirlwall's attitude was that of the rude English autocrat who believed the Welsh were beneath his notice.[17]

However much he was daunted by these events, Walters had sufficient courage (if that is the right word), to continue with his exploration of these issues, and to do so in public. Four years after the Ollivant debacle, he was mounting a campaign to ensure that Welsh-speaking chaplains were appointed to the prisons at Swansea and Cardiff. When the new prison regulations came into force in 1858-9, requiring full-time chaplains, the Glamorgan magistracy decided that a knowledge of Welsh was not a requisite for their nominees. Two English-speaking chaplains were appointed. Walters, with others, took the matter up, held public meetings at Swansea and elsewhere, and pointed out that at Cardiff Prison 409 Welsh-speaking prisoners had been admitted during 1857-8. They also made the point that Glamorgan was as much a Welsh-speaking county as an English one, with 61 English places of worship and 449 Welsh. Walters even managed to persuade Bishop Thirlwall of the rightness of the cause, for the bishop refused to licence a chaplain for Swansea gaol until provision had been made for its Welsh prisoners. But even this concession did not satisfy Walters. It meant another chaplain would have to be provided, paid for by the rate-payers. Bishop Ollivant's comments in a letter to the Glamorgan bench also came under severe stricture. The bishop had argued that the post at Cardiff needed a man of superior ability and actual experience, but he admitted it would be difficult if not impossible to obtain a Welshman with such qualifications. Walters's comment was scathing and tells us much about the man and his causes: "[t]here is an idea prevalent among some people that native Welshmen are not eligible for offices of trust and importance." There were two Welshmen who were candidates for the Swansea chaplaincy who more than satisfied the requirements mentioned by Ollivant. Public pressure eventually forced the magistrates to rescind the appointments they had made and to appoint Welsh-speaking clergy. "It is not too much to say", wrote a columnist in the *Weekly Mail* of 1875, "that the appointment of Welsh-speaking chaplains for the county prisons of Glamorgan is entirely due to Dr Walters and to a few other equally prompt and resolute spirits who acted with him at the time."[18]

It could hardly have been expected that Walters would have refrained from comment on one of the *causes célèbres* of the nineteenth-century Church in Wales. This was the appointment by the dean and chapter of Gloucester of the headmaster of their cathedral school to the benefice of Cowbridge, of which they were patrons. Mr Starling did not speak Welsh, and the bishop of Llandaff, Richard Lewis (Ollivant's successor), claiming Cowbridge was a benefice where a Welsh speaker was required, was not prepared to accept Starling's claim that he could employ a Welsh-speaking curate while he himself made some acquaintance with the language. The bishop of Gloucester was annoyed at the action of his episcopal colleague who had just been appointed to the bench, but the law was on the side of the Welsh bishop. Walters jumped in, guns blaring. It was deplorable that the English bishop should browbeat a new colleague who was simply upholding his duty. Rather than casting reflections upon the Welsh clergy he should have examined his own heart. How would his people react in his own diocese if he appointed a monoglot Frenchman to a parish? The Welsh people saw their language as the language of religion, and these Anglo-Welsh appointments had been one of the principal causes of dissent. It was appalling that a man who could not fully perform his duty should be permitted to hold a preferment which properly belonged to the Welsh clergy.[19]

There was another controversy in 1890. In that year a suffragan bishop was appointed to the diocese of St David's, in order to assist the now elderly Bishop Basil Jones. He was blessed with the title of bishop of Swansea. John Lloyd, the new suffragan bishop, who was in his early forties, had been appointed the previous year to the vicarage of Carmarthen. Walters strongly protested about his appointment and also started a vigorous controversy in the pages of the *Cambrian* newspaper. The correspondence was subsequently published as a pamphlet. The editor, in his introduction to this pamphlet, wrote:

> That the thoughts and feelings so frankly expressed by Dr Walters will meet with entire assent is, of course, not to be expected. The timid will deprecate, the time-serving will look askance, the self-conserving will be silent, and the indifferent will smile; but there will be large numbers of clergymen and laymen who, whatever they may say or leave unsaid, will feel that the standpoint taken by Dr Walters is that of a strong, fearless and outspoken man.

Walters made it clear that he had no wish to disparage the new bishop personally, and wished to give his diocesan bishop full credit for good intentions, but he suggested nevertheless with more than a touch of maliciousness that Lloyd's chief qualifications for the post were his youth and inexperience. Until the previous year he had not even had the experience of supervising a curate or of having worked in a non-rural area. The bishop had not consulted his diocesan advisors, so the appointment had come as a complete surprise to them, especially as two years earlier the bishop had rejected the idea of a suffragan bishop, turning down an offer of £1,000 per annum promised for such a post. The lack of funding would mean that the suffragan bishop would need to be appointed a residentiary canon of the cathedral in order to obtain a stipend for his post. But the appointment was symptomatic of another issue, namely the arbitrary nature of the bishop's appointments. These seemed to be "dictated by eccentric capriciousness, uninfluenced by any consideration of a personal character, and quite oblivious of all recompense due to past services, and of all regard for generally admitted public usefulness." When "round" men were pitchforked into "square holes", and there was no recognisable system of patronage, the loyalty of clergy to their bishop was placed under severe strain. Walters continued:

> The effect, in my opinion, is most disastrous. It tends to demoralize the clergy and to make them careless and indifferent

whether they work or not. They see young, and comparatively untried men promoted over the heads of older and more experienced persons who have laboured hard and faithfully and grown grey in the service of the Church. Men whose ministries are highly valued and prized by the general public, are left out in the cold and disregarded. It is most distasteful to the working clergy and laity of the Church. Public opinion cannot, in these days, be ignored with impunity, and such a system of patronage will, I fear, culminate in a general dissatisfaction throughout the Diocese. In that case the prosperity and welfare of the Church will suffer as a matter of course. I think that the welfare and even the existence of the Church in Wales, as a useful and prosperous Established Institution, depends, humanly speaking, upon a wise, judicious and equitable disposal of patronage.

Walters's main plea was that an equitable system of patronage should be established whose rules would be clearly understood by all. Furthermore, he added, it was a sad reflection upon the administration of the diocese that all too often the bishop had to go outside it in order to obtain clergymen to fill positions of trust and importance. This was all the stranger when, as he wrote in an additional letter, five episcopal appointments had been filled from clergy who were then serving in the diocese of St David's. The bishop, who had little experience of parochial life and did not readily mix with his clergy was not, Walters felt, a fit judge of men. Denying that his assertions were due to disappointment ("my life-long and self-denying labours ought, I think, to free me from any such unjust reflections"), he ended by asserting that the new suffragan bishop was a man more to be pitied than blamed.[20]

Walters's action in the above controversy was consistent with his long-expressed opinions about the Welsh Church. Speaking at the Swansea Church Congress of 1879, he said, "I submit with all respect that the treatment of Welsh clergymen engaged in purely Welsh parishes has been neither respectful nor considerate". Men endowed with gifts and power who were able to influence the minds of the Welsh people and to command their sympathies "have been denied Episcopal favour in the shape of ecclesiastical dignity." Such a system could only "damp the zeal, cool the courage, and chill the ardour of the Welsh clergy."[21]

Ten years earlier Walters had spoken about another but related difficulty faced by Welsh-speaking incumbents to the annual meeting of the CPAS in London. Too often the minority English-language speakers of a parish demanded preferential treatment from their clergyman. He continued:

> One of the chief causes [of the difficulties in the Welsh Church], perhaps, is the co-existence and general use of the two languages in the same locality. That entails the necessity of providing a double number of services to what would be otherwise required. In Wales the gentry and the higher classes of society speak the English language only, whereas amongst the great mass of the population Welsh is the prevailing language. The English portion of the community, which is by far the most influential as to wealth and position, requires that the ministrations of the Church should be performed in the English language; whilst the Welsh, which is by far the most numerous, on the other hand requires that the services should be performed in the Welsh language, and the clergyman is consequently often placed in a very awkward predicament. The social rank and position of his English parishioners entitle them to the most favourable consideration as to the time when and the place where the English services shall be performed. The time and place for holding the Welsh service is therefore made subservient to the convenience of the English, and in too many cases by far the Welsh service is performed at a most inconvenient hour in a most uncomfortable schoolroom, and the result is, that the Welsh people, rather than contend with those who rob them as they think of their heritage and birthright, quietly abandon the Church and provide religious accommodation for themselves outside its pale. A very foolish and senseless cry is often made against the Welsh language ... but as the Welsh language is at present the only medium of communication, the only language adequately understood by eight-tenths of the population, it is our duty to meet things as they are, and not as we would wish them to be. The people must be ministered unto in their own tongue, and wherever this is not duly and properly attended to the people are driven from communion with the Church and sent elsewhere to seek the Bread of Life.[22]

Many of these controversies in which Walters was engaged indicated an increasing division between the Welsh *gwerin* clergy and the Anglicised university men. The Welsh were given the poorly endowed but large and scattered valley parishes. The English, by comparison, tended to obtain the richer parishes, and in particular the urban livings. There was jealousy on the part of the Welsh, pride on the part of the English. These conflicts tended to manifest themselves in particular during the election of proctors for the clergy to Convocation, the so-called "parliament" of the Church. Electioneering was the order of the day, and frequently the candidates issued manifestos and their friends drew up campaign plans. Convocation must have been quite an anti-climax to those who were elected to it.

Walters had tried for election to Convocation in 1874, being nominated as a last-minute replacement for Canon E. O. Phillips, vicar of Llanbadarn Fawr, who had withdrawn his candidature. On the other hand he had retired from the election in 1870 in favour of Latimer Jones, then vicar of Carmarthen. On this occasion Walters had strongly advocated the necessity of electing Welsh-speaking clergy to Convocation who could speak of the needs and condition of the Welsh Church from first-hand knowledge rather than hear-say evidence. He said much the same in 1874, writing: "It is impossible for those who are not identified with Welsh interests, who have no experience of the Welsh character, and who do not know the Welsh language, to be acquainted with the wants of the Welsh people." Richard Lewis, later bishop of Llandaff, had in very poor taste ridiculed these Welsh pretensions, and was much criticised for his "claptrap" by various writers in the press. But in the subsequent election for two proctors Latimer Jones had 175 votes and Archdeacon de Winton 120, while Walters had 65 votes. His defeat, Walters wrote, was not only because his was a late entry, and people had already pledged their votes, but also because the archdeacons of St David's and Cardigan had circulated the clergy asking them to vote for de Winton. As a result many of the clergy had stayed at home rather than incur their archdeacons' displeasure by voting for Walters. One may detect a note of bitterness in Walter's words: "[t]his is another result of the systematic and questionable policy of appointing to high places in the Church men of anti-Welsh sympathies, who seem, for their want of acquaintance with the religious life and language of the Welsh people, to have an instinctive dread and abhorrence of every movement tending to promote the welfare of the Church in the Welsh-speaking portion of the Principality."

A further election took place in January of the following year due to de Winton's death. Canon Williams of Llanelli was suggested as a suitable candidate, but others demurred and argued that Walters would make his voice heard in London, whereas Williams was not an effective speaker. Others were promoting Dr John Griffiths of Llandeilo. Walters promised to withdraw his candidature in favour of Griffiths if Williams's supporters did likewise, arguing that Griffiths's age and service to the Church merited consideration, but also wishing to save the clergy from having to travel to Carmarthen at such an unseasonable time. For some it meant a three-day stint away from home. Eventually Williams was selected, but Walters was eventually successful on three separate occasions during the 1880s. It was an honour he much appreciated.[23]

Walters's obituary described him as a great defender of the Church.[24] This was true, for Walters's latter years saw the intensification of the campaign to disestablish and disendow the Church in Wales. But defence to Walters did not mean disparaging the Nonconformists, but rather speaking honestly about the difficulties and situation of the Church and endeavouring to correct and reform them. Speaking at the CPAS annual meeting of 1882 Walters drew attention to the destitution of the Church in Wales. Though the Church might be flourishing in the rural parishes, it was appallingly weak in the larger populous districts. If she could not hold the masses in these places her position as an Established Church would soon be gone. He continued: "[t]he great dangers we have to meet with are in the populous districts – where the elements of all influence for good are fast drifting away from our reach – and the attempts made here are now all inadequate to reclaim the people from sin and ignorance and secularism." Describing the parishes of Swansea and Ystradyfodwg, where the increase in the population had been phenomenal, he argued it was hardly fair to expect their incumbents to provide on their own and from their own resources the spiritual wants of their parishes. It was enough for them to minister to their ordinary congregation. Such men needed assistance: "how gladly then do we greet a helping hand and a word of sympathy extended to us down from such a centre of civilisation as London." Even better than a word of sympathy was a willingness to use new ways and methods in the Church in order to meet the needs of these "newly founded colonies". Glamorgan, he pointed out, had the largest increase in population of any county in England and Wales. The Church, thought Walters, should have the freedom to act where there was a need, rather than having to wait for lengthy and costly procedures to take place before it could respond. He thus wrote:

"[w]henever a new colony of people is formed a clergyman should be sent to minister among them at once. The Church should be the first to step in, and not be, as it generally is, the last, and after the ground has been preoccupied by others. I am afraid the people, if they had waited for the Church to provide for their spiritual wants, would, in many cases, be but little better than heathen."

But there was another factor, one unique to Wales. This was the bilingual position, which needed not only tolerance in arranging services to the satisfaction of both languages, but also required clergymen "well up in both languages". But not only did this involve double duty; those who gladly undertook this work had to face a hostile Nonconformist press: "[t]hey ridicule the ritual of the Church; they ridicule the position of the Church; they ridicule the very existence of the Church as by law established ..." But in spite of these difficulties he believed that there was a growing spirit throughout Wales in favour of the Church.[25]

Walters could see the other side too, and was ready to co-operate with Nonconformists in every possible way. He accepted that without their contribution the condition of Wales would have been deplorable. Unlike the hierarchy he was able to recognise Nonconformity's contribution to the spiritual life of Wales. Not all Nonconformists were hostile to the Church, he noted, and many of them (as well as churchmen) were tired of the continual political agitation which had by now taken the place of religion. Walters was thus ready to say to them "[g]race be with all who love the Lord Jesus Christ in sincerity". But, on the other hand, this did not mean that he would refrain from defending the Church against the attacks of Nonconformists.[26] He did so, for example, by defending the tithe against Abel Thomas, in a prolonged newspaper controversy. It commenced by quoting authorities against one other, but ended up, in Walters's words, by "bantering personalities and evasive quiblings" on Abel's part. Abel was equally annoyed that Walters continually dragged the larger issue of disestablishment into the argument, accusing him and his colleagues of "downright robbery". But Walters was surely right to emphasise that it was only when the Church had awoken from its lethargy that Nonconformity seemed determined that it should no longer "peacefully pursue its high and sacred mission", and instead wished to cripple "her means of usefulness".[27] Walters also defended his fellow clergy against Lord Aberdare's assertion that they had greeted the development of the new college at Aberystwyth with "ill-disguised hostility". However, Lord Aberdare had the mastery of him on this issue, arguing that the clergy had refused "to promote objects of general Welsh interest" which lay outside the interests of the Church.[28] Walters also joined forces with J. D. Llewellyn of Penllergaer in defending the Church against "iconoclasts" such as John Griffith, the rector of Merthyr Tydfil. Griffith had spoken in favour of the disestablishment of his own Church at a Liberationist meeting at Swansea. Watkins was also involved in a correspondence about the British school at Neath, which was said to have given the church people there great satisfaction.[29] There were many other controversies not noted here for Walters was not a man to sit still while his Church or his principles were attacked.

His defence of the Church was also practical. The Church press was weak, Walters argued, and was unable to effectively counteract the "bitter and intolerant spirit" of some of the Nonconformist papers. At the Swansea Church Congress of 1879, of which he was the local honorary secretary (no mean position) he emphasised this concern, and a meeting was held to try and establish a good Welsh newspaper which would give information on the Church and its events. But in spite of a generous offer by a publisher to start such a paper if a subscription of £5 a week was guaranteed for two years, the attempt came to nothing.[30] Concerned about the inability of Welsh-speaking men to obtain the necessary monies for their ordination training, and recognising that as a consequence many had entered the Nonconformist ministry "not by choice but necessity", Walters wished to establish a new theological college in order to provide a free education for these men. The problem (as he saw it) was that the Welsh-speaking men did not have the resources to obtain a university education, while those who had the resources generally lacked a knowledge of Welsh and preferred to work in an English-speaking area. As he wrote: "between these two stools, as it were, the Welsh Church goes down."

It is not surprising therefore that Walters was later to be one of the founders of the Welsh Clerical Education Aid Society. Its aim was "to increase the efficiency of the Established Church among the Welsh-speaking population, by adding to the number of its ordained ministers such persons, from their decided piety, natural talents and abilities, as well as general aptitude for the work of ministry, it may be deemed advisable to support." As such the society offered grants towards the cost of ordination training to Welsh-speaking men who wished to serve in Wales.[31] These men needed to be good preachers as well, for Walters, with many others, thought that effective preaching alone would secure "the sympathy, co-operation, and love of the people", for whoever was able to "arouse the feelings, arrest the attention, and enlist the sympathy of his fellow-men for good, possesses the happiest influence over them." But the liturgy too needed to be simplified; it was too complicated, and more simple and plain services were required. Until this was done the Church's mission to the working classes would remain unfulfilled.[32]

Walters wrote extensively. He was the author of a confirmation catechism, many tracts, and of a sermon preached before the University of Cambridge.[33] Equally well-known as a lecturer ("Jones of Llangan", "The Coal-field of South Wales" and "The Ancient British Church" were his more popular ones),[34] Walters was appointed a canon of St David's in 1887. A freemason, and like many of the Welsh clergy, a Tory in politics, Walters was recommended on two separate occasions to prime ministers as a possible candidate for a vacant Welsh see. In the St David's vacancy of 1874 Godfrey Morgan of Tredegar recommended him, and in the 1889 St Asaph vacancy he was recommended to Lord Salisbury by Sir Michael Hicks-Beach, Mr J. D. Llewellyn and Sir R. Ellis, MP. How far Walters was considered is not known. There were certainly voices raised against his nomination. In 1874 Lord Dynevor, noting his controversy with Bishop Ollivant, suggested he was not a man of good repute, and Dean Bonnor added that his anti-ritualism was such that he feared he would become "an evangelical Pope", so creating party spirit rather than the reconciliation required. He quoted two examples of this anti-ritualism: his protest at the singing of a processional hymn at the opening of a church, when he remained in the vestry, and his finding fault with clergy for turning to the east in the creed.[35] Besides by that time his health was not good. His second wife had died after a long and trying illness in 1890, and one son had had to retire through ill-health to the Hawaiian islands. These concerns, together with the oversight of one of the largest parishes in Wales at that time, so taxed his strength that he retired at the then early age of 69 (presumably having the resources to do so) and died shortly afterwards in late 1892.[36]

Such was Thomas Walters. He was a man who coped with substantial, demanding and what must have been at times demoralising parishes, and brought new life to every one of them. But he was also a man who could not avoid pitching into any quarrel that was around. Thankfully, he knew his subject, was a good controversialist, and had no phobias about bishops. He presents us with an alternative picture of the Welsh Church far more revealing than its hierarchy would have wished to see in print. It is a much more varied picture, warts and all. And yet, in a sense, Walters too joined the number of the elite. Clergy were gentlemen, and this man rose to the occasion, made the best use of the opportunities which came his way, and from a *gwerin* background, ended life as a manorial lord. At least that was as ironic as many of his pet foibles.

ENDNOTES

1　WM, 30 July 1884, a cutting in John Griffith's Scrapbook at South Glamorgan Library, Cardiff, MS. 5.157.

2　*Weekly Mail*, 23 June 1875, p. 4.

3　Owain W. Jones, "Thomas Walters", *Brycheiniog* 21 (1984-5) 64-8, especially p. 67.

4　Ibid., and *Weekly Mail*, 23 January 1875, p. 4; CMG, 2 March 1866, p. 8; 8 October 1853, p. 4; *Haul*, 1874, pp. 36-8.

5　Jones, *Walters*, p. 64.

6　The papers of the Ecclesiastical Commission for the parishes of Ystradgynlais and Llansamlet are in the possession of the Representative Body of the Church in Wales. In the 1832 parliamentary return (enclosed in the above papers) it is stated that the income was £200, but the parish was served by a curate who received £50 per annum plus fees. The church held 450 people.

7　EC papers, particularly letters of 7 July 1865, 1 February 1866, 21 November 1866, 2 August 1867, and a return of 1863. In 1868 the EC was prepared to augment the benefice with an income of £17 per annum provided an identical sum was obtained from a non-ecclesiastical source. It could not be found and the augmentation was lost. The English language services, says a newspaper report of 1865 (contained in South Glamorgan Libraries, MS. 2.245, John Griffith's scrapbook) were resumed "through the kindness and unwearied exertion of the worthy rector." Its writer hoped that Walters would soon be able to have a curate to continue this good work.

8　QAB papers for the parish (as for EC papers). The patron probably gave the land as a benefaction. QAB gave a mortgage for its repair.

9　EC papers, especially its letter to Walters, 10 April 1856.

10　For the old church see Jones, *Walters*, p. 66, and Theophilus Jones, *A History of the County of Brecknock* (Glanusk edn., Brecon, 1930), IV 90.

11　*Weekly Mail*, 23 January 1875, p. 4; CMG, 24 December 1859, p. 7; For Thomas Levi see *Dictionary of Welsh Biography*. See also T. G. Davies, *Howel Gwyn of Dyffryn and Neath* (Neath, 1992), pp. 98-9, and his *Neath's Wicked World* (Swansea, 2000), p. 194. Davies, in the former, suggests that Walters wrote to the press under the pseudonym of "Anglo-Catholic Presbyter". This is most unlikely, as Walters was a convinced evangelical.

12 WM, 14 July 1876, p. 6; CPAS Report, 1869, pp. 15-16.

13 EC letters and papers; WM, 3 May 1878, p. 4; Brian H. Jones, *Llansamlet Parish Church: The First Hundred Years* (1979), pp. 3-12; Letters of E. Lloyd Davies, dated 1873-4, Church in Wales Records, NLW, SD/LET/286, 289. A short description of the church is given in W. Samlet Williams, *Hanes a Hynafiaethau Llansamlet* (Dolgellau, 1908), pp. 70-1.

14 According to a return made to the EC of 1887, the income of the parish comprised tithe rent charge of £40, £52 from stock invested by QAB, and an EC Grant of £201.

15 Jones, *Llansamlet*, pp. 11-13; EC papers; *Church Builder*, 1881, p. 32; Albert Jordan, *History of the Church and Parish of Llanbadarn Fawr [Radnorshire]* (Brecon, 1926), pp. 101-2.

16 CPAS Annual Report, 1882, pp. 21, 24.

17 NLW typescript, "Letters from Llanbadarnfawr Parish Chest", pp. 120-53, 169-76. Bishop Ollivant's privately published letter, without title, is dated December 1884.

18 CMG, 29 January 1859, p. 6; 26 February 1859, p. 8; *Weekly Mail*, 23 January 1874, p. 4. See also Joan N. Harding, "The Welsh Chaplains" in *Minerva* 6 (1998) 10-14.

19 *Guardian*, 26 September 1883. For the background see my article, "Pastoral Problems and Legal Solution in the Established Church in Wales", in Norman Doe (ed.), *Essays in Canon Law* (Cardiff, 1992), pp. 7-24.

20 *The Rev. T. Walters Interviewed: The Appointment of Suffragan Bishop of Swansea (sic)*, pamphlet, published by the *Cambrian* newspaper, Swansea 1890, *in passim*, quotations on pp. 1, 9, 15. The vicar and rural dean of Swansea, J. Allen Smith, defended his bishop, arguing that when a man entered the ministry "he has surely far higher motives and grander aims than preferment and promotion.": p. 18.

21 *Report of the Swansea Church Congress*, 1879, pp. 367-8. In 1869 Walters hinted that much of the problem lay in the appointment of Anglo-Welsh bishops: CPAS Report, 1869, p. 19. He may have been gratified by the appointment of Joshua Hughes as bishop of St Asaph in 1870, but probably had to admit that this appointment intensified rather than solved these problems in that diocese.

22 CPAS Report, 1869, pp. 17-18.

23 WM, 23 January 1874, p. 6; 16 February 1874, p. 4; 26 February 1874, p. 6; 19 May 1874, p. 7; 21 May 1874, p. 6; 22 January 1875, p. 6; 1 February 1875, p. 8; 12 February 1875, p. 6.

24 *Bye Gones*, 24 August 1892, p. 368.

25 CPAS Reports, 1869, pp. 19-20; 1882, pp. 23-4; cf. his speech at the Swansea Church Congress (*Report*, p. 368), where he noted that for many years he had both the co-operation and the sympathy of Nonconformists

in his parishes. While they might be envious of the Church's established position, they were not violently hostile towards it.

26 CPAS Report, 1882, p. 21: WM, 27 November 1874, p. 5.

27 *Tithes: Was there a Tripartite Division of Tithes in England and Wales: Correspondence between The Rev. Thomas Walters and Abel Thomas, Esq.* A pamphlet published by the *South Wales Daily News*, January 1884. Quotations are from pp. 23, 26.

28 *The Letters of Lord Aberdare* (privately published, Oxford, 1902), II 30-2, dated 29 June 1875.

29 *Weekly Mail*, 23 January 1875, p. 4; WM, 30 July 1884: a cutting in John Griffith's papers, MS. 5.157.

30 *Report of the Swansea Church Conference*, pp. 583, 602-3; CPAS Report, 1869, pp. 19-20.

31 CPAS Report, 1869, p. 18; *Weekly Mail*, 25 January 1875, .p. 4; Jones, "Walters", p. 65, quoting *Y Haul* for July 1869. Walters hoped that CPAS might be able to grant-aid such an institution.

32 *Report of the Rhyl Church Congress*, 1891, pp. 136-7.

33 *Weekly Mail*, 23 January 1875, p. 4.

34 *Weekly Mail*, 23 January 1874, p. 3.

35 The "Bishops and other Clerical Appointments Book", contained in the papers of the third marquess of Salisbury at Hatfield House, used by kind permission; Godfrey Morgan to Disraeli, 18 May 1874, Lord Dynevor to Lord Barrington, 24 June 1874, R. M. Bonnor to Sir Watkin Wynne, 26 May 1874, Bodleian Library, Oxford, Disraeli Papers, Dep. Hughenden 157/4/245, 297 and 157/2/147-80. See also the letter of a "Disinterested Vicar" in WM, 1 February 1889, p. 4, who recommended Walters for a bishopric. He noted his exemplary life, his powers of organisation, his successful bilingual preaching, and surprisingly claiming him to be a man of moderate views, safe and sound.

36 *The Rev. T. Walters Interviewed*, p. 3; WM, 5 April 1890, p. 2. His first wife was Caroline, daughter of Benjamin Rees of Dowlais, and sister of Thomas Rees, vicar of Llanishen near Cardiff, who died in 1863. Six of their children were buried at Ystradgynlais. His second wife was Lydia, daughter of William Richards of Swansea. One son served in the administrative service at Honolulu, and another, Walter, was rector of Trefgarn in Pembrokeshire from 1893 until his death in the late 1920s. His successor at Llansamlet, John Williams, a former schoolmaster at Llanbrynmair, died in the West Indies where he went for the benefit of his health: *Bye Gones*, 29 April 1903, p. 88.

LLANDRILLO CHURCH, COLWYN BAY
from a postcard of the 1900s

9

DISESTABLISHED BEFORE HIS TIME:
W. VENABLES WILLIAMS AND THE CREATION OF THE PARISH OF COLWYN BAY[1]

William Venables Williams, the son of a rector of Llanhychan, and a Master of Arts of Jesus College, Oxford, became vicar of Llandrillo-yn-Rhos in 1869. It was to be an eventful incumbency, to say the least. Williams had served for the previous ten years as vicar of Llangedwyn. His new parish was large in size though small in population. Its eleven-hundred-odd population could not, however, be accommodated in the parish church, which in 1901 could seat 306 people, of which 200 seats were available free of charge.

From 1759 until the death of Bishop Carey in 1846 the Llandrillo-yn-Rhos rectory was held *in commendam* by the bishops of St Asaph (who, from the income, paid a curate to undertake the duty of the parish). In that year the rectory and its income had been taken into the care of the Ecclesiastical Commission. This meant that the parish was able to make a so-called local claim for assistance from the commissioners, who wished to act as good landlords of their estates, especially by supporting the local churches. Consequently, when the rectory was taken over by the commissioners, they allowed £395 of its annual commuted tithe income of £640 to be set aside as an endowment for the new district of St Catherine's, Colwyn, which was partly formed out of the parish of Llandrillo-yn-Rhos. It is important to note, however, that the commissioners acted as rectors of the parish only in so far as they claimed the rectorial tithe; the actual pastoral and parochial work was undertaken by its vicars.[2]

****

In 1870 Venables Williams wrote to the commissioners and pointed out that much of his income as vicar was obtained from tithe rental charges which came from a number of adjacent parishes. In addition to the vicarial tithes of Llandrillo, valued at £272, he received tithes from the parishes of Llansanffraid (£76), Llaneilian (£35) and Llysfaen (£14). The vicars of Llandrillo, as an acknowledgement for the tithe income, paid to the incumbents of these parishes the sum of one pound each, in lieu, it is thought, of an annual sermon. Venables Williams wrote that he felt diffident about receiving tithes from parishes where he did no duty, and wondered if these tithes could be restored to their respective parishes. In return he suggested he should receive the whole or major part of the rectorial income of his parish, which he estimated at £600 per annum, plus a small field of three acres. His net income was not more than £300, for the poor rate was five shillings in the pound, and though his population was about one thousand, it was growing rapidly as his parish was being developed as an important bathing place. His existing glebe of two and a half acres was in another parish (apparently in the new Colwyn district), and this also included a quarter right to the salmon tithe. In order to possess the whole of this particular tithe the vicars had paid the rectors, from time immemorial, the sum of three guineas per annum.

Some question arose as to whether the annual one-pound fees should be retained or not, but Venables Williams suggested that if they were retained the anomaly would be even greater than at present. It was decided, therefore, that such payments should cease, and the income from the various tithe rent charges were returned to their original parishes. In return the vicar of Llandrillo was compensated for the loss of this tithe rent income by being given an equivalent amount (£125 per annum) of the tithe-rent-charge held in his own parish by the commissioners in their rectorial capacity. Venables Williams's costs were reimbursed, and his subsequent request that the two guineas given annually by the bishops for the sacrament wine of the parish should be deducted from the three guineas he paid for the salmon tithe was allowed. The extra guinea too was allowed him "for his trouble". Although Venables Williams hinted that the commissioners could be more generous in their allocation of their rectorial tithe income, they replied that his income of £300 plus for a population of one thousand meant that any further augmentation was against their rules.

Consequently, Venables Williams tried another approach in order to obtain further assistance from the commissioners, although he claimed he was merely following the suggestion of his bishop, Joshua Hughes. In this large bilingual parish, he wrote, he had to give two services each Sunday in both languages, the services probably alternating between Welsh and English, though in 1851 both services were conducted in Welsh. The bishop, duly impressed by the necessity of an increase in the number of services, had urged him to make an appeal to the commissioners for assistance with the stipend of a curate on the grounds of a local claim.

His first request, in 1870, was turned down, and accordingly on 14 March 1872 he wrote again, this time giving more details about the growth of his parish. One part of his parish, three miles from the parish church, was rapidly becoming a small town. This, of course, was the area now known as Colwyn Bay. During the last summer he had held services every Sunday in a carpenter's shed, the success of which was far beyond his most sanguine expectations. The attendance had been between 150 and 200 people, but being single-handed he had had to give up taking these services as he also had two full services in the parish church. The result was that the dissenters had taken up the challenge and were now building two chapels in this new area. A curate was needed for the mission church he intended to build there, for he would be unable to take its services in addition to his own services at the parish church. This curate, he implied, could also be responsible for an additional Welsh service. Williams's application was endorsed by the bishop, who pointed out the need for these additional bilingual services. Once again the commissioners replied they could not assist, as the income of the parish was too large and its population too small to merit assistance.

A further request in August 1880, when Venables Williams mentioned his two churches with five Sunday services, was also turned down for the same reason. His reply, when he heard this news, on 17 January 1881, was to express astonishment at the commissioners' decision. He had two churches (a mission church having been built at Colwyn Bay), four services, a large Sunday school, and an additional service in the summer, whereas when he was appointed in 1869 he had but one church with two services. The population was then one thousand; now the area of Colwyn Bay alone had a population of 800 and an additional 1,200 summer visitors. He felt he was more entitled to a grant than the parish of St Asaph with a population of under 2,200. Yet that parish had received a grant of £120 for a curate, even though it had four vicars attached to the cathedral who only did duty in the parish church once a month. That grant given them (he moaned) was simply in order to gratify a whim for providing a lecture on Sunday and Wednesday evenings.

A more elaborate statement accompanied his renewed application of 10 May 1881. The population of his parish was 700 in the Llandrillo area and 1,030 at Colwyn Bay. In addition there were many furnished rooms let for the use of summer visitors, many of whom came from the Liverpool and Manchester areas. Nineteen houses were being erected which would command rents of between £20 to £50 per annum, and another 18 had already been sanctioned by the local council. The commissioners took out their maps, and discovered that Colwyn Bay was closer to the new district of St Catherine's Colwyn than Llandrillo. Perhaps, they suggested, Colwyn Bay could be linked with that parish instead? The bishop replied to this query. He had visited Colwyn Bay and reported that the new church there was one and a half miles from St Catherine's, but the development was towards the Llandrillo end, rather than towards Colwyn itself. As the incumbent of St Catherine's already had two English and two Welsh services each Sunday he could not cope with another church. Though Colwyn Bay might form a new district or parish in the future, it was better in the meantime that a grant for a curate be given to Venables Williams upon the distinct understanding that he should give one Welsh and two English services each Sunday at Colwyn Bay, and one English and one Welsh service at Llandrillo.

And thus a curate came, Richard Jennings, a nephew of Archdeacon Jennings[3], together with a grant for his full stipend from the commissioners on the basis of a local claim. As a deacon he was only entitled to £110, but his vicar made it up to £120 himself stating that £110 was too little for a man to live on. If there was kindness to begin with, there was conflict thereafter. Venables Williams was clearly not an easy man to live with. By 1884 Williams was demanding Jennings's resignation, on the grounds that he was allowing Nonconformists to enter and teach at his Colwyn Bay Sunday School. The real issue appears to be that Jennings had become very popular and as such obtained a power-base in Colwyn Bay which disquieted Williams. In a significant phrase, Williams demanded that he should be master in his own parish. Jennings refused to resign and the bishop supported him, claiming that no reason had been given for his dismissal. Furthermore, Bishop Hughes appealed for common sense to prevail, arguing that Williams's actions could only widen the breach between himself and his parishioners. As he pointed out, the Colwyn people supported their curate; they were later to present him with a "handsome" testimonial. The vicar took no notice of his bishop's advice and matters became even more heated. Jennings was ordered out of the vicarage and told not to call again, and Williams publicly wrote that he would not acknowledge him in the street. The situation was only resolved when the bishop arranged for Jennings to take another curacy at Disserth, and even then Williams expressed his anger because this meant that Jennings could not give him the statutory three months' notice, and he would have to work the parish on his own for that period of time. He even appealed to the archbishop of Canterbury over this matter![4]

Another bitter dispute arose between Venables Williams and his bishop during 1885. The bishop, Joshua Hughes, was the first native Welsh speaker appointed for nearly 150 years to a Welsh diocese, and he accordingly took his linguistic responsibilities seriously. On 11 December 1885 Venables Williams wrote to the commissioners that his bishop had refused to sign the necessary certificate that his then curate had performed the required duties. Without the bishop's endorsement the commissioners' grant could not be paid. The bishop had told him he would decline to sign it until Welsh services were held on Sunday evenings at Colwyn Bay in addition to an afternoon service at Llandrillo. This, Williams argued, would be a suicidal policy. The Welsh service was held in the evening (5.45pm) at Llandrillo, and was attended by about 50 people. There was no call for such a service at Colwyn Bay. When the parish church had been closed for repair and services transferred to Colwyn Bay some 12 years earlier, only about 20 to 25 people had attended this Welsh service. Besides this, he had four services in the winter months plus the Sunday schools, and seven in the summer months. He was giving more services than when the grant was made, and there was not one word in its documentation about two Welsh services being required. Indeed, as he argued later, there was not a word in the correspondence stipulating a Welsh service.

The bishop argued that the curate's grant had been made under a local claim on behalf of Colwyn Bay. Furthermore, the bishop claimed that as two-thirds of its inhabitants spoke Welsh they were entitled to a Welsh service at a convenient time. However the bishop refused to hold a commission into the liturgical and bilingual requirements for Colwyn Bay, and Venables Williams was informed there was no appeal against the alleged injustice of the case. Without the bishop's sanction no grant would be paid.

Although no sequel is recorded, it seems that Williams won his case against the bishop, who appears in this instance to have been more concerned for the Welsh language than with the practicalities of administering a bilingual policy in the parish of Llandrillo. The bishop, it seems, allowed a compromise solution, which Williams reluctantly accepted, by which the Welsh service was transferred from the parish church to Colwyn Bay. When, two years later, an enquiry was held into the linguistic provisions of the parish, on the complaint of one William Price of Rhos Abbey Hotel about the lack of Welsh services, Williams offered this episcopal compromise as justification of his policy.[5]

The curate's grant, as we note later, was transferred to form an endowment for the new parish of St Paul's Colwyn Bay, and this was gazetted on 17 June 1893. To the controversy surrounding this we now turn.

****

St Catherine's Church in what is now described as Old Colwyn was built in 1837 as a daughter church of the parish of Llandrillo. It became the parish church of a separate district in 1844. By the 1880s the new area of Colwyn Bay was becoming a large and distinctive community, although D. R. Thomas, the historian of the diocese of St Asaph, remembered that when he passed through it in 1857 there was but a solitary cottage and a toll bar.[6] The first services in Colwyn Bay were held on 18 June 1871, using as a venue the carpenter's shed already mentioned, and were attended by a nucleus of 70 people. A year later a mission room was opened. It cost £170 and had room for 150 people. This in turn was replaced by an iron church which opened in June 1880.

Venables Williams had endeavoured to persuade the commissioners to offer him a grant for this building on the now familiar ground of a local claim. It cost, he wrote, £800, and he had already received £20 from the Incorporated Church Building Society, £10 from the Bishop of St Asaph, the same from himself, £150 from G. A. Langley, a local landowner, and £25 from the diocesan Church Building Society. Not to be outdone the commissioners added their name to this list of subscribers in a sum of £20. They were none too pleased when they discovered that this building would not be a permanent structure. In fact, it appears that the grant was never paid because of the difficulties caused by the site being vested in the bishop and incumbent rather than in themselves.

Tragically this iron church burnt down on 31 October 1886. Williams hinted at one stage that he believed it had been deliberately fired by one of the anti-tithe agitators.[7] It was resolved almost immediately to build a stone structure and to use the insurance money of £1,350 as a nucleus for this work. Venables Williams accordingly wrote to the commissioners on 2 December 1886:

> Now that the temporary iron church at Colwyn Bay has been totally destroyed by fire, I think it a fitting opportunity when contemplating building a permanent stone church, to separate Colwyn Bay from the mother church of Llandrillo-yn-Rhos by forming it into a distinct and independent parish.

The bishop of St Asaph, writing the following day to the same commissioners, noted the circumstances, and added:

> And it has occurred to him [the vicar] that this may be a good opportunity of separating Colwyn Bay from Llandrillo and forming a separate district.
> This has been my earnest desire for some time. The rapid growth of the population, the importance of providing suitable accommodation for divine worship, and the impossibility of working Colwyn Bay satisfactorily while held in conjunction with Llandrillo, appear to me to form a very strong reason for the proposed arrangement. And if their Lordships would be kindly disposed to deal with Colwyn Bay as they have dealt with Rhosddu by Wrexham, I think it would very materially strengthen the Church in that district. I heartily recommend the proposal to their Lordship's kind consideration.[8]

The commissioners replied stating that the local claim had already been extinguished, so they could not offer any additional grant. The suggestion was made, however, that the grant of £120 for the Llandrillo curate could be transferred to form an endowment for the new district (thus forming a stipend for the new vicar), provided that its patronage was placed into the hands of the bishop.

Meanwhile an appeal had been launched for the new church building, while the congregation worshipped in a local public hall. This was over-crowded, and many were turned away for lack of room, their number including many summer visitors. Venables Williams also claimed that he was paying its weekly rent of 20s. from his own pocket, and this was for Sunday use only. The church to be built, the appeal letter declared, would be worthy of this favourite summer resort and equal to the accommodation required. It would seat between 800 and 1,000, and cost £7,000, though this sum did not include the tower, porch, vestries and chancel which would be built later. Subscriptions and the insurance money amounted to only £2,000.[9]

It was made clear that this new church would become the parish church of a new district, and as such the plans were approved and the eventual building inspected by the commissioners' architect, Ewan Christian. He noted in his report that the building was suitable for a parish church, even though the chancel was a temporary structure. As the conveyance of the site had been sorted out at some cost, and as the vicar and wardens had had to pay over £18 to redeem the tithe-rent-charge on the property, Venables Williams requested that the commissioners should not only reimburse him for these sums but also allow him the grant awarded in 1880, but which he had never claimed. He suggested it was for £35, but an observant clerk noted it was for only £20. In this he was successful, but the records are silent as to the former.

The new church, dedicated to St Paul, was opened on 8 June 1888. Only the nave and north aisle of the planned structure were built; the chancel was a temporary structure. A deed transferring the patronage from the local incumbent to the bishop was signed a fortnight or so before the church's dedication. It was clear that the bishop's intention was that the church should be made the parish church of a new district as soon as possible. Writing to the commissioners on 4 June, the bishop wrote:

> It is of utmost consequence that Colwyn Bay should be so far endowed, that it could be held by a separate incumbent, and not as now proposed, be held with Llandrillo. It was that district, of which Llandrillo forms a part, that furnished Mr Osborne Morgan with his most virulent attacks upon the Church.[10] I am happy to say that, very nearly, in every case, by a change of incumbency, the spiritual aspect of that District is changed, and if I could appoint an efficient clergyman to Llandrillo another very important link would be added to the chain which I trust, in time will restore the people to the Church.[11]

With the backing of the historical researches of the archdeacon of Montgomery, D. R. Thomas, the bishop endeavoured to suggest that Llandrillo was the mother church of Llansanffraid. The tithes of this latter parish were still in the keeping of the commissioners. The bishop hoped thereby to establish a local claim for Colwyn Bay upon the expectation he could obtain an augmentation from the Llansanffraid tithes for its future incumbent, thus giving the new parish a "fair start". But the argument, devious in any case, failed to convince the sceptical commissioners, who merely replied that all they could allow was the transfer of the curate's grant of £120 from Llandrillo to the new parish, having noted that it had been given to enable services to be held at Colwyn Bay.

Unfortunately this matter was left in abeyance due to the long and lingering illness, and subsequent death, of Bishop Hughes. The new bishop, A. G. Edwards, revived the matter, and thus on 11 May 1889 Venables Williams wrote to the secretary of the commissioners noting their suggestion about the transfer of the grant and pointing out that the church had been consecrated and its patronage assigned to the bishop of St Asaph and his successors. A commission appointed by the late bishop had assigned the townships of Rhiw and Llwydcoed as the extent of the new parish, which would be entirely taken out of the parish of Llandrillo. He continued: "I have had an interview with the present Bishop, who is quite prepared to proceed herein, but wished me to put myself in communication with you with a view to your bringing the subject under the consideration of the Ecclesiastical Commissioners so as to have it finally decided, and at as early a date as possible."[12]

The commissioners, in their reply to the diocesan registrar, R. J. Sisson, on 25 June 1891 (for the matter lingered), said that as the proposed district was to come out of one cure only

> it is competent to the Ecclesiastical Commissioners, with the consent of the Bishop alone, to recommend to Her Majesty in Council the assignment of a District Chapelry to the Church in question, with authority to the Incumbent of the new cure to perform all Church Offices, and to retain all the Fees arising therefrom, subject to his paying over the whole of those emoluments to the Incumbent of the Mother Cure, until he either voluntarily surrenders them or avoids [*sic*] his living.[13]

****

The only "right" allowed the incumbent of the "mother" parish when part of his parish was made into a new district was to retain for himself the fees of the new parish. This was seen as a form of compensation for the loss of a part of his freehold income. Courtesy dictated, however, that after his consent had been given to the separation, he should be consulted about the various other steps required in the creation of a new district, such as its territorial area, the financial arrangements, and the appointment of a new "vicar". In some cases the latter was protected by allowing him the first nomination to the parish.

It was the lack of this consultation that caused Venables Williams to create a great row about the formation of this new parish. It appears that at first he was more angry with the way this was done, rather than with the principle involved to which he had consented beforehand and also to an extent initiated. In the final arrangements he was neither consulted nor even informed as to what was happening, while an appointment was made without any reference to him whatsoever. What made the situation more poignant was that the late bishop had promised to present him to the new benefice, and had arranged for him to hold it in plurality with Llandrillo. It may even have been the case that Williams had agreed to give up his moral "right" as the incumbent of the mother church to appoint the new vicar in return for the bishop's promise to appoint him instead, as ecclesiastical law forbade a patron to present himself. Bishop Hughes may also have been favourably disposed to Williams as his share of the pew rents of the Colwyn Bay church contributed £100 to his stipend, although this does not appear to have been mentioned in the correspondence until a much later date. Knowing Williams's explosive temper it is hardly surprising that the controversy received substantial press coverage, and eventually became the subject of parliamentary interest, with the result that the House of Commons ordered that the correspondence relating to the creation of the new parish should be printed as a white paper.[14]

Had the bishop absolute power, asked Venables Williams on 4 November 1892, to "carve out" any portion of his parish and assign it to St Paul's without his consent? He understood that the deed which had assigned the patronage to the bishop and his successors, instead of the incumbent of the original parish, would only come into effect upon the next avoidance, that is, allowing him the right of the first nomination. He may have been mistaken here, possibly forgetting that he may have given up his right of appointing the first vicar in return for the understanding already mentioned. The commissioners explained the matter to him as they had done to the bishop earlier, informing the aggravated vicar that while his request that the draft scheme be sent him had been noted, they were not required to obtain his approval to it. On 2 January 1893, in answer to his request for information as to the "status quo" of these arrangements, he was sent in reply a copy of the letter finalising the arrangements addressed to the diocesan registrar, H. A. Cleaver. While Williams desired that the surplice fees should be reserved for him in the eventual deed, he also sent the commissioners on 7 January the following statement by way of explanation:

My Lords and Gentlemen,

I am vicar of Llandrillo-yn-Rhos in the Diocese of St Asaph, in the county of Denbigh. I was appointed by Bishop Short in the year 1868. The population was then about 900, and there were only two services on a Sunday morning and evening (English and Welsh). There was then no such place as Colwyn Bay, which began to grow in 1871, when I commenced an additional service in the afternoon in a carpenter's shed, kindly lent me for the purpose by a Nonconformist parishioner, the late Mr Abel Roberts. This shed being no longer available in 1872, I built, at a cost of £200, what is known as the Mission Room, capable of seating some 230 persons, the first sod was cut on the 20th May. Bishop Hughes opened and preached in it 18th June.

The Mission Room becoming too small in 1880, I erected an iron church, at a cost of £1,200, and capable of seating 530 persons. The late Dean Edwards preached at the opening. This church was insured for £1,350 (including the organ), the whole of which was paid by the Alliance Insurance Company when the church was destroyed by fire, 31st October 1886. I at once took active steps to repair this terrible loss, as church-goers were left, so to say, "houseless". For 18 months or so services were held in the Public Hall close by. The present noble and stately edifice (St Paul's), capable of seating more than 1,000 persons, was built and consecrated in about 20 months from the burning of the iron church, viz, on the 13th July 1888, by Bishop Hughes.

The cost was between £6,000 and £7,000, raised entirely by my own exertions. The site of the church, given by Sir Thomas Erskine, Baronet, was conveyed by him to the Bishop of the diocese and the vicar of the parish (Llandrillo). It was re-conveyed to the Ecclesiastical Commissioners. Previous to the consecration, Bishop Hughes suggested to me the desirability of settling the patronage of the new church, which I consented to,

and signed the deed of settlement of patronage, dated 24th of
May, 1888. I venture to point out that there is nothing on the face
of that deed intimating that by signing it I gave any power
thereby of assigning a district to St Paul's, Colwyn Bay; indeed, I
may say that Bishop Hughes was most anxious, in recognition of
my having built the church, if a district were assigned, that I
should hold the two benefices together, by licence or
dispensation of the Archbishop of Canterbury; this was partially
arranged and only broken off by the sudden illness and
subsequent death of Bishop Hughes. Some two years ago the
present Bishop of St Asaph asked me to go to the palace to
discuss the question of assigning a district to St Paul's, when I
told him that the appointment of a vicar of St Paul's apart from
myself would be like the loss of the apple of my eye. The matter
then dropped, and I heard nothing more about it until the 13th
October 1892.

Venables Williams went on to note the correspondence between
himself and Bishop Edwards. His letter to the bishop of 18th October
1892 assented to the proposal for a new parish, but only on the
understanding that he should be presented to the new incumbency and
hold both livings by licence of the archbishop of Canterbury: "[t]his
was the arrangement agreed to by the late Bishop Hughes, and would
no doubt have been carried out but for his illness." The registrar
wrote stating that the bishop could only reiterate the reply he gave at
a previous interview when Williams had laid down his terms, namely
that he would do what he considered best for the parish.

Further letters followed from Venables Williams, asking if the
bishop would let him know what advantage would accrue to St Paul's
Church by having a district assigned to it. He eventually managed to
see the bishop, after the intervention of his wardens and much
obstruction from Bishop Edwards, and was told by him that "he
would hold his hand with the proceedings, waiting to see what course
I would pursue." This he assumed meant the provision of a Welsh
service in the parish church (which Bishop Hughes had asked him to
transfer to Colwyn Bay), and which had now been provided. He thus
continued:

I therefore was much astonished to receive intimation from the
secretary on the 4th instant, that the assignment of a district to St
Paul's Church has been decided upon and is being carried out.

I earnestly entreat the Ecclesiastical Commissioners and Her Majesty the Queen in Council not to consent to an act which at once would deprive me of an income to the amount of £105 a year.

The population of the parish is now 4,000, and between the two churches (the parish and St Paul's) there are provided every Sunday eight services and a Sunday School; and during the summer months there are two additional services and daily morning prayer.

Throughout the year there is early celebration every Sunday at 8. There are also Wednesday and Friday evening services.

In the year 1891 the congregations at all the services numbered 62,000, while the communicants were 3,500.

During my incumbency I have raised in this parish, for church purposes, something like £17,000. There are no landed proprietors to help me, the largest subscription I received being £150, and only two or three of this amount, so that the above-named £17,000 has been raised by dint of hard and incessant work. I have also had erected in St Paul's Church the finest and largest organ in North Wales at a cost of £1,070, all of which except some £500 ("Building" and "Organ" funds) have been paid off.[15]

By the date of this letter the local controversy had become linked with the proposed Suspensory Bill of the Liberal government. This bill was regarded as a preliminary move towards the disestablishment of the four Welsh dioceses from the Church of England, and by its terms any new incumbent would be prevented from obtaining a vested interest in his new appointment. Venables Williams, known as a supporter of disestablishment, was probably astute enough to see the possibilities of aligning his cause with this, and accordingly he obtained the support of J. Herbert Roberts, MP, the liberal member for Denbigh West. Roberts thus wrote to the Lord President of the Council forwarding a petition from Venables Williams and the statement presented above, together with his own comment:

I may point out to your Lordship that the opposition to the above assignment of district is taken not only because it involved a personal hardship to the present vicar, but also on the broader grounds of principle that such a step, involving as it does the creation of a *new cure* and therefore of a new ecclesiastical vested interest, cannot be justifiable immediately preceding the passing of a Suspensory Bill (announced in the Queen's Speech) to prevent the creation of new vested interests. I trust, therefore, that your Lordship will see your way to deprecate such a step being sanctioned by an Order in Council.

The scene moves to the board room of the Ecclesiastical Commissioners, where during a general meeting held on 9 February the above letter and the statements and appeal of Venables Williams were read out, together with a supporting petition signed by 582 people. Mr Leveson Gower, MP, one of the commissioners appointed by the government, stated that he was authorised on behalf of Her Majesty's government to deprecate, in view of contemplated legislation, the assignment of any new district within the Welsh dioceses. The commissioners thought otherwise, and with the single objection of Leveson Gower, resolved that they did not "feel justified in withholding their sanction to the scheme on the general ground specified by Mr Roberts." Nevertheless they were prepared to consider the objections to the scheme made by the vicar of Llandrillo, and referred the matter to their estates committee.[16]

Leveson Gower's objections caused a considerable storm in the press. *The Times* editorial condemned Leveson Gower for his statements, while the Lord Chancellor was quoted as denying that a church estate commissioner had any right to influence the commissioners in the name of the government. The lord president, Lord Kimberley, was forced to deny that the government was trying to influence an independent body. Lord Salisbury, as the opposition leader in the Lords, protested about the conduct of the government in dealing with the four Welsh dioceses as though the Suspensory Bill had passed into law. The Liberal home secretary, Asquith, speaking in the House of Commons accepted that until the Suspensory Bill had been passed the government had no power or authority to prevent the creation of new ecclesiastical interests in Wales, otherwise than by the votes of those members of the government who acted as Church commissioners.[17]

The matter was regarded as of such importance that the Church Defence League actually issued a penny pamphlet on the subject, *The Government and the Suspensory Bill for Wales: Speech by Lord Salisbury*. It was a lively performance, but a hollow victory for Williams, for Bishop Edwards was not prepared to let the matter rest. The bishop wrote therefore on 13 February denying that Venables

Williams would lose any part of his stipend by such an assignment, and added these words: "I beg leave to say that in the spiritual interests of the whole parish, more especially the Welsh-speaking portion of the parish, it is imperatively necessary that the scheme for the assignment of a district to St Paul's, Colwyn Bay, should be carried out."

A letter of Edwards, dated 22 February and from the Athenaeum Club, offered further reasons why the division should go ahead. The sentence of consecration of the new church mentioned that it was intended that a new district should be assigned to it. Before his predecessor had consented to consecrate the church he had insisted on its patronage being vested in him, and both he and the vicar had agreed upon the plan for the division of the parish. He believed that it was absolutely necessary for the spiritual benefit of the parish for the division to take place, and if the living of Llandrillo was vacant now, he would insist upon this division before a new appointment was made. He continued:

> The population of the parish is about 4,000 (this is the Vicar's estimate). The Welsh-speaking people form two-thirds of that population; the endowment of the parish exists for the benefit of the regular inhabitants. There ought to be two Welsh services on Sunday in the parish church and two at Colwyn Bay, and these services ought to be held at hours convenient to the people. The rural dean stated that when he officially visited the parish on the 17th November 1892 there was no Welsh service at all in the parish church, and frequent and continual complaints have come to me from the parishioners as to the absence of any Welsh service in the parish church and the inadequacy of the services in Welsh at Colwyn Bay, which are given in a small mission room at most inconvenient hours. I called the vicar's attention on several occasions to these facts, and to the complaints which reached me on the subject, but without effect. I must, therefore, put clearly before the Ecclesiastical Commissioners the fact that in this parish, with a population of 4,000 people, two-thirds of whom are Welsh speaking, there are two churches, viz, the old parish church of Llandrillo and the new church of St Paul's, Colwyn Bay, and that there is no Welsh service held in either of these churches. The extremely small number of Welsh communicants and the small number of baptisms and confirmations (both only a third of the average for the rest of the

diocese), the giving up of the day schools, the small attendance at the Sunday schools, and the contribution of only £5 to foreign missions (from a parish where the offertory exceeds £500 a year) these and other facts connected with the parish prove to my mind that the division of the parish determined upon by my predecessor ought to be carried out in the interests of the parish with the least possible delay.

Claiming once more that the stipend of the vicar would not be affected, the bishop also argued that as the commissioners were not being asked to give any further endowment to this district beyond what had been already given (that is the curate's stipend), "[t]here would therefore be no creation of a new or additional vested interest."[18]

The commissioners agreed at their meeting of the 2 March to accept the bishop's recommendation, with Leveson Gower alone dissenting. Gower argued that a revocable and conditional payment, such as a curate's stipend, could not be a life interest, whereas the endowment of a parish would be, and in this he was surely correct.

While this correspondence was taking place, Archdeacon D. R. Thomas was casting doubts about Venables Williams's claim that Bishop Hughes would have instituted him to the new benefice and permitted him to hold it in plurality with Llandrillo. In a letter to the *Standard* Thomas noted that the bishop had been most anxious to establish a new parish at Colwyn Bay, and he [Thomas] had assisted him in the attempt to gain an endowment for it, but he could not believe that the bishop was "anxious" for Venables Williams to be the new incumbent. He concluded: "I am fully convinced that Mr Williams is labouring under a misapprehension in this respect, and that the Bishop is only carrying out his predecessor's intention."

Venables Williams replied to this assertion with interest. His letter to the *Standard* of 1 March was as follows:

> In reply to the letter of my old school fellow, "D. R. Thomas, Archdeacon of Montgomery" (high up according to his statement in the opinion of Bishop Hughes) who casts serious doubts on my veracity, a compliment which I reciprocate with compound interest, I will ask my quondam friend whether he is still willing to say that he "cannot believe on anything short of the clearest documentary evidence that Bishop Hughes was anxious that I should hold the two benefices by licence of the Archbishop of

Canterbury or by any other method"?

If so I am prepared to produce such incontestable "documentary evidence" in the full light of day. I most confidently affirm that I am not "labouring under a misapprehension in that respect", and that I am in the proud position of being able to prove beyond the shadow of a doubt that the present Bishop is not "carrying out his predecessor's intention."

At first Thomas was not convinced, for in a letter to the commissioners of 4 March he indicated that Bishop Hughes had spoken to him several times about the arrangements for Llandrillo. The bishop had been most anxious that while Colwyn Bay should be formed into a separate parish, Venables Williams should not be in charge of it. "There was more than one deputation, too, from the parish that pressed strongly for the same course", he added in confirmation of his assertion. Five days later Thomas wrote another letter to the commissioners. Since that date he had seen some further correspondence which revealed that Bishop Hughes had agreed to the proposed arrangement to allow Venables Williams to hold both benefices, "and it is only right that I should withdraw my letter, though it is quite accurate as to the tenor of these conversations."[19]

Venables Williams was wise to have retained these letters which convinced Archdeacon Thomas of his mistake and possibly of Bishop Hughes's double-dealing. He sent the letters on to the commissioners as well, hoping, no doubt, that they would influence the final decision in his favour. The first letter from Bishop Hughes was dated 21 March 1888. In it he noted his belief that there was a substantial sum available from the local claim to the Llandrillo tithes held by the commissioners, and if this allowed a sufficient stipend, then

> I had no hesitation in acceding to your proposal to institute you to the new benefice. This would be the best and only satisfactory arrangement. As things now stand, it is questionable that it would be an advantage to form a separate parish. Do you think that a fair sum might be collected to offer as a benefaction to the Ecclesiastical Commissioners, which they would meet with a grant, or can you make any other suggestion? The case is urgent, and the bi-lingual difficulty very serious. I believe that the neglect of the Welsh masses by the Church will be the strongest argument for disestablishment in Wales.

By early April the bishop had accepted that the only endowment available was the £120 stipend paid to the curate, though he now suggested that there could be a transfer to Colwyn Bay of the £125 formerly assigned to Llandrillo from the rectorial tithes:

> This would make the endowment £245 [with] Llandrillo being about £300. After the transfer a house would have to be provided, which, judging by the success of your efforts as regards the church, would not be a serious obstacle. I merely mention this as the only chance which occurs to my mind of realising the scheme you at first proposed to me. Failing this, might I hope that if the church is consecrated, and a new district is formed, you will engage a curate for Llandrillo, and another for Colwyn Bay? I am very anxious that there should be a morning and an evening Welsh service at Llandrillo, and another in Colwyn Bay. I believe that the Church in Wales is already among the breakers, and the neglect of the spiritual wants of the masses is the rock on which its greatest danger lies.

A letter of 26 April indicates that Bishop Hughes felt uneasy about forming a new parish with such a small endowment, but on the whole considered it might be better to proceed. The matter of a dispensation was also taken in hand, so enabling Venables Williams to hold together the two livings, and matters got as far as the archbishop's secretary agreeing that there would be no legal impediments to its granting. In his covering letter (which enclosed these letters) Venables Williams concluded by stating that Bishop Hughes's last public act was the consecration of St Paul's Church. Had he not died, he proclaimed, "there can be very little doubt that I should now be vicar of both benefices by dispensation under the Pluralities Act Amendment Act."[20]

An appeal was also made to Archbishop Benson of Canterbury. On 18 February 1893 Venables Williams wrote to him describing the work and labour he had put into building up the new parish, as well as noting the intention of the late bishop to institute him as its first incumbent. Two years before, he wrote, when the matter had first been raised by Bishop Edwards, he had replied that losing Colwyn Bay would be like losing the apple of his eye, but matters had then dropped. More recently the bishop's secretary, rather than the bishop (which he felt was very discourteous) had communicated with him about the bishop's proposals, but his churchwardens had failed to obtain any satisfactory answer to their queries, and when they had exhausted all possible means of conciliation with the bishop he (Williams) had appealed to the government.

In reality Williams was fighting for his bread, as he would find himself in a lamentable position by the loss of an income of £105 per annum which derived from the pew rents of the new church. He could not make ends meet already with the cost of the vicarage and parish and he had informed the bishop that he would be the first victim of disestablishment and disendowment in the Church in Wales. Besides this he was now aged 64, his wife had been in delicate health for a number of years, and his eldest son aged 37 had recently died as rector of a parish in Wiltshire.

The archbishop investigated, or at least his secretaries did so, and the bishop of St Asaph replied. The position of the parish was most unsatisfactory, claimed Edwards. It was too much for one man, and church needs were insufficiently catered for at Llandrillo, especially in relation to the Welsh services. A comment was made by the archbishop that it seemed that Williams's principal objection was about his loss of income. The comment was a little unfair, as Williams had not until this point made it a feature of his case.

This particular correspondence was not printed in the parliamentary report, but one letter from Venables Williams to the archbishop of 7 March *was*. Enclosing the correspondence between himself and Bishop Hughes, he commented that this made abundantly clear that "his intention was to allow me, by your dispensation, to hold the two benefices, Llandrillo and Colwyn Bay." The archbishop, wrote Williams, may have remembered that Bishop Hughes had spoken to him about it, for the archbishop had advised the bishop to communicate with his legal secretary about the matter. He concluded: "Bishop Hughes's intentions, as expressed in these letters, bear the solemn impress of his last Will and Testament, and as such ought to be most religiously and faithfully carried out."[21]

As this correspondence was pursuing its course, Venables Williams received some support from the ecclesiastical press. The *Weekly Churchman and Reunion News* in an editorial on the case stated:

> There is, in the first place, no doubt that in a very large number of cases such sub-division leads to the impoverishment of the clergy. The advantage gained by making two districts, each of which is fairly manageable in respect of size and population, in

place of one which must overtax the powers of any conceivable priest, is too often more than compensated for by the fact that two priests are left in the two districts without means of a reasonable livelihood. Nor is even the advantage we have just mentioned always secured. The incumbent of a new and unworked district of two, or three, or four thousand is certainly no better able to cope with his work than the incumbent of the parish from which the district has been separated was to meet the spiritual needs of a parish with a population of eight, or ten, or twenty thousand – the more especially as in many cases he finds himself in his new district, cut off from the support of the parish church and without a nucleus of workers. Sub-division of a parish only too often tends to clerical impoverishment, while it increases inefficiency ...

The particular circumstances, moreover, of the case of Llandrillo-yn-Rhos, as we have said, show a particular grievance and provide a further argument against the separation by the Commissioners of that part of the parish which is known as Colwyn Bay, and which is in proximity to the Church of S. Paul in that watering-place ... We think that our readers will feel with us that, in the twenty years following his appointment, the Vicar of Llandrillo is open to no charge of neglect as concerns the fabric of the buildings at Colwyn Bay. Other figures show that his efforts were rewarded with success.

After noting the eight Sunday services, the large number of communicants, and the raising of a sum of £20,000 for church purposes during that time, the editor continued: "Making all due allowance for the great influx of visitors in the summer months, we must say that this is a good record and one which entitles Mr. Williams to much consideration." But this was not all, for the editorial went on to speak of Bishop Hughes's efforts to obtain a dispensation for Venables Williams to hold the two benefices in plurality. Having noted that the bishop had made some of the arrangements before he died, the editor continued:

This we take to be a pledge which in any other sphere than the Church would be held to be absolutely binding on the honour of his successor, and if the facts are correct, and unless the Bishop of S. Asaph has some overwhelming weighty matter against Mr. Williams personally, we must regard it as such. The latter, after many years of hard and, it would seem, faithful work finds himself, at an age of not less than 65, in imminent danger of having his income reduced from £325 to £220, "with the entailed cost of maintaining an expensive vicarage", and is, as he says, "fighting for his bread and cheese", and justified, as we think, in taking, with the support of both his churchwardens, the "extreme step of appealing through the present Government, to her Majesty in Council not to consent to an Order which would inflict upon him a flagrant injustice." Nor is it a light grievance that the Vicar of Llandrillo should have wrested from him all the associations which must have gathered around his work at Colwyn Bay, or that Churchmen in that place should unwillingly suffer such a disturbance as is involved in the action of the Commissioners.[22]

The Colwyn Bay *Weekly News* also gave its support to Venables Williams. The bishop had acted in an inhumane way by depriving the poor vicar of all that made life worth living for him. He deserved much better for his years of strenuous effort, and surely, the editor suggested, it would have been better to have let nature take its course, for he was now an elderly man. But, the editor thundered, was this a representative action of the rule of the Church of England in Wales, "that noble institution that the Archbishop of Canterbury came from the steps of the Throne of Augustine to Rhyl to defend"?[23]

Archbishops normally follow the advice of their local suffragans, and so it was in this case. Edwards was not one who was willing to be bound by his predecessor's intentions, many of which he privately despised. In this case, however, he argued that when his predecessor was alive the population of the parish was 1,603, whereas it was now 4,000. "My predecessor pointed out the great necessity at that time for making due provision for the Welsh people of the parish. If the necessity was great then, it is much greater now. My predecessor also pointed out that there should be two curates for the parish. But there is and has been only one, and that curate is paid wholly by the Ecclesiastical Commissioners," Edwards wrote in his letter of 9 March 1893.

All this may have been true, but nothing is noted as to Bishop Hughes's intention to present Venables Williams to the new living. Nevertheless, Edwards' won his case as his episcopal statements were believed, and thus on the 9 March the commissioners wrote to the vicar of Llandrillo and informed him "that after a most careful review of all the circumstances of the case, the Commissioners have come to the conclusion that it is desirable in the interests of the parish of Llandrillo-yn-Rhos that the sub-division should take place." The grant of £120 would be transferred for the endowment of the new parish, though the surplice fees would be reserved to him as long as he held the vicarage of Llandrillo.[24]

The last card had been played and lost, although the sympathy of his parishioners was clearly with Williams. When Bishop Edwards came to preach at Colwyn Bay the members of the choir absented themselves from the service because of his unjust conduct towards their previous vicar.[25]

In his farewell letter to the Colwyn Bay parishioners, dated 25 May 1893, Venables Williams described it as a "final blow" to have to say farewell to them and sever himself from "a very loved portion of my labours in this parish." Hoping he would not be considered egotistical, he wrote that without his labours there would not have been a new parish or even church at Colwyn Bay. When the final certificate had been given by the architect for £700 there had not been a penny in the bank to cover it, and he had to offer his own securities for that amount in order to save the credit of the parish. Now he was required to make way for someone who would reap the benefits of his labours. "I feel," he wrote, "very keenly and bitterly the having to give up my ministrations at St. Paul's. I think that the Division of the Parish need not have been so cruelly and relentlessly carried out (no reasons being assigned) during my life-time." He had intended coming to them on Whitsunday to bid all an affectionate farewell, but his heart was too full to come.[26]

As it may be expected from his previous track record, relationships between Venables Williams and his bishop became extremely strained by this controversy. Williams was not a man to treat fools lightly. An account of his interview with Edwards on 29 November 1892 was later published in the press, although it is true to say that the bishop did not consider it a fair account. It was as follows:

In the course of the conversation, the Bishop said he would hold his hand in the matter, as he had a large tender place in his heart for the Vicar for having built the Church (St Paul's) but charged him with not being *"loyal to the Church."* On the Vicar asking him what he meant, he said, "Oh, you understand, you are sharp enough." The Vicar replied that he might have some amount of sharpness, but not sufficient to understand innuendoes. "Well then," the Bishop asked, "Will you have a Church Defence Meeting in Colwyn Bay?" At once the Vicar said, "Not wise, most impolitic. My motto is *Quieta non movere*, i.e., 'Let sleeping dogs lie.'" Angrily the Bishop remarked, "That is the very policy which caused Cornwallis West to receive only one vote in ten against Herbert Roberts." The Vicar merely said that was a question he could not pretend to discuss, but added that if the Bishop insisted to have [*sic*] a Church Defence meeting in Colwyn Bay, he would consult six, nine, or twelve laymen, and, if they thought it advisable, he would at once acquiesce, whatever his own individual opinions were. There the matter ended, and the Vicar invited the Bishop to give him his reasons for acting so cruelly towards him. The Bishop then said, "That letter of yours, it can't be forgotten." The Vicar replied, "I made the *amende honourable*." "That is impossible," was the hard reply. The Vicar said, "There is a good old proverb, 'Let byegones be byegones', but the best part is to come, and which is not generally known." "What is it?" asked the Bishop. "And fair play for the future," the Vicar replied, "but evidently with you it is not 'Let byegones be byegones' nor 'fair play for the future.'"

The Bishop then urged upon the Vicar that, for his own sake, he should have a sphere of less labour. The Vicar replied, "I hope there is a lot of life in the old dog yet." The Bishop then suggested that the Vicar should present himself to Old Colwyn, which would soon be vacant. The Vicar said, "My Lord, the suggestion is so grossly indecent; I must decline to discuss it."

Venables Williams was patron, as vicar of Llandrillo, of Old Colwyn, but its incumbent, Pryce Jones, had no intention of resigning, and Williams was quite correct about the impropriety (if not the illegality) of appointing oneself to a parish in one's own patronage. The letter which had caused so much offence was an anonymous one, written under a Latin pseudonym, which had appeared in the *Liverpool Courier*. It had suggested that the youthful and former Nonconformist John Owen, who had just been appointed by Edwards as dean of St Asaph, had never been episcopally confirmed. Venables Williams, after a threat of legal action, apologised publicly for writing it, and later suggested that his information had come from Canon Richardson of Corwen, who was bitterly hurt that he had not been appointed himself to that deanery.

****

Venables Williams expressed his bitterness and anger in a number of letters to Edwards, which were also published in the local press. There was anger that Edwards had cancelled one of his most important episcopal functions, namely a confirmation at Colwyn Bay, in order to attend the meeting of the commissioners in London "for the sole purpose of damning and deposing me from my legitimate position as Vicar of Colwyn Bay." There was equal anger that he had not been permitted to put his case to that meeting. It was an "impertinent slander" that Edwards had inferred to a deputation from Colwyn Bay that he, Williams, was spiritually unfit for that living. Yes, he was fit enough for Llandrillo or Old Colwyn, but not for Colwyn Bay!

When he read the parliamentary report on his case Williams's anger knew no bounds. While the bishop was offering him comfortable words that the case had not yet been determined, he had already written to the commissioners asking if he could proceed with the new district without his consent. He had told further lies about the extent of the Welsh population of Colwyn Bay, and had said there was no Welsh service at Llandrillo at a time when he knew that Williams had recommenced these services there. He had written about the complaints he had received about the lack of these services, but at no time had he given him the chance of defending himself against "common informers". Equally, he had claimed that there would be no financial loss and that Williams would lose "not a penny of the endowments", while he was aware that the wardens of Colwyn Bay paid him an annual grant of £105 from the pew rents. Edwards had not only told lies to get his own way, he had also acted privately and secretively behind his back.

If this was true of one parish, it was equally true of the diocese. Williams was giving the first inkling of what would became a major dispute in the diocese some years later, relating to Edwards's use of his extensive patronage. One of the leaders in the subsequent agitation was Archdeacon D. R. Thomas, along with Venables Williams. "The shuffling of the cards in this Diocese during the last four years has been somewhat remarkable," Williams wrote, "and must be exposed, however unpalatable to the occupant of the Episcopal Throne." The bishop had a perfect mania for moving the clergy about, while his distribution of patronage reminded Williams of the children's game of "General Post". Quoting from Edwards's speech to the Manchester Church Congress (some time before he became bishop), Williams noted his claim that a bishop should be the pastor of his clergy, visiting them in their parishes and homes as a brother labourer, and thus removing their feeling of isolation and remedying their lukewarmness. Archbishop Maclagan of York, 23 years older than Edwards (and two years older than Williams) had visited all but two parishes in the archdeaconry of York within a year, but Edwards had done nothing similar. At a clergy meeting at Bala he had had lunch with some young baronet while the clergy had been left alone, dispirited and isolated. "The fact is," he continued, "having been a schoolmaster for 10 years, the Bishop treats his Clergy as so many school-boys, and I, as a rebellious cleric, am now suffering from the weals of the St Asaph Episcopal Birch-rod!!"[27]

The bitterness remained. During the spring of 1894 the evangelical weekly, The *Record*, published letters from a substantial number of Welsh incumbents in response to a request for information as to the probable consequences of disestablishment in their parishes. Venables Williams responded in this way:

> Having been myself disestablished and disendowed by the Bishop of St Asaph, the so-called champion of Church Defence, I am myself a determined advocate of Disestablishment and Disendowment. *Fiat justitia ruat Ecclesia.*

Three weeks later a letter from his pen appeared in the same paper. He took exception to some comments made about his statement, namely that it was too personal to be acceptable. Williams wrote that he had believed for many years that disestablishment was in the interests of the Church itself, and for holding these views he had been personally charged in December 1892 with not being loyal to the Church. As justification for that statement the bishop had said he had refused to have a Church defence meeting at Colwyn Bay. As a result the bishop had disestablished him in his own parish, making representations to the Ecclesiastical Commissioners which in an ordinary court of law would have carried no weight whatsoever.[28]

The same allegation was repeated in letters to the commissioners during 1895, when he queried the boundaries of the new parish, stating, correctly, that the commissioners had not followed the boundaries agreed to by himself and Bishop Hughes. They argued that they had been unable to find these particular boundaries on the ordnance survey maps, and in any case they had sent him the copy of the scheme which he had acknowledged. His reply, of 1 February 1895, indicated that he had acknowledged the receipt of the scheme believing, in the absence of any contradictory notice, that it was the same scheme as had been agreed. He believed, however, that the boundaries had been altered by the "whims and caprices" and "the back-stairs influence" of his bishop who had no wish to see the School Board included in his parish. "Let him deny it if he can," he concluded. The circumstances of the school board are not known, though it may have been an allusion to the long controversy between church and state education.

****

In conclusion, we need to make some evaluation of this controversy, and note some of its results.

Venables Williams was certainly a man to speak his mind. His refusal to give in to the demand of his tithe payers for a 25 per cent rebate, during the tithe wars, was so strongly worded that he received an anonymous letter threatening to blow up his vicarage.[29] His action with regard to Dean Owen was impulsive and silly. The reply he gave to Archdeacon D. R. Thomas, noted earlier, was hardly diplomatic. He was one of the leaders of the opposition to the appointment by Bishop Hughes of the south-Walian David Howell as vicar of Wrexham in 1875, claiming it was not "sour grapes" on his part as he had told the bishop he had no wish to leave Llandrillo. W. Walsham How, later the first bishop of Wakefield, and then an incumbent in the diocese of St Asaph, took the bishop's part and heavily criticised these "memorialists". Venables Williams was scathing in his condemnation of How. It was very amusing, he wrote, to find a man taking "such a high view of the duty of waiting until an offer of preferment comes, when he is himself holding the richest living in the diocese, purchased with gold!" Rather, Walsham How should be more ashamed of retaining a living which his father had purchased for him than condemning "his brethren who have the honesty and courage to speak out against an act of the bishop that is universally condemned by both laity and clergy." He also poured scorn on the poor curate of Abergele who asked his name to be withdrawn from the list of objectors, hoping, said Venables Williams, to be promoted to a better curacy.[30] During 1897, when a "Memorial" was presented to Bishop Edwards against his patronage policy, signed by a considerable number of his clergy, the bishop regarded Venables Williams as one of its instigators. During this controversy the bishop unwisely referred to Williams's previous comments about Dean Owen, and his retraction of them. Williams thus replied in characteristic style:

> My Lord, – I am really thankful to you for giving me, in your speech at a well-whipped-up and carefully packed meeting of the "faithful laity" and the sycophants of the diocese, a longed-for opportunity of defending myself against your most unworthy attack upon me. I wish to inform you of that which should long ere this have been patent to you, that my reason for making what you are pleased to call an apology was that my information was not first hand, my part in the affair being "circulating" or "publishing" a statement made to me in the presence of witnesses, at my own table, concerning a person whom I did not know, and at that time had never even seen. I may tell you I have never ceased to regret having signed that apology, to which you so jauntily refer: far better for me to have faced an action at law for the so-called libel. If I had had "the ablest lawyer" in London at my elbow, he would have advised me to do what I did. I gave you the names of those who were my informants, both of whom, instead of either prosecuting or persecuting for the alleged libel, you promoted to archdeaconries. Could I have foreseen the unwarrantable and most inexcusable use you are now making of the vaunted apology, I would not have made it, in the face of the fact that I was not the originator of the so-called libel. You are quite at liberty – indeed I invite you – to publish this letter. You descended, in your infuriated speech, to personalities with the highly characteristic schoolmaster's birchrod in hand. We, the memorialists, studiously avoided personalities; we are quite satisfied with our gentlemanly behaviour. I can only hope that you now, after a little calm reflection, can look back without any misgivings to your bitter but most unbecoming episcopal invectives of Thursday last.[31]

The diplomacy which wins friends and gains battles was not in the make-up of Venables Williams. In this he was his own worst enemy.

His track record as the vicar of a growing parish was impressive. The *Weekly Churchman* was fair and objective in its comments about his pastoral ministry. He had built up a new district and run a successful parish. But the hint is given time and time again that his primary parochial concern was more for the occasional holiday makers than the resident Welsh people of the parish. It may be that he was a typical man of his age who had little time for the Welsh language. His actions certainly suggest this may have been the case. In 1894, for example, his bishop served a monition on him that he should hold a Welsh service and sermon every Sunday at the parish church at Llandrillo.[32] For Venables Williams the future of Wales lay with the English language. Such an attitude was bound to cause conflict with his diocesan bishops, especially at a time when the Church's failure to promote the Welsh language in the past had prompted the taunt that it was an alien Church.

We may note, too, he was a rebel. Or, perhaps, more fairly, he was prepared to take on causes which were unpopular. Was this because he was a bishop-baiter, or because he felt that bishops were not above the law? His involvement in the appointment to Wrexham, and in the disputes with Bishop Edwards over his patronage during the 1890s, and his preference for disestablishment, all stood against him in the eyes of his bishops. With Bishop Edwards he was a marked man, for Edwards had made his aggressive anti-disestablishment policy a test of loyalty to the Church, and failed to understand that some clergymen had an honest conviction that a Church freed from state restraints could be a growing and vigorous body. Those who opposed Edwards's policy on disestablishment felt the weight of his episcopal power, as did David Howell, D. R. Thomas, and many others. Venables Williams's comments about Edwards's bias against him may have been exaggerated, but at least there was some foundation in fact for them. His willingness to help Nonconformists in his parish, as, for example, by allowing the local English Congregational Church to meet in a room at Rhos Abbey Hotel until they built their own church, or laying a foundation stone of St John's English Methodist Church, would not have been found pleasing by Edwards either.[33]

Edwards came into the diocese sweeping with a new broom. Bishop Hughes too often had taken a charitable view of a particular situation, as he probably did in allowing Venables Williams's wish to remain incumbent of both parishes. But Edwards could see, as the vicar of the parish could not, that change was necessary. No one man could do justice to two such parishes. We have hinted already that Venables Williams had probably concentrated his energies on serving the wealthy holiday makers rather than the indigenous and not-too-rich Welsh-speaking inhabitants, but the hint is also given that he was too parsimonious to employ an additional curate. The responsibility for finding the stipend of £120 per annum was that of the incumbent, and it may be that Venables Williams, unable to manage on his existing income, either felt unable to go to the additional expense of funding this stipend, or was unwilling to press his parishioners into more money raising. It has always been a familiar situation. But that he failed to obtain the services of an additional curate was clearly held against him by his bishop.

If the archbishop was a little unfair when he suggested that Venables Williams's main concern was the loss of part of his income, Edwards was equally misleading when he claimed that he would lose nothing financially by this division. Certainly Venables Williams's financial assertiveness comes out strongly in his appeals, but there was also the feeling of pastoral attachment as well. The loss came from the pew rents of St Paul's, which secured him an estimated £105 per annum. We may be charitable and suggest that Venables Williams was in financial difficulties. There are two indications of this, namely the state of the vicarage when he died and the charges he imposed for the right to erect monuments in the churchyard.

Williams's successor, Enoch James Evans, discovered that the vicarage was in a state of absolute decay. The building had been built in 1762, alongside the church, and when he came into the parish Venables Williams had had to take out a private mortgage of £264 from Sir John Morris of Elmsdale near Wolverhampton in order to add a dining room and an additional bedroom.[34] After his death Venables Williams's estate was assessed at £191 for dilapidations on this building. At first his executor, his wife, Alice Venables Williams, then living at Swallowbeck, Lincoln, claimed that his estate was tied up with private trusts and there would be a great delay before a settlement could be made. But before long it was clear that he had died hopelessly insolvent, and in addition to these dilapidations there was an outstanding balance of £98 from the offertories and £40 collected towards the building of a mission room unaccounted for and accepted as claims against his estate. The money was not forthcoming, and Queen Anne's Bounty was unable to assist Williams's successor with a grant to meet these dilapidation costs (a standard procedure under such circumstances), as the income of the parish was over £200. In 1909 Evans was astonished to receive £107 of this dilapidation money from Williams's executors, which appears to have been tied up in chancery, and resolved to use it to rebuild the outhouses. He was not too amused when the diocesan registrar and the bishop's secretary now claimed from him their expenses for the original survey of the property and their subsequent work, amounting to £13 in all, especially as he had had to meet the surveyor's claims previously under threat of legal proceedings.[35]

The vicarage was rebuilt, and in the papers of the commission investigating Evans's application for a grant it was remarked that the surplice fees of £150 for the previous year were quite exceptional. This was because the new incumbent had lowered the fee for erecting monuments in the churchyard and many had taken advantage of this in order to put up gravestones. Nevertheless that return indicated that the income of Llandrillo was not inconsiderable. Although the tithe-rent-charge had sunk considerably in value, being £193 as against a commuted value of £370, the letting of the glebe, an income of £69 from the redeemed tithe, and £36 in pew rents, procured a gross income of £415 and (after expenses and the £80 rent of a temporary vicarage while the new one was being built) a net income of £297.

The *Weekly Churchman* made the point that a new district could often be underfunded and subject to considerable difficulties with the loss of support from the parish church. That the latter did not happen is a tribute to Venables Williams, but the former was certainly true. The new vicar, Canon Hugh Roberts, who paid tribute to the work of his predecessor at his first service (possibly a diplomatic move as well for his son, Dr Montagu Williams, was his organist),[36] had letterheads printed which had pictures of the church as it was and as it would be when fully completed, together with the statements that the only endowment was the £120 granted by the Ecclesiastical Commissioners (which had been transferred from Llandrillo), and that the church needed £14 per week to meet expenses. It appears that he had ended the system of pew rents. Two curates had to be employed at a time when grants for their stipends were unavailable, and there was no vicarage. Instead the congregation assisted him with the rent of a house at £80 per annum. Though he had Easter offerings of £41, the fees were reserved for the incumbent of the mother church. Eventually, through hard work, the church was completed, a new vicarage built, and a Welsh church and hall erected as well. A new parish undoubtedly released new energies and offered new opportunities for leadership, but there had been much financial difficulty along the way. But this work could never have been accomplished while Colwyn Bay was still part of the parish of Llandrillo, and as such it more than justified the bishops' desire to make it a separate parish.

And thus a new parish was formed. But the insensitive way it had been done left a nasty sting in the minds of many. It was not an auspicious start, and it almost appears that one result of it was that Venables Williams regarded his parish thereafter as a pre-retirement post and lost all interest in it. Nevertheless, the local papers spoke of him in high tones as a widely known, efficient parish priest, a man of wide sympathies, and as one who had acted for many years in a public capacity as chairman of both the Colwyn Bay and Abergele petty sessional benches and also the Conway Board of Guardians. It may have been significant that in order to bury him in Llandrillo Churchyard his grave had to be blasted out of the rock.[37] That at least formed an apt if symbolic illustration of his life.

ENDNOTES

1 The papers of the Ecclesiastical Commission for the parishes of Llandrillo and Colwyn Bay, used here, are in the custody of the Representative Body of the Church in Wales.

2 D. R. Thomas, *History of the Diocese of St Asaph* (2nd edn., Oswestry, 1913), III 210.

3 Archdeacon Jennings, a former pupil of Ystradmeurig School, became archdeacon of Westminster and an influential figure in the church of his day.

4 NLW, Church in Wales records, SA/DR/51, fol. 123, and SA/DR/46, fol. 373. It is stated that this correspondence was printed as a pamphlet by Venables Williams.

5 *Byegones*, 20 April 1887, p. 293; *Report into Tithe Rentcharge in Wales* (London, 1887), pp. 121-2. It was falsely claimed during this enquiry that there were no Welsh services in the parish, which Venables Williams was able to show was totally untrue. He had conducted a Welsh service every Sunday since his induction.

6 Thomas, *St Asaph*, III 202.

7 *Report into Tithe Rentcharge in Wales*, p. 121.

8 *Copy of the Correspondence relating to the creation of a New Benefice in the Parish of Llandrillo-yn-Rhos (Colwyn Bay), Denbighshire, and of the Minutes of Proceedings of the Ecclesiastical Commissioners relating thereto*, 17 April 1893, p. 3.

9 There is a printed appeal in SA/DR/50, fol. 256, which is endorsed by Bishop Hughes with the words, "I strongly recommend this appeal".

10 Osborne Morgan, son of a vicar of Conway, was liberal MP for East Denbighshire, and a leading campaigner for disestablishment, although a churchman. He used his "inside" knowledge of the Church to considerable effect in his attacks on the Church establishment.

11 The letter is in the EC files, and not included in the published correspondence.
12 *Correspondence*, p. 5.
13 Ibid.. p. 5.
14 For the full title see reference 8 above.
15 *Correspondence*, p. 15-16.
16 Ibid., pp. 17-19.
17 *Times*, 17 February 1893; *Morning Post*, 16 February 1893, both in the EC files.
18 *Correspondence*, pp. 20-1.
19 Ibid., pp. 22, 24, 27. The letter from the *Standard* is pasted into the records of the Ecclesiastical Commission for this parish.
20 *Correspondence*, pp. 24-6.
21 *Correspondence*, p. 26; Lambeth Palace Library, Benson papers 120, fols. 119, 121, 128.
22 *Weekly Churchman*, 25 February 1893, p. 99.
23 *Colwyn Bay Weekly News*, 8 June 1893 in SA/DR/54, fol. 428.
24 *Correspondence*, pp. 26-7.
25 *News of the Week*, 19 August 1893, p. 9.
26 The letter is printed in Norman Tucker, *Colwyn Bay: Its Origin and Growth* (Colwyn Bay, 1953), p 182.
27 SA/DR/54, fols. 428-35. This includes the cutting from the *Colwyn Bay Weekly News* of 8 June 1893.
28 *Record*, 2 March 1894, p. 201, and 22 March 1894, p. 281.
29 Instead he offered a ten per cent rebate to those in distress. See SA/DR/46, fols. 528 and 722; and *Report on Tithe Rentcharge*, p. 121. The subsequent tithe disturbances at Mochdre in his parish were caused by the refusal of the Ecclesiastical Commissioners to reduce the tithe rent charge by 25 per cent. Venables Williams was an innocent victim of the commissioners' policy: see Ivor Wynne Jones, *Colwyn Bay, a Brief History* (Clwyd, 1995), pp. 88-90.
30 *Wrexham Guardian*, 13 March 1875, p. 7, and *Wrexham Advertiser*, 3 April 1875.
31 *Carnarvon and Denbigh Herald*, 21 January 1898, p. 6, and see also regarding the 1897 rebellion, George Lerry, *Alfred George Edwards* (Oswestry, 1939), pp. 57-76.
32 *Record*, 16 February 1894, p. 164.
33 *Colwyn Bay English Congregational Church, 1882-1932* (1932), p. 10; Dilys Thomas, *Memories of Old Colwyn* (Wrexham, 2000), p. 151. She notes he had given up his National School in favour of the Board School.
34 SA/LET/396, a letter of Venables Williams to Bishop Short of St Asaph, 2 April 1869, pointing out the need for an extension to the vicarage with its two reception rooms and four bedrooms, and noting his hope of a mortgage from the Bounty governors.
35 The new vicar described the vicarage house as old, small and low, with the bedrooms only seven feet high, and the servants' bedroom in an attic

difficult of approach; the water from the churchyard alongside ran into its foundations, making it also miserable and unsanitary. A growing neighbourhood demanded a vicarage of good appearance, he wrote to the Ecclesiastical Commissioners, appealing for financial assistance. The necessity of building a parochial room and establishing new schools meant that he could not raise sufficient money in the parish, and the subsequent loss of the dilapidation money had caused even more anxiety. Sir Edward Langley gave a site, next to the existing house, and the commissioners allowed the sale of the glebe field for £1,200, while a loan of £1,000 was obtained from Queen Anne's Bounty. Nevertheless the architect, Douglas Marshall of Chester, had to scale down the plans to fit the funds available. Although the bishop wrote to the commissioners, appealing for funding under a "local claim", stating that the vicar was beset with great financial difficulties in the parish, they had to report that all such monies had been long extinguished. Its final cost was £2,210.

36 *Record*, 23 June 1893, pp. 616-7.

37 *Bye-Gones*, 14 November 1900, p. 496: *Colwyn Bay Weekly News*, 8 June 1893. Venables Williams described the work he had done in his parish in his book *Llandrillo yr Rhos* (reprinted, 1993), pp. 43-4. He also gave good service to his community. By requiring the London and North Western Railway to pay the full rates in 1871, increasing their value from £125 a mile to £950 per annum, Venables Williams considerably improved the fortunes of Colwyn Bay. As a result the local rates were reduced by over 50 per cent: Jones, *Colwyn Bay*, p. 10. Williams also built a road from Llanrhos Road to Llandrillo Road, no doubt of benefit to himself but of equal value to the community. To offset its costs he established a toll gate: A H Stamp, *Penrhyn Bay* (Conwy, 1996), pp. 102, 556.

LLANVAPLEY CHURCH
in the early 1900s

10
MR TOWNSHEND AT LLANVAPLEY

TOWNSHEND, Rev. Edward Mansel, M.A. (Cantab.); *R.* Llanvapley, Abergavenny, from 1898; *b.* Feb. 3, 1860, at Bath; Ordained 1889; chiefly known for his fearless activity in getting things done that everyone else thought hopeless and impossible; helped to found the Clare College Camb. Musical Society, 1882; was College Sec. to C.M.S.; won a cup in Lent Trial Eights, 1883, and wrote the first Univ. letter to C.M.S.; founded a Y.M.C.A. with hall at Tewkesbury; preached before Archbishop Magee at Avranches, and gave 30 addresses a week for two-and-a-half years to some 10,000 East-End folk, during which he re-organised the London Clerical and Lay Unions, preparing way for National Church League, and was first Vice-President, Prot. Defence Brigade. By a resolution on General Committee (against Board of Missioners' proposals), saved £90,000 for C.M.S., and soon afterwards exposed the grotesque school history manual of a Cabinet Minister, and laid Mr Gladstone's late Home Rule Government in the dust in the *Times*, for the neglect which blew up all their Army and Navy's cordite; met Archbishop Benson, and extracted from him a pastoral against Ritualism; invited, 1896, to meet Lord Salisbury and his Cabinet while still a Curate; prepared the outline of the Church Discipline Bill, and launched it on an astonished House of Commons in 1898; historic debates followed. For 11 years was engaged in the repair of his Church and Rectory, in memory of Dean Williams, but contrived to get published the 6th Book of Hooker on "Confession"; sent great Petitions to Parliament on King's Declaration; supplied a Reformation Programme for the Church Pageant; produced expositions of Ornaments Rubric, endorsed by Archdeacon Sinclair and Sir Ed. Clarke, K.C., and was thanked by Chairman of Royal Commission on Disorders, for letter to Archbishop of Canterbury, and by Church Association for Address to the Speaker; during the war, invented a Tank, pressing it, and armour protection (personal and battleship), and Irish Industries, with effect; finally proposing in the Press two years before Armistice, a great National Thankoffering of 200 millions for Christian Work for raising Ministers' stipends to "a living wage" in all denominations.[1]

Thus reads the entry for Edward Mansel Townshend in the 1920 edition of *Who's Who in Wales*. Clearly, he was a man of some ingenuity who was not prepared to be modest about his achievements. And yet he remained as rector of Llanvapley until his death in 1947.

There was no further preferment within the Church he served, and no recognition by the State.

****

The induction of Edward Mansel Townshend to the Gwent parish of Llanvapley took place in 1898, and was conducted by the rural dean, A. J. Hogan, rector of Llantilio Pertholey. Townshend had been previously instituted by the bishop of Llandaff at his palace. He wrote in his memoir of this induction:

> It was a Homely function, with the little group of rustic Villagers. He made me unlock the big Door - the Key turning the wrong way, and then lock myself in, and Ring the Church Bell, come back and unlock the Door and invite the people to enter.
>
> This, and the conduct of a short Service and Sermon, formed what was then known as an Induction Service.
>
> In those days, other Clergy were not invited, Mr Pinney alone being present, nor was there, as now, any general Entertainment and Tea.[2]

The family had arrived at Llanvapley in an ancient four-wheeled fly, which had been almost upset by the bad ruts in the lane leading to the rectory. Townshend was to remain as rector of this small parish until his death at the age of 87 in January 1947.

Born in 1860, a direct descendant of Colonel Richard Townsend[3] of Castle Townshend, Co. Cork, and a relation of General Townshend of Kut, of First World War fame, Townshend was educated at Clare College and Ridley Hall, Cambridge. Ordained in 1886, he had served a first curacy at Tewkesbury, a chaplaincy at Avranches, followed by curacies at Stepney Causeway (where he was chaplain to Dr Barnardo's Homes), Spitalfields, Waltham Abbey, Harrogate, and Reading. In 1898 he was preferred to Llanvapley by the then patron, the marquess of Abergavenny, who was (wrote Townshend) a pronounced "Protestant" and vice-chairman of the Church Association.

His appointment to the parish came about in this way. A letter Townshend had written to the bishop of Gloucester had been drawn to the marquess's attention by his cousin, Sir William Harcourt, with the suggestion that the writer should be offered some kind of preferment. Although Townshend does not mention the subject of this letter, which was probably published in a newspaper, it might well have concerned the Church Discipline Bill. Townshend claimed he had successfully drawn the proposals for this bill to the notice of the House of Commons, while his other "protestant" work had included exposing some incautious developments within the Church Missionary Society, and helping to form a National Church League and the Protestant Truth Society.[4] In addition Townshend's cousin, the Revd John Hume Townsend, who was vicar of St Mark's, Broadwater Down, Tunbridge Wells, was friendly with the marquess, and had put in a good word for him.

As a result of these moves an interview took place with the marquess, during which Townshend was told that he would be expected to retain a man at the rectory and keep a horse-trap, even though the stipend was not particularly good. This man had been employed by the previous rector, and functioned as rectory gardener, farm labourer and coachman, bell ringer, sexton, gravedigger and the carer of the church stove. Gilbert Harris, the marquess's chief agent, drove Townshend by trap to inspect Llanvapley, where he found the church was small and "we barely looked at it". There were no schools, for which he had little regret, writing: "I was glad to be saved from what is always a heavy responsibility and worry". The rectory, he discovered, was most attractive but in a sad state of disrepair.

The parish he entered as rector was as small in income as it was in population. In 1832 the then rector, Thomas Williams, later archdeacon and dean of Llandaff, returned in a parliamentary enquiry that he served a population of 109 people, all of whom, and 11 more, could be seated in the church. There was one service on Sunday which alternated between morning and evening, which seems rather strange as Williams had no other parochial cure, unless he helped out at a neighbouring parish as an unlicensed curate. But there was an evening service with sermon on Fridays. He reported that he had just rebuilt the glebe house or rectory, for which he had taken a mortgage out from Queen Anne's Bounty of £466 at an interest rate of three and a half per cent. His average income was £231, and this came from the rent of the glebe lands (some of which he retained in his own possession, keeping a smallholding and land for pasturing his horse), the tithe rental charge of £141 5.s, and the surplice fees of two to three shillings each year. There were no Easter offerings.

Another parliamentary return completed by Williams's successor and Townshend's predecessor, John Lloyd, in 1887, noted that he let 54 acres of glebe land for a sum of £101 15 s, keeping four and a half acres for his own use and one acre for gardens. The tithe rent charge, now commuted at £160, brought in £157 in 1884 and £145 in 1886 – it was a time of considerable agricultural depression. The rectory house was valued at £40 per annum. Outgoings including tax and rates on the tithe, the poor rate and the collection of the tithe by a solicitor, amounted to just over £30. With no further sources of income but rent and tithe Lloyd returned his income as £216 per annum. Two years previously it had been £236, a drop of just under ten per cent.

On his arrival in the parish Townshend was informed that his stipend was £180. This he considered to be a great improvement over his curacy, the stipend of which was only £150 per annum. At first he feared that his predecessor might take one third of that sum as a pension for his retirement as he was entitled to do so. He did not do so, however, but nevertheless Lloyd threatened to take this pension if Townshend made any difficulties over the dilapidation charges on the rectory house. These charges were for putting the house into good order for a new incumbent, and were the responsibility of the outgoing rector. This threat annoyed Townshend considerably, for John Lloyd was a wealthy man who could afford to keep a carriage and pair, as well as men-servants, while his brother was chairman of the local quarter sessions. "Such meanness seems incredible towards a humble curate of such limited means," he wrote later, with "a young wife and family of four to provide for".

Luckily Townshend was able to use the interest from a legacy of £1,000 which had been left him for a number of costly items he was forced to purchase, as well as for the cost of work required on the rectory house. A secondhand dogcart cost £20, a secondhand Princess pony phaeton with a back seat and dark green morocco cushions cost a further £40, while a coal cart cost £12 (for the coals had to be collected from Abergavenny). Townshend also had to purchase a horse for £23 which his man trained. These carriages and the employment of a manservant, he wrote in his memoirs, meant he could order out the dogcart or the pony carriage at any hour of the day, and be sure "of punctual appearance and perfect attention". Another £15 paid for the cost of removal and the purchase of some items of furniture. Townshend rejoiced that he was able to manage such purchases without having to use the capital of that legacy, whose interest enabled him to pay his man's wages of 18s. a week and an additional 10s. for his wife who did the washing of the family. So anxious was she to secure this post that she offered to come at sixpence a day in order to exclude competitors.

****

As we will note time and time again, Townshend's limited private means were never sufficient to offset the small income of his living. The Ecclesiastical Commissioners disliked assisting parishes in private patronage, and always required a benefaction of equal value to any grant it might offer such a parish. Besides, their remit was populous parishes, and Llanvapley could hardly be placed in that category. In addition, by the 1900s the commissioners were not in favour of endowing small livings, feeling that they should be united to form larger benefices and so provide a decent stipend with their combined incomes. The other main source of ecclesiastical funding, Queen Anne's Bounty, was unable by its rules to offer grants to parishes with incomes over the sum of £200. However, Townshend managed to obtain a small grant from Queen Anne's Bounty of £100 in return for an augmentation of the same amount, which he was able to find through a legacy received on his mother's death. It added £9 to his income. He argued at that time that as he intended to remain in his parish for his lifetime it was better to use the legacy in this way, even if he only had a life interest in it, than to invest it and pass it on to others after his days.

During 1918 a valuation was made of the living. This was a particularly good year in one sense as the First World War had brought about agricultural prosperity, so those clergy whose income depended in part on the tithe or on agricultural rents benefited correspondingly. On the other hand inflation was high. In that year Townshend's income was returned at £102 for land let out, and £160 for the tithe rent charge, a considerable increase over the rates which prevailed in the 1880s. On the other hand outgoings were equally high. Rates and taxes on the glebe lands and tithe income cost £40, the collection of the tithe by an agent cost another £20 (although Townshend may well have put this in as a charge for his own services in order to reduce the gross income of the benefice), 18s.6d was paid for insurance, and as rector he had to pay an average of £10 per annum towards the chancel repairs for which he was responsible. This brought his income down to £196 per annum. Nevertheless from this Townshend had to pay £82 for the wages of a man, the upkeep of a horse and the maintenance of the grounds of the rectory. His man, he explained later, was no luxury, for his task was to cultivate a garden of vegetables and fruit, look after a cow and a number of pigs, "the produce on which my very large household of eleven persons (three at school) *very largely* exist, and supplemented by gifts of clothing from a society." Was this special pleading on Townshend's part, or an indication that his private resources had been exhausted?

Queen Anne's Bounty required the rector of Llanvapley to pay one guinea each year as his "tenths". Although the sum claimed was not substantial, being based on a 1535 valuation, it was still an annual imposition on poor incumbents, and the governors of the Bounty had the power to make a grant to cover this payment for poor benefices. Townshend applied for such a grant in 1904. Claiming in his application that his gross income was £206 but the net income £174 (he had deducted repairs to the rectory at £25 as well as other items) Townshend argued that he had to pay out of this smaller sum £40 per annum for a life insurance policy, £10 in various annual subscriptions incumbent upon him as rector of the parish, and interest of £4 19s.6d. on a loan of £180 he had taken out for repairs to the rectory. The grant was allowed, but was withdrawn in 1918 due to the considerable increase in the tithe rent charge of those years. The grant had come as a great blessing in 1904, however, for it was a struggle "to maintain and rear respectably a family of six to eight children" on a pittance of less than £200, and its granting had put an end to the many anxieties he had suffered in case it was not allowed. Townshend went on to suggest that the governors should offer 50 grants of £50 each year to rural parishes whose clergy "isolated and unknown" found it difficult to obtain an augmentation which they could offer for a grant, whereas large town livings with substantial populations found that task comparatively easy and as a result obtained the majority of the grants available each year.

In late 1918 a piece of good fortune came Townshend's way. Lord Llangattock, who had died in 1912 – he was the father of C. S. Rolls of Rolls-Royce fame – had bequeathed a sum of money to the diocese of Llandaff in order to assist poor parishes. Townshend was later to claim in a letter to the commissioners of 31 July 1919 that he had played no small part in initiating the original bequest. In 1918 the bishop of Llandaff indicated that he would offer £500 from this fund for the augmentation of the living of Llanvapley, and expressed the hope that the commissioners might respond to this benefaction by providing an equal grant. This was immediately after the end of the War and nine months before the date of disestablishment, so there was a great rush of applications from Welsh parishes to both the

Ecclesiastical Commission and Queen Anne's Bounty for assistance before time ran out, for after disestablishment neither body would be able to assist the Church in Wales. Townshend's application joined a long list of potential grantees.

The bishop's kindness to Llanvapley came about because of the failure of a proposed plan which would have given Townshend a substantial increase in his income. A local incumbent had accepted a war chaplaincy. All had been arranged for Townshend to take over his parish, presumably in plurality with his own, adding another £100 to his stipend. But the plans fell through as this clergyman came back after a month and resumed duty, and as his resignation had not been filed there was nothing to prevent him doing so. But on the expectation of that increased income Townshend had sent two of his younger children to good boarding schools at Monkton Combe and Weston. His appeal to his bishop for assistance in these trying circumstances was met by the offer of this benefaction.

The bishop's offer came, as he wrote to the commissioners, at an opportune time. He was £300 overdrawn, with a heavy doctor's bill to pay of £38, and as much "in other directions to pay off"; he had a large rectory and family to provide for, while his wife had been invalided "more or less by war effort". He begged them to make a grant to him in return for this benefaction from the bishop. This was written on 16 July 1919. He repeated the same request on the 31st, when he pointed out that such a grant, together with the augmentation, would raise his income by an additional £40 to £50 per year. Another list of woes was now added to augment his appeal. His son had been invalided home from Mesopotamia the previous year after three and a half years of service, and had to go to the seaside, and he, that is his father, had to pay these additional and unexpected bills.

Townshend's letters of request continued. He had three boys away at school, and they were now at home on holiday (an expensive time), while their sisters were working for the war effort. In the previous autumn, his eldest son, an engineer on £400 per year working on a project putting up a rest camp for 10,000 American soldiers in Liverpool, had had to work all hours on it without even a Sunday free, and was now at home with a nervous breakdown. Townshend had had to find £15 for his medical expenses, for the company he worked for still owed him money. The war grant he had received from the commissioners had gone on these school and medical fees, and he was now overdrawn to the sum of £344, so there was no possibility of a family holiday. His need for money was so desperate that he even asked if the interest on the £500 held by the commissioners from the benefaction could be allowed him, as that would help him to keep going.

The commissioners regretfully pointed out that the bequest had only just been transferred, and in any case they did not allow the interest on such sums to be returned. More hopefully, his grant was gazetted on 11 August 1919 and it included a return grant from the commissioners. The benefaction would produce a sum of £20 per annum, which would be paid quarterly, but the commissioners' grant of £26 per annum would be paid half yearly. And thus Townshend's total income became £309 less £72 in allowable expenses, or £237 net.

In 1920 there was better news. A benefaction from the same source, the Llangattock bequest, was given. It was for £1,000. There is some uncertainty whether this received a grant from the commissioners, for the date of disestablishment had passed before the benefaction was finalised.

The news came at a time when Townshend was querying an income tax deduction, and was anxious about the continuation of his war bonus grant. This was a grant given to clergy, whose income was under £350 and whose tithe-rent-charge was under £150, in order to meet the increasing prices caused by the war. Townshend had received £40 in the previous year (1919), but with disestablishment on the near horizon there were doubts if the scheme would continue for the Welsh clergy. Nevertheless he felt he had a strong claim to its continuance for himself as it was of vital importance to his financial stability. His boys' school fees were "closely and directly dependent on it". Some weeks later he wrote in despair, having discovered that the Welsh Church was not going to pay these grants. As a result he was "in a very great hole". True, his income was on the borderline for the grant, but he had been given the benefit of the doubt because he had a large family, a very small income and three children at school. As a result of this grant he had just been able to pull through. Had he applied for this grant in 1918, when it was first given, he would probably have received it. Might the commissioners now credit him with this grant as an oversight? He felt he had some claim on this fund, adding, "perhaps I may be allowed to say something?"

This "something" was his claim that in 1916 he had started a movement for clerical relief whose aim was to have all income "levelled up" to £400 per year. The kind sympathy of the archbishop of Canterbury, the bishop of London and *The Times* had been obtained, and that paper had agreed to co-operate. When the Armistice came he had prepared a letter which he had the privilege of sending to the king. His letter had "evoked a most kind reply". This matter was presented by the king to the prime minister in a letter which "presented the clergyman's need in some striking phrases and was accompanied by a most earnest letter from Bishop Boyd Carpenter." The eventual result of all this activity was the war bonus scheme. Such was his involvement. But, Townshend wrote, "it seems a little hard that the neighbourhood whence its effect commenced should be the one to be first deprived of the Bonus at a very critical moment ... and that the man who I believe worked harder at it than any other man in Wales, should be reduced to great straits in consequence."

If Townshend felt sure he would receive their "kindly sympathy", he also threatened to start a newspaper campaign in the *Western Mail* to have these grants restored for Wales. It was to no avail. The commissioners wrote in reply that they had no power to make grants, retrospective or not, to benefices in England or Wales. Indeed, they may have wondered why a person so well acquainted with the scheme had failed to make application for it in 1918!

The income of the benefice was now £352, but Townshend's memoirs record grave disquiet about the result of disestablishment on his small income. The Welsh Church Commissioners, appointed to take control of the assets of the Welsh Church, sold most of the glebe land of his parish at a low value – at a time when prices were artificially low – and so reduced his income to £309. This would have been ancient glebe, given before 1662, and so confiscated by the Welsh Church Act. Although life interests were respected by this act the Church in Wales resolved at the time of disestablishment to permit any incumbent with a life interest to receive either the amount of the life interest or the assigned stipend. This was fixed at an average of £310 in 1925 but none were to be less than £250 in value.[5] The value of ancient glebe was excluded from this provision of life interest.

Worse was to come, for the commissioners, according to Townshend's account, in spite of promises to the contrary, confiscated the eight acres of curtilage land attached to the rectory, which was also ancient glebe, and required him to pay £12 a year rent, 10s. in tithe and 30s. in land tax with £7 10s. as an annual charge towards repairs. He required this land for growing food for his family and for pasture for his horse, so his income was now effectively reduced to £287 10s. These outgoings, he wrote, with the cost of his man and the feed for the animals – two sows and two cows – were just about covered by the value of the dairy produce and vegetables the land produced. In 1939, according to the Church in Wales *Handbook* for that year, his income was still £300 per annum, although most incumbencies in his deanery were at £350, but the population of the parish was only 87 and his quota – a charge imposed on each parish in Wales after disestablishment – a meagre £6 11s. per annum.

****

When Townshend came to inspect the parish in 1898 he found that while the rectory house was most attractive, possessing a spacious and picturesque appearance, it was in a bad state of repair. Only the garden, which had been laid out by his predecessor, was well kept. Approached by a carriage drive, with an "American" garden, small orchard, summerhouse, vegetable and fruit gardens, and a large tennis lawn, the house had views in all directions to the Sugar Loaf Mountain and other rural scenes. The wide creeper-covered front of the rectory, with its deep-set eaves, looked upon the lawn and garden "with a benign expression of comfort and quiet dignity". Indeed, Townshend claimed that these grounds had been described as the loveliest in Monmouthshire. The rectory house possessed a large back yard, with a good-sized coal-cellar, a large dairy, coach-house, cart shed, stables and loft, cow-shed, and nearby the "big rectory hay stack". All this, however, was little compensation for the problems of the rectory house, whose front had been rebuilt by Dean Williams but whose rear still bore traces of its previous existence as an old cottage-farmhouse.

Several floors had to be renewed, a water supply found, roofs and windows made good, painting and papering done everywhere. There was a hole in the schoolroom floor in which two men could stand, and the kitchen range was almost in pieces. Doors and gates too had to be replaced. What made it worse was that his predecessor had obtained a dilapidations certificate in 1895 from the diocesan surveyor, John P. Seddon (having paid £36 5s. for the repairs required by his survey), which exempted him for five years from any charges for which he would otherwise be liable. Thus Townshend could not obtain any compensation for the state of the house from his predecessor, who was relieved of all responsibility, but instead had to meet these charges from his own pocket. Writing to the governors of the Bounty in April 1904 Townshend maintained that the surveyor should have assessed these repairs at a sum of at least £400 to £500, which he, "a poor man, is unable from his own pocket to satisfactory meet". Although he wished to question the circumstances under which this certificate had been given, feeling there could not have been a proper survey, he was informed, as we noted earlier, that if he did so a pension amounting to a third of the value of the benefice would be applied for by his predecessor. It was cheaper to pay for the repairs than to have such a permanent charge upon on his income.

Lord Abergavenny's carpenter, Thomas Williams, "a genial, cheerful, good natured man", saw to the repairs, and a water supply was provided by a hydraulic ram purchased for £5 from Merryweather's, linked to a large supply tank placed near the village spring. The Crawshay Bailey trustees, owners of this property, allowed Townshend to wall in the spring (a very powerful one) for a peppercorn rent, but he was required to provide a handsome reservoir basin made of terracotta, a gargoyle for the overflow and a large brass tap for the purposes of the villagers. The overflow from the spring went to the ram some 20 yards lower down. This reservoir was presented to the village by Townshend in memory of "the glorious sixty-four year reign of Queen Victoria" – a characteristic gesture on his part. It cost £27 but the cost of piping the supply to the rectory over a distance of 1,300 feet, and raising it to the four storage tanks holding 1,400 gallons of water, added another £43 to the bill. In all it appears that the water supply and its necessary parts cost £192, and this, together with other work, was the object of an appeal launched in 1904.

This appeal was to restore the church, repair the rectory house, and put in this water supply. In case people thought this was a selfish desire on his part (as most of the villagers lived without this amenity), Townshend claimed it would allow water to be piped to it for fire prevention purposes. He admitted in his memoirs that the aim of this appeal was not only to restore these two buildings, but also to bring attention to past neglect. The church roof was an utter disgrace. Slates had been "stuck in" to make good the existing stone tiles. A most unseemly patchwork had resulted. The chancel roof had fallen in nearly three feet and was in a dangerous state. The interior of the church, he wrote in a letter of 18 April 1904 to the governors, had been painted and treated in a white and yellow wash.[6] Donations to this fund had been received from such individuals as Lords Tredegar,

Llangattock and Abergavenny, Colonel Mansel and Sir Henry
Jackson, clearly indicating that Townshend had acquired the art of
writing persuasive begging letters. Archdeacon Bruce backed the
appeal and the *Western Mail* placed it on its front page. Alas, the
bishop, a man of £20,000 a year, wrote Townshend in his memoirs,
was a very pronounced High Churchman, and though by that time
Townshend had described his fund as a memorial to Dean Williams
(who had restored the bishop's cathedral and helped revitalise the
diocese), he offered him only half a crown: "It was enough to make a
man, like myself, almost wish for disestablishment." This was Bishop
Richard Lewis of Llandaff who died in 1905. Townshend's bank
manager had actually laughed at the hopelessness of his task.

In April 1904 an appeal for financial assistance was made to the
governors of Queen Anne's Bounty. Their reply was chilling, although
Townshend had mentioned the circumstances of that unfortunate
dilapidation certificate. Grants were not given for the cost of repairs,
they wrote, nor could money be lent for dilapidation charges which
had occurred during an incumbency of such a short extent. The letter
concluded by stating that the bishop, if the house was inspected by
the diocesan surveyor, might require the work to be done whether the
loan was granted or not.

The general application was dropped, and instead during July of
the following year Townshend requested the governors' assistance
towards the cost of the water supply and for repairs to the coach-
house. Against the cost of this work, £192, he offered a benefaction
of £128 arising from the monies left over from the appeal after the
work had been completed on the church. Townshend hoped to receive
a grant of £64, that is, half of the benefaction, the usual amount of the
grant awarded. But the governors now insisted that a legal document
granting a legal right to this water supply should be supplied them
before they could consider this request, to which Townshend could
only reply that it was a public right. Receipted accounts were also
required as the work had already been carried out. Many of the
payments had been given in cash, Townshend replied, and the
building firm which had undertaken the work had been taken over by
a Mr Haviland, who had mislaid the books. Specifications were
demanded, but could not be supplied.

Eventually some printed accounts for 1900-01 were made
available, but as they included other items of expenditure the
governors found them very misleading. It turned out that these
accounts had been produced for another appeal, for £100, and which

was called the New Century Appeal. Townshend's predecessor had contributed £25 to this appeal, which he said had helped to relieve him of a burden "impossible to sustain". When the matter was eventually sorted out the figures given them seemed to indicate that only £158 out of the £192 could be accounted for by the accounts, which in any case had not been audited. The governors also argued that some of these costs were for dilapidation charges for which the incumbent was personally liable and which could not be assisted by grant money. They also pointed out that the work, which had been done unsupervised, had cost far more than it should have done. In his reply to the commissioners' allegations Townshend wrote that the contractor, Thomas Williams of Abergavenny, had waited patiently for payment and had made some substantial reductions to the scheme, but the plant had worked successfully day and night without intermission, even through two frosty winters, and had piped over 100,000 gallons of spring water to the rectory.

The governors eventually replied it was not their practice to make retrospective grants for work which had been carried out before an application had been made. They could not assist. Townshend was bitterly disappointed, especially as he claimed that the secretary of the Bounty had encouraged his application by stating that such grants were sometimes allowed. He had had to spend a considerable amount of time getting the details they required while he was busy organising a large bazaar, involving an immense amount of labour, though thankfully it had raised sufficient funds to meet the outstanding debt. His parish had no large landowners or resident gentry in it and it was hard to obtain support. But perhaps in the heat of the moment he forgot the substantial assistance which the local peers and squires had already given him and whose names he had so readily divulged to the governors as apparent supporters of his work. Townshend signed his name with the ascription "with profound dissatisfaction" for, as he put it, after all the trouble he had been put to by the governors they had not expressed "one particle of regret".

The governors replied. He had been warned about the outcome, but they had considered his case. Their answer was sufficiently open for Townshend to try and obtain the reimbursement of the two guineas he claimed it had cost him to make the first application. His request was declined. Yet if he claimed in self-defence that the cost of the works had been found by subscription and through a bazaar, there is also a suggestion that he was forced to borrow £180 to complete this work from a private source at an annual charge of nearly £5. Possibly this was paid off as the subscriptions came in.

****

A further application was made to the governors in March 1909. This was in order to provide a good-sized room for the Sunday School and for parish use. An outbuilding attached to the rectory, damp and with moisture everywhere and incapable of repair, had been previously used for this purpose. It needed to be rebuilt, linked onto the rectory, and a much-needed additional bedroom placed above it. This work was urgent, for the room was also used as a day nursery, school-room and playroom by his children, though it was most unsanitary as a leaking house drain flowed under its floor and the resulting stench was almost unbearable and even found its way into the rectory. The building would need to be removed in order to repair the drain. In addition other improvements were required at the rectory. The principal sitting room needed to be extended and a bathroom and extra bedrooms provided. Townshend thus applied for a loan by way of a £500 mortgage, hoping to find another £250 towards the work from sales of work, concerts and Lenten lectures. It would take three to four years to raise this amount unless a patron came forward with an offer of assistance, but as this was unlikely Townshend wanted to obtain the governors' approval for the improvements in order to start raising funds immediately.

The governors replied expressing their reluctance to lend money for such a purpose. Parish rooms were the responsibility of the parish and not of the incumbent. They wondered if the income of the parish could bear a mortgage of that amount, for the annual payments could well become a burden. But above all the governors felt that the population of the parish was small and that it was unfair that such small parishes should compete with larger parishes for the limited funds available. Was it not possible to unite this benefice with another?

Townshend obviously felt a fuller explanation was required, and he gave this in his reply of 10 March 1909. He was fearful of incurring dilapidation charges on that schoolroom which was a part of the rectory curtilage, and so its repair would be an advantage to his pocket now instead of increasing his future liabilities. The parochial room would be as convenient to him as to the parish as it would be used as a school-room for his family. Besides this it would be useful for fund-raising events which would benefit the parish as well as himself, and could equally be used for ruri-decanal meetings. .

He was met by a similar reply. A parish room was the responsibility of the parish. As the income of the parish was under £200 the governors could not allow it to be burdened with a loan. Consequently in his reply of 5 May Townshend changed his tactic. He now dropped the idea of a parish room and instead asked for assistance with providing a better sanitary scheme for the rectory and for help in rebuilding part of the house. Once more the governors suggested it might be wiser to unite with another parish. The benefice was really too small for assistance to be given it. Nevertheless, they suggested he send them his plans.

The plans were being prepared, Townshend replied on 8 May, but he added, "[o]f course this is a small parish. But are the souls in a small parish of *less* value than those elsewhere?" Larger parishes had more and wealthier people who could assist the Church. His parish, by contrast, had a large proportion of Nonconformists, and the only private house in the parish, the Court, was owned by a lady living in Ireland "who keeps up with the Roman Catholic families" and was "absolutely hardened against our people and our church." From this small parish Archdeacon Williams had gathered the funds for the rebuilding of Llandaff cathedral and the reconstruction of the diocese, claimed Townshend, adding that "it seems a bit hard that his old Parish and Home should be regarded in this way, when we come to you for help." Neither had he been idle, for on his small income he had raised over £1,500 for societies and towards the repair and expenses of his church. Besides, obtaining such a sum was not beyond the ability of his parishioners. They had raised £200 last year, less about £35 in expenses. The smallness of the parish should not be an obstacle. Rather it should be the reason for their assistance. It was impossible to unite the parish with another as the governors had suggested. The others were too far distant. Many came to his church from outlying areas of other parishes, as his church was easier of access and had good roads to it. Three of these non-parochial attenders were farmers who were also among his principal tithe payers, including the brother of Archdeacon Watkins of Durham. There was also an inn, close to the church, frequented on Sunday evenings by about 20 lads, some of whom came to church, and many of whom, it was hinted, lived in these outlying parts. Perhaps, he suggested, these areas could be added to his parish? He would be sad to see any other church added, for he felt he had enough to do already and his people would be dissatisfied with a single service.

Whether the governors were impressed by Townshend's arguments
we do not know, but their architects suggested a much-reduced
scheme for his consideration. It did not meet with his approval.
Although it gave him an additional bedroom and extended the
"morning room" as a place where teas could be served, he felt it
would cost as much as his own plans. Yet this concession on the part
of the governors gave Townshend further encouragement to request a
grant of half the costs up to £400 together with a loan of £100,
provided he could continue with the original scheme, albeit with a
few modifications. He would give a statutory undertaking to be
responsible for the remaining costs and the repayment of the loan
before leaving the parish. Townshend also promised to increase the
endowment by £100, half to be raised from local church funds and
half chargeable to his estate, but the governors could retain half of the
loan as a guarantee of this! His mother, aged between 70 and 80, had
told him she hoped to leave him between £4,000 to £8,000 (now in
the hands of trustees), while he had a £1,000 insurance policy and his
own estate was worth £3,500 besides. Faced with this knowledge the
governors might well have asked him why he was applying for a loan
in the first place. As they were gentlemen, they did not. But Mr Le
Fanu, secretary of the Bounty, was not obliging. His former
comments still applied. Nevertheless it was at this point that
Townshend appears to have passed over to the governors the sum of
£100 as part of a future benefaction in return for a grant. This sum
probably came from his own private resources, for he stated that as he
was living "hand to mouth" it would never be paid otherwise.

Although Townshend must have been aware by this stage that only
a modified scheme could attract grant aid, the scheme he now
presented to the commissioners could hardly warrant this description.
The morning room was to be extended by taking in the hall and
staircase, so that it would be 39 by 20 feet, so allowing two new
bedrooms above and an attic room. This concept of a hall-room had
been borrowed from his friends at Dingestow Court, the Bosanquets,
who used it (he wrote) to entertain the people of that parish, when
their vicar was able to address them. As a result there was a large and
loyal congregation in that parish with very few Nonconformists.
Obviously Townshend hoped for similar results for, as he wrote to the
governors in his defence of this scheme, "in this place a little homely
hospitality goes a long way." His 25-foot-long dining room was too
small for these purposes. His predecessor but one, Dean Williams, a
wealthy man though a "bit old-fashioned high church", had given

much employment to Nonconformists and, claimed Townshend, was accordingly much loved. He for his part could only influence them with hospitality, but for this, of course, he needed a suitable room. This work was proposed as yet another memorial to Archdeacon Williams. As such it was announced in the 12 February 1909 number of the evangelical weekly the *Record*. The paper reported that a fund for £1,000 had been established in order to restore the nave of the church, restore the rectory house and create a parish room for Sunday School and missionary meetings.

Townshend obviously anticipated that the governors would support his scheme to honour the late dean. The governors thought differently. However desirable a memorial to the late dean may have been, they replied, it had no bearing on the question of the proper size of a house in which future incumbents would have to reside. Several protests were penned by Townshend, but in the end he had to accept that the plans would have to be substantially reduced. The morning room was now to be 18 by 16 feet only, and the costs were restricted to £360. If the plans were approved by the governors' architects it was agreed that Townshend would be offered a grant of £100 to meet his own benefaction of £200, of which £100 was in hand. But once again Townshend saw this "concession" as a guarantee of assistance for more substantial work.

As a result new plans were drawn up for the rectory in July 1910. The new plans allowed for a morning room extended by another 7 feet with a bay window besides other additions elsewhere. But the governors' architect noted a defect: there was no cloakroom or water closet downstairs and without such provision the plans could not be accepted. Townshend's mother died in the following month and anticipating some legacy from her estate he offered an additional benefaction of £200 if the governors would meet it with a further grant and thus allow the staircase-hall-morning room he so desperately wanted. This facility, he pointed out, was very common in new country houses and would bring into his darkened rectory house some much-needed light. Alas, the governors were not helpful. The plan could not be approved as it lacked a toilet downstairs, and although the bay in the morning room and the link between that room and the staircase-hall would be allowed, they could not permit the extension to the study. While he could retain the previous grant of £100, he could also apply for a larger grant, for which no pledge could be given as the governors still considered that the benefice was too small to be burdened with a loan. Townshend accordingly applied for this larger grant, though he stated that his entertainments committee would find the money for the study extension.

Writing in January 1911 Townshend noted a reverse in his fortunes. His mother's estate had not produced what was anticipated. He was to clarify this in a later letter. He had sacrificed his claims on her estate in order to provide for an invalid sister, who was so ungrateful (he hinted), that she was unwilling to assist his scheme. Now, in order to obtain this additional £200 he had had to sell several articles and he hoped his sacrifice would be respected by the governors. Another £50 would be needed for fittings. He then added an intriguing aside, "[m]y picture, Lady Jane Grey, is in the *Sphere* this week".

March came and with it yet another larger scheme, based on an estimate of £450. A second bedroom was to be placed in the attic, one bedroom was to be divided into two, an additional bath-tub put into a dressing room, the staircase-hall to be extended outwards so as to be in line with the remainder of the building, new hot water and heating apparatus provided together with a water-closet on the first floor, and the outside coal store rebuilt. The governors were clearly amazed and perhaps a little annoyed. Their approval could extend to only a few alterations and to the sanitary and heating arrangements. But even this work, they expostulated, would cost more than the earlier scheme they had rejected. The first grant of £100 against his benefaction of £200 was confirmed, but if more was required it could not be found from the limited funds at their disposal. This meant, in effect, that Townshend could only do the work which they had allowed and some of that would be at his own expense. The governors justified their action by pointing out that they needed to protect the interests of future incumbents, as well as to ensure that parsonages were not built or extended so they became larger than livings could afford.

Townshend's reply was the reply of a man whose dream had been shattered by reality. He had been utterly taken aback by their attitude. The governors' requirements had already doubled the costs of the original proposal for work which would be of little use to him. He had offered more than one half of the total cost if the governors could meet the other part, and after all the trouble he and his architect had taken this refusal was all the more "startling and tragic". His own means were now at breaking point. The governors replied, in effect, that he had been warned this might be the case. His scheme was far more costly than the one originally agreed, and he could still continue with the alterations and improvements they had accepted. Although

Townshend tried his luck again by offering an additional £200 for an equivalent grant if the modifications he wanted were allowed, generating much correspondence, the governors held firm to their refusal.

But Townshend was not to be outdone, and so a different tactic was tried. In December 1911 he requested a grant of £30 to £40 towards an underground water tank to hold 3,000 gallons together with a hydraulic ram as the existing supply depended on a water windmill. The available water supply was only sufficient for drinking and washing purposes, but was insufficient for the purposes of bathing or cleaning. Unable to obtain detailed estimates for this work he offered to pay £25 himself if the governors would offer a similar sum. This appears to have been acceptable to them, or at least Townshend believed this to be the case.

At this stage the governors were still pressing Townshend to supply the amended house plans for inspection, pointing out that they would not allow any work to proceed or any grant to be paid until the plans had been approved. Two years went by, and in September 1913 Townshend reported that his architect, a Mr Francis, was spending all his time in public houses, but he felt unable to pursue him into these places. In any case he was not happy with his work and these delays were increasing the costs of the scheme. By April 1914 Townshend was still complaining about his architect, but a contractor from Abergavenny, a churchman, had estimated the work at £590 rather than the original £520. Towards this sum Townshend was able to offer his own benefaction of £100 which he had paid in 1911, his promise of an insurance policy valued at £145 which would mature in 1914, and an additional £25 he had offered, together with the governors' grant of £125 (which included the alleged small supplementary grant for the new water supply), gifts of £32 promised from others, and a further promise of £50 if the governors would increase the supplementary grant of £25 to £50. The total, even with the anticipated supplementary grant, was still short of what was required.

Townshend supported this application for an increase in this "supplementary" grant with two "personal considerations". His wife had had a bad accident which had resulted in a miscarriage, two operations had been required and he had had to find £100 for medical expenses, and his eldest son had had a mental breakdown. He had been "doing so nicely" in the office of the chief engineer of the Manchester Ship Canal and had partly designed the entrance to the new great dry-dock there. The premium for his "apprenticeship" had been found through a friend and this was an additional anxiety. It was a hard time, and he hoped that the governors would allow him the additional £25. They did not.

During 1914 the governors continually requested sight of the plans and specifications. These requests were made against the backcloth of Townshend's letters announcing that he was hoping to find another £100 to make a total benefaction of £345, in the continuing expectation that the governors would deal with him as "liberally as may be in their power" with an additional grant. These letters spoke of modifications which may well have seemed to the governors to be additions: for example, a landing space on the hall staircase allowing a sort of balcony over the morning-room-cum-hall, and the upstairs lavatory to be placed in another position so that it might not be seen from the hall – "a very important consideration". To offset some of the costs the proposed alteration of the backstairs would be abandoned and he would provide at his own expense linen presses; old doors would be reused and dark-stained pine cornices would be erected instead of plaster ones. The scheme would continue to provide a spacious hall-cum-morning room, with a bedroom and an attic over it, in place of a small and insanitary schoolroom. Adequate drainage could also be provided.

The marquess of Abergavenny had offered £25 towards this work to avoid Townshend's encroaching on his (Townshend's) proposed gift of an external recreational room and library for the use of the village lads, to be termed the King Edward Memorial Room. This particular gift of Lord Abergavenny prompted Townshend to request an equivalent grant to meet it from the governors, as additional help from others as well as the sacrifices he was making would be required to meet the increased building costs being incurred by the war. This was written on 29 August 1914.

The governors still requested sight of the plans and pointed out that a letter detailing the specifications was not sufficient. If the plans were approved then the governors might be prepared to make an additional grant to cover one half of the cost of the rainwater storage only. It was a hesitant response. The next letter in the correspondence is of 1916, when Townshend wrote to say that Mr Francis the architect had joined the army and C. E. Bateman of Birmingham – a former president of the Institute of Architects – had taken his place. Alas, the delay of two years had meant that the "goal posts" had changed, for the governors wrote in reply that they were not favourably disposed to sanction any new building during the war save what was absolutely necessary. They would also insist that the money was in hand to meet the costs.

The plans were not available until 1919, although Townshend recited the history of the works from 1914 in order to justify his slow response, including the endless delays caused by the intemperate Francis. The builder who had repaired the church and would have done the work on the rectory had refused to take that work on due to irregular payments. Another builder had been found, but was too busy to submit an estimate, while a third man had been approached but his price was higher and before any contract had been signed war had broken out. Prices were now one hundred per cent higher, with disestablishment on the horizon. The governors, wrote Townshend, had shown great kindness to him in the past over this scheme, in what had been "not very easy circumstances". Nevertheless, he wondered if they could continue their kindness and he his indebtedness to them. If he managed to raise another £500, could they meet it with an equal grant, for this, with the £200 in hand, would equal £1,200. This £200 probably consisted of the money he had given in 1909 together with the £100 grant allowed him. One assumes that the various gifts given in the past and the other sums he had mentioned were now included in this £500 offer. But it was all a little vague and uncertain.

Townshend believed he could obtain this £500 almost at once. Furthermore, if they were able to use ferro-concrete blocks, which could be made on the site, savings could be made. For an additional £200 he could create a small Sunday School building standing a little apart from the rectory. His engineer son had prepared a design for this much needed facility. The room could then be made available for Bible and confirmation classes, parish meetings and a Sunday school, as well as for a lads' night school and club. The Sunday school was now being held in "our kitchen" and the lads' club met in the old coach-house. It may well have seemed to the governors that they were being taken back to stage one of the scheme.

A decisive reply was given by the governors. In view of the Welsh Church Act the governors had decided not to give any further grants to Welsh benefices. As a result of this letter Townshend went on the defensive. The scheme had already been approved and he had £200 in the Scottish Provident Institute intended for it. If a small ground floor extension was built for the Sunday school the upper story could be completed later. The quantities for the work had been supplied and paid for, probably (if this was not bluff) from some of the gifts he had mentioned previously. The governors made very short shrift of these arguments. The amount in his account with interest stood at £220 12s.7d. It is clear from this statement that the additional £25 Townshend believed had been awarded him had never been allowed. The governors were required to transfer an income of between £10,000 and £12,000 to the Welsh Church at their own expense. They felt this was the extent of the help they could offer to the Welsh Church. While they would allow him the £220 to complete the original design, after 31 March 1920 the funds would be transferred to the Representative Body of the Church in Wales to which he would need to apply for any additional grant. It almost appeared that the governors were not unhappy that his file was being transferred elsewhere!

As a result of this information Townshend protested that the £100 he had given to the governors for safe keeping in 1909 should now be worth much more. He quibbled too that although the general interest rate in 1920 was five per cent he was only being allowed four per cent, while he expressed his annoyance that before 1917 no interest had been allowed on grants for building purposes. Had this money been properly invested it would have accumulated to a considerable sum. But the governors replied that they were trustees not speculators and were limited by legal restraints, while any money invested by them was at their own risk and not at the risk of the beneficiary. The reply seems to have satisfied Townshend for he now wrote a more conciliatory letter which hopefully gratified the governors, who must have been well used to his constant requests and importunities: "I cannot tell you how sorry I am to be, without my wish and will, transferred out of the English Church. You have always met me kindly and helpfully ..." However, as he believed that both his bishop and archdeacon were friendly to him he still hoped something might be done. This letter closes the correspondence file with the governors, but his memoirs note that the diocesan boards of finance, of Llandaff possibly, and certainly of Monmouth when that new diocese was formed in 1921, fulfilled all his proposals, for one of their first duties was the repair of parsonage houses and the provision of an adequate water supply for them. One assumes it was a limited scheme, but one satisfactory to him after so many years of patient waiting and abortive proposals!

****

Townshend's parish was a small one. One wonders how he managed to spend his time when he had one church, no school, and only 30 families all-told. Some hints are given in the Bounty papers that he ran Bible classes, bazaars, lads' clubs and Sunday schools. His memoirs indicate he was much given to hospitality – which he wished to extend to his parishioners as well – and was a frequent guest at the big houses of the neighbourhood: Nevill Hall with the marquess of Abergavenny, Hendre with the Rolls family, the Jacksons of Llantilio Crossenny Court, the Mansels of Maindiff Court, and especially the Bosanquets of Dingeslow. The latter, he wrote, were nearer to him in "Protestant principles" than any other family in the neighbourhood. Most of these families had left the area by 1920. Mrs Carlisle of Llanvapley Court was the local landowner, but his relationship with her was not so friendly. She was high church, and though she offered him £600 towards the repair of the church she insisted that it be met on his part by high church services and a surpliced choir. The offer was declined. Instead she gave the money to Abergavenny Cottage Hospital in memory of her husband. While Townshend allowed chairs for her and her friends in the chancel he felt insulted when her guests turned east for the creed. The chairs were accordingly removed. Mrs Carlisle later married an Irishman and on moving to Ireland sold her home to Reginald Herbert, a devout Roman Catholic, with whom Townshend had a good social but not pastoral relationship.

The memoirs of his life extend to two large typewritten volumes for the earlier years, but the third volume, on Llanvapley, was never completed and its 30 or so pages merely record the first few years of his ministry in that parish. These years were given up to what Townshend was pleased to describe as "Protestant agitation", which was, after all, the reason for his appointment to that parish by Lord Abergavenny in the first instance. His lordship was a vice-president of the Church Association, and Townshend became its local secretary.

It is not surprising, therefore, that his memoirs speak more about this work than about his parochial activity. He helped persuade Walter Walsh, "the gifted author of *The Secret History of the Oxford Movement*", to give a public lecture at Abergavenny Town Hall. His own conference sermon at the Church Association at Gloucester was warmly complimented by Archdeacon Taylor of Liverpool. When Lady Wimborne spoke at Monmouth the Church Union people of Cardiff, led by a Mr Kirk, attended, and Kirk responded by quoting Reformation scholars who, he said, were in favour of the confessional. Townshend followed this up and discovered that he had misquoted all his references. After a lengthy newspaper controversy Townshend discovered that the sixth book of the Tudor theologian, Richard Hooker's *Of the Laws of Ecclesiastical Polity* contained an able and scholarly refutation of the confessional. He therefore persuaded the National Church League to reprint this book, the cost of which was met in part by donations from Lady Wimborne and Lady Llangattock.

More exciting times came in the "Khaki" election of 1900. Townshend discovered that the Conservative candidate for Monmouth, E. M. Underdown, refused to give his support to the Church Discipline Bill, which endeavoured to regulate the ritualistic practices of the high church clergy, even though he had been sponsored by Lord Abergavenny, one of the bill's principal sponsors. But Underdown's decision was given at the last moment when he believed it would be too late for his opponents to give any publicity to it. The Liberal candidate, Reginald McKenna, supported the bill. As two-thirds of the government candidates had already been elected, posters were rapidly prepared and posted all over the constituency stating that the Conservative candidate opposed this bill and that it was perfectly safe for conservatives to support the Liberal candidate on this occasion. Mr McKenna, he gleefully reported in his memoirs, doubled his majority. Townshend's deep distrust of the ritualistic movement also emerges in his memorial sermon to Queen Victoria, included in these memoirs. What was the reason for the greatness of her reign? It was, he retorted, her simple Christian faith: "There you have it! No sacerdotal rubbish! No ritualistic paraphernalia!"[7]

His wife Jessie, daughter of a Warwickshire vicar, died in 1933 at the age of 64. The year before her death she had organised a sale of work and fête for the repair fund. It had been opened by General and Mrs Tullock. Sunday school teaching, playing the organ, attending to the choir, providing hospitality and bringing up a large family of four sons and five daughters had been her lot. She was also the leading light in the Llanvapley branch of the Women's Unionist Association. Her memoir by her husband, printed from a newspaper account, is a genuine tribute to her companionship and love over years of difficulty and strife, as well as being one of the few such published accounts of a clerical wife which has survived from that period.

E. Mansel Townshend, as he appears to have described himself, was a man whose energy needed more substantial outlets than a small rural parish could provide. His appointment to his parish was probably to enable him to engage in "protestant" work locally and within a diocese where Anglo-Catholicism was on the decided increase. A large family, as was then customary, and a small income, appear to have exhausted his private resources and made him bold in asking for assistance. An eternal optimist, there is, one feels, a certain importunity and naiveté in his frequent alterations of the building plans for the rectory as well as in the claims he made for himself, particularly in his *Who's Who in Wales* entry, which clearly suggests he felt acutely his lack of recognition by his superiors. The papers he left and the records which remain in the various church archives indicate a not too untypical story of clerical life at the time, but also note his desire to rebuild his parish spiritually and materially, as well as to do something for the village folk. That he completed this task under the circumstances of his life was no mean achievement.

ENDNOTES

1 *Who's Who in Wales*, 1920 edition, pp. 477-8.

2 The memoirs of the Revd E. Mansel Townshend are used by courtesy of Mrs Janet Skinner, of Plymouth, wife of Richard Skinner, his youngest grandson.

3 Most of the family had changed the spelling of their name at the suggestion of the Marquess Townshend in 1870.

4 According to the obituary of his wife, reprinted from a newspaper report of 1933, and see also the *Who's Who in Wales* entry at the head of this chapter.

5 *Welsh Church Handbook*, 1925, p. 65.

6 Extensive repairs to the church were undertaken in 1911 at a cost of £150.

7 Townshend's concern regarding ritualism surfaced during his only known speech before the Llandaff Diocesan Conference: *23rd Report*, 1906, p. 48. In it he noted the impact ritualism and its doctrines had on Nonconformists who, as a result, desired to see the disestablishment of the Church.

EPILOGUE

We may look back to the Victorian age as an age of large congregations and considerable church progress, but it was not the golden age we tend to assume it was. It is probably true that no age can be described as such. Each age has its own difficulties, problems, tensions, as well as opportunities and gains.

The clergy depicted in these pages are there because there was sufficient material found about them which enabled me to write their lives and assess their characters. With perhaps two exceptions, namely the last two depicted, their names will be familiar to most students of the Victorian Church in Wales. Many achieved high office, or turned it down, as did Constable Ellis, and as such we have to admit these men were the exception. Because the sources are limited the stories of the more "run of the mill" clergy are unknown, and their lives and ministries remain unrecognised. The life of Edward Mansel Townshend provides one exception. In his life we sense the strains and stresses of a rural ministry, lived as far as we know with little recognition or encouragement from the wider Church. In his life too we can note some of his family concerns, a feature which is often missing in the lives of the other clergy depicted. We know that for many clergy, whose incomes depended on the tithe, its depreciation due to the agricultural depression of the 1880s caused significant loss, nobly borne, no doubt, but not the least trying for that. There were other clergy who gave a significant rebate on their tithe rental during those years, feeling they had to suffer along with their parishioners.

Many of the men depicted in this book were pioneers. Constable Ellis and George Huntington were some of the earliest leaders of the Oxford Movement in Wales. William Leigh Morgan was another, though his theology was far different and he worked within an inner city area. Thomas Walters and Venables Williams were church builders, while John Griffiths and Robert Wickham endeavoured, as archdeacons, to bring reform and new life into the Church of their day. Several were engaged in controversies about nationality and language. Each had to face many problems in common, such as the difficulties of raising finances for the work of church extension, coping with the pastoral challenges of their parishes, and within the wider Church, facing the prospect of disestablishment. And each had their own private concerns: Huntington with the difficulties of living in an inadequate house, Townshend with the costly demands of a large family needing a good and expensive education. Though Walters appears to have become a wealthy man, Venables Williams died in straightened circumstances, and the widow of George Huntington appears to have needed the help of charitable trusts for the needs of her old age.

We live in a very different age, with our own set of problems and opportunities. Yet the Christian ministry is still seen as a vocation, and the Church continues its commitment to worship, mission, and social concern, though there is one difference. We are now more committed to unity with the other churches of our land, a matter barely accepted in those earlier days, although there were some far-sighted men, such as Archdeacon Griffiths, who were prepared to hold out a friendly hand and greet as Christian brethren those whom others of his generation would unchurch.